Self and Image
in
Juan Ramón Jiménez

Self and Image
in
Juan Ramón Jiménez

Modern and Post-modern Readings

John C. Wilcox

University of Illinois Press
Urbana and Chicago

This book is printed on acid-free paper.

Library of Congress Cataloging-in-Publication Data

Wilcox, John C. (John Chapman), 1943–
Self and image in Juan Ramón Jiménez.

Bibliography: p.
Includes index.
1. Jiménez, Juan Ramón, 1881–1958—Criticism and
interpretation.   2. Self in literature.   I. Title.
PQ6619.I4Z95   1987   861'.62   86-1460
ISBN 0-252-01331-X (alk. paper)

To
the memory
of
Carrie Chapman
(1884–1960)

Contents

Preface

The Spanish poet Juan Ramón Jiménez was born in 1881 in the Andalusian village of Moguer. He died in 1958 in Santurce, Puerto Rico.
His first poems were written in the late 1890s, and his last during the
mid-1950s. His range is immense. His early style is typical of *fin de
siècle* verse—mournful, decadent, and sentimental. His middle and
late styles—taut, elliptical, and unsentimental in the extreme—have
similarities with such contemporary Europeans as Yeats and Valéry.

Jiménez had a strong personality; his work is extensive and it underwent a profound change and evolution. Many consider him to be the
most important Spanish poet of this century. His reputation always
seems to precede him: both the poet and his *Obra* ("Work") never fail
to provoke in readers ardent admiration and/or strong dislike.

As a way of introducing the present study, let me attempt to describe—briefly—a few of the major presuppositions which I believe
readers bring to Jiménez and his *Obra*, all of which underlie this study.
These presuppositions are, I freely confess, my "narrative" of Jiménez's
"Work," the "fiction" I need to represent in order to frame my reading.

A major presupposition is that Jiménez is a poet of light, balance,
harmony; a poet of firm vision and aesthetic resolve; a master of the
poetic word. In taste he was fastidious—concerned with the beauty
and perfection of a moment in time. That, certainly, is one image of
Juan Ramón which is frequently represented by historians and critics
alike.[1] In this study, I label it his "solar" image, and I characterize it as
his "Dr. Jekyll" mask.

Another presupposition is that Juan Ramón is an effete and languid
melancholic, a doubter, lost in darkness, overwhelmed by negative
psychic forces, unable to resolve the antinomies of day and night. This
aspect of the poet was glimpsed by Rubén Darío in 1904 (in Albornoz,

Jiménez Escritor 27–32). Following Darío, I call this mask Jiménez's "lunar" self and characterize it as his "Mr. Hyde" persona.

Jiménez's "solar" self receives continual critical assessment. His "lunar" self, however, has received much less attention. In addition, students accept that Jiménez, like other Modern poets, selected word and phrase with particular care and precision (see Gullón, *Estudios* 131–38), but few readers are prepared to specify the distinctive linguistic modernity that constitutes the "poems" themselves.

Hence, the present study, which addresses the manner in which both "lunar" and "solar" self-images compete for dominance of the "Work," also describes in as much detail as possible ways in which linguistic, rhetorical, and semantic features combine in selected "poems" to constitute "modern" poetic texts. In general, my reading of these poems starts by focusing on structure and syntax: phonology, suprasegmentals, parts of speech (the conjunction "y" in particular); it proceeds to analyze figures of speech; it then moves on to interpret the semanticization of the particular distinctive features that were foregrounded in the initial stages of the analysis.[2]

A further presupposition—discussed in chapters 1 and 7—is that Jiménez's *Obra* falls into two or three periods. Sánchez-Barbudo's studies divide the work into two epochs: "la primera" (1900–1915) and "la segunda época" (1916–53). Sánchez Romeralo (*Poesías últimas* 10–37), in accordance with the poet's notes, divides the work into three "tiempos": 1895–1913, 1914–30, 1931–56.[3] I too find three phases in Jiménez's poetry, although my dates are somewhat different. For me, Jiménez has a pre-Modern (that is, a late-romantic, *modernista-simbolista*) phase (1900–1913); this is followed by his Modern phase—with a capital "M"—which begins around 1914.[4] A third phase, his post-Modern impulse, begins after 1936 (the year the Spanish Civil War obliged Jiménez to leave Spain) and runs concurrently with the Modern impulse until the "Work" ends. The first phase is written under the enthrallment of the 'dark', the "lunar" mask. Jiménez's "Mr. Hyde" is the main protagonist of these years. The second phase is the domain of the 'bright', the "solar" mask. Jiménez's "Dr. Jekyll" is the exclusive actor during this time. In its third impulse the *Obra* attempts to blend lunar and solar aesthetics, but the 'darkest' voice of the "lunar" persona, "Mr. Hyde," dominates what might be Jiménez's final poem, the third and final fragment of *Espacio* (1954).

In order to question and illustrate the above presuppositions I have selected five poetic texts on selfhood from the three impulses I respond to in the Jiménez *Obra*. Three of the texts are poems which range in length from fourteen to twenty-eight lines;[5] another is an eight-hundred-line prose-poem. A fifth is a sub-text: manifestations of negativity which are scattered throughout the *Obra*'s first phase.

The texts analyzed are those in which the speaker is concerned with images of selfhood. They confront, that is, the enigma of *desdoblamiento*, the multiplicity of poetic selves, at three distinct phases in the poet's life (mid-1900s, 1916–19, 1941–54).[6]

As I explain in chapter 1, I have opened each text to what I call *modern*, *post-modern*, and *specialist* readings. *Modern* readers utilize insights developed and refined by Anglo and American Formalist critics and by European structuralists; *post-modern* readers are more influenced by post-structural reading strategies developed over the last fifteen years (semiotic, psychoanalytic, deconstructionist). A *specialist* responds principally to the *Obra* and the criticism it has inspired.

The texts selected for analysis in each chapter have, by interaction with *modern*, *post-modern*, and *specialist* readers, appropriated, applied, and developed a variety of contemporary techniques for critical reading, the general characteristics of which may be briefly indicated as follows.

Chapters 2 and 3 study the early, pre-Modern poetry. Chapter 2 analyzes the manner in which *actants* function in a poem from the 1904 volume *Jardines lejanos*: "¿Soy yo quien anda esta noche, / por mi cuarto, o el mendigo / que rondaba mi jardín, al caer la tarde? . . ." The latter, which has never ceased to intrigue Jiménez's readers, is a traditional poem (a "romance"), yet it does not resolve its paradoxes. To explain the enigmatic but innovative ways it poeticizes time and space, the analysis resorts to the narratologists' distinction between "story" and "plot." To explain the indeterminacy of the text's concluding stanzas, the analysis avails itself of the post-structural concept of *différance*.

I argue that the text evolves into a struggle between two actants: one 'bright', the other 'dark'. The 'bright' actant is an innocent pantheist, the earliest manifestation of the "Dr. Jekyll" persona, who will evolve into a Modern poet. The 'dark' actant, who ruminates and broods, is the earliest manifestation of the "Mr. Hyde" persona. The 'dark' actant foregrounds negative insights and comes up against a condition of *différance*; its destablizing views will undermine the spiritual optimism of its 'brighter' other. It is the 'dark' actant which later acquires a post-modern impulse and threatens to undermine the perfection and beauty of the Modern poet's *Obra*.

Chapter 3 studies not a poem, but a neglected sub-text from the first, the pre-Modern phase of the Jiménez *Obra*: the intrusion, although constant suppression, of dark, uncanny, ominous, and negative attitudes to life, to love, and to poetry. This text is dispersed throughout the 1900 to 1913 phase of the "Work"; it is therefore a text the speaker refused to confront as a whole. My argument is that this text is manifest in the constant but intermittent use of the nouns "sol" and "luna," "perro" and "pájaro," "tronco" and "árbol," "hombre enlutado, fantasma, sombra, mendigo" and "poeta melancólico." In my analysis, I apply the term "lexeme" in opposition to the positive, Modern term "symbol." Such nouns as "sol" and "luna," I argue, are negative *lexemes*, which are plurivalent and contain three or four *sememes*. The negativity studied is repressed by Jiménez in the second phase of his "Work" but resurfaces, in the same negative lexemes, in its third and final phase.

Chapters 4 and 5 focus on the second or middle phase of the poetry, the Modern impulse. They show how a 'bright' Modern aesthete resists randomness, chaos, lack of control; how he labors to construct a world of sunlight, a world in which all will cohere at a central point. The Modern aesthete is the text's 'brighter' actant who reaffirms the onto-metaphysical postulates on which its formation and civilization's depend. This actant, rather than embrace *différance*, suspects that vision, image, representation, and self are constituted by sameness and difference; that they exist and emerge as part of a web or network of that which is established, recognized, secure, and traditional, and that which has not yet been formulated or canonized.

To advance these arguments, chapter 4 studies actantial oppositions in "Golfo," the next important text on selfhood in the Jiménez *Obra*. It appeared in the *Diario de un poeta reciéncasado* (1917), the volume that established Jiménez as the major Modern poet of the Hispanic world. Its particular focus is on rhythm as a textual actant, especially on rhythmic contrasts, because "ritmo" is one of the highly significant distinctions between Jiménez's second and first phases. The analysis links rhythm to lexematic oppositions which foreground semantic differences. Though these oppositions are still unresolved by the end of the text, where a state of indeterminacy prevails, it is argued that the meditative, even depressed (Predmore 106) speaker in this text is moving toward the conclusion that self must contain disparate urges, must blend the contraries of negativity and positivity.

Chapter 5 develops the notion of actantial oppositions in "Yo y Yo," from *Piedra y cielo* (1919), by studying the text's explicit and implicit use of first and second person pronouns. "Yo y Yo" is exemplary of a Modern Jiménez poetic text, hence particular attention has been devoted to specifying—in much detail—ways in which it poeticizes *langue*. The text reveals a 'brighter' actant questing after a self that will make all cohere, a self that will contain all. But that self contains an even 'darker' actant, its own post-modern shadow, which doubts and which will undermine all idealistic notions of self and *Obra*.

Chapters 6 and 7 study the *Obra*'s post-Modern phase. Chapter 6 is a study of "narrative topics" and lexematic oppositions in the prose-poem *Espacio* (1941–54). *Espacio* is an obscure text and the chapter's focus is to understand it as a synthesis of the *Obra*. The negativity, which is pervasive throughout the *Obra*'s first phase but rarely in evidence in its second, reappears in *Espacio*. In this phase, the self is seen disintegrating, but the "Dr. Jekyll" in the speaker struggles to fuse negative with positive thoughts and feelings. He succeeds in this until *Espacio*'s last sequence of one hundred lines, where the speaker's darkest post-modern voice cries out its despair. The 'dark' actant therefore reappears in the *Obra*'s third phase. One part of it recognizes the dynamics of sameness and difference as constitutive of reality; but another part of it faces up to the condition of *différance* itself: that there is no absolute, all-embracing reality that resolves all enigmas and dilemmas and reassures all subjects; that there is no single self that can emerge, pristine and transparent, no pure and authentic voice that penetrates enigmas back to origins and illuminates all, in short, that there is no hegelian ontology inexorably progressing toward a more refined state.

Chapter 7 contrasts the pre-Modern, Modern, and post-Modern visions in the *Obra*, by focusing on the *Obra*'s basic narrative topics ("la mujer, la obra, la muerte"). This chapter also analyzes manifestations of these visions in the *Obra*, especially in Jiménez's final collection of poetry, *Leyenda* (*1896–1956*), which was published in 1978. The argument is again advanced that Jiménez's Modern persona is fully articulated in a rather limited number of his books.

The postscript assesses the insights these *modern*, *post-modern*, and *specialist* readings have had on the Jiménez *Obra*.

Acknowledgments

These readings, which have taken their own good time to evolve, would not have been possible without the encouragement of colleagues and friends to whom I owe a debt of gratitude.

My thanks to J. A. Pritchard, Master at Liverpool Collegiate, for first teaching me about I. A. Richards; to Paul Olson, for his lecture on Juan Ramón at Bristol University (1965), which opened my mind to Jiménez's complexity; to Ricardo Gullón, for his guidance and patience as I first got to know the *Obra*; to Francisco Hernández-Pinzón Jiménez, the poet's nephew, and to Raquel Sárraga, librarian of the Sala Zenobia-Juan Ramón Jiménez at the University of Puerto Rico, Río Piedras, for the help they extended me in my initial investigations of Jiménez; to Edgar Slotkin, for his seminar on contemporary literary criticism, at the University of Cincinnati (1977–78); to Graciela Palau de Nemes and Howard T. Young, for numerous ways in which they have encouraged and helped me over the last few years; to Margo Persin, Martha LaFollette Miller, and María Stycos Nowakowska for allowing me to share and to continue to learn from their critical, professional, and personal commitment to Modern Spanish poetry.

I wish to thank Andrew Debicki, not just for the model he provides in his *Poetry of Discovery*, but for his constant encouragement over the last five years. He heard a paper I gave, an early version of chapter 5, urged me to develop it, and suggested the possibility of constructing a book around detailed analyses of Jiménez's poetry—which is precisely what I have tried to do here.

Some of the ideas in chapters 2, 4, 5, and 6 were originally addressed in papers given at various conferences and symposiums, and I wish to acknowledge the encouragement I received from those who heard them. In particular, I want to thank Aurora de Albornoz, Antonio Ca-rreño, Biruté Ciplijauskaité, Javier Herrero, John Kronik, Paul Olson, Antonio Sánchez-Barbudo, and Antonio Sánchez Romeralo.

I also want to thank my editor, Carol Bolton Betts, for her thoroughness, for her tact and humor, and for her sound judgment and advice.

This book would not have seen the light of day without the help of the CYBER computer at the University of Illinois (Urbana-Champaign). I thank Professor Brian Dutton for his patience in teaching me to "word-process" on it, as well as John Cull and Ed Dewan for their frequent help.

I also thank the Research Board of the University of Illinois for the grant they awarded me for the preparation of the manuscript.

I am most grateful to the Center for Advanced Study at the University of Illinois (Urbana-Champaign) for awarding me a fellowship for the spring of 1984, which allowed me to complete the manuscript.

I extend my gratitude also to don Francisco Hernández-Pinzón Jiménez for permission to quote from the works of Juan Ramón Jiménez, and to the Sala Zenobia-Juan Ramón Jiménez for allowing me to reproduce the Sorolla portrait of Juan Ramón that appears on the dust jacket of this book.

To Marvin Lewis, friend and colleague, my sincere thanks for his unfailing moral support.

To my wife, Julie, my deep gratitude, for reasons she well knows.

Abbreviations used for collections of Jiménez's poetry (full details in Works Cited)

LIP I   *Libros inéditos de poesía*: I
LIP II   *Libros inéditos de poesía*: II
LP   *Libros de poesía*
PLP   *Primeros libros de poesía*
SA   *Segunda antolojía poética*
TA   *Tercera antolojía poética*

1

Modern and Post-modern Readings for Jiménez and his *Obra*

Readers

Jiménez's "Work" is a complex text that evolves through various phases and moods: it begins with nostalgia and melancholy, moves on to affirmation and jubilation, and ends with euphoria and doubt. Accordingly, if readers wish to do justice to its variety, they will need to develop more than one reading strategy.[1] That, at least, is what happened to my reading, the more I confronted the *Obra*'s different phases. My response gradually split into three distinct gestures, a triad I have called *modern*, *post-modern*, and *specialist* readers. These readers are, in effect, "reading strategies" which read the texts concurrently, and whose genesis lies in the impact structural and post-structural methodologies have had on Formalist ideology and practice.

Expressed in the discourse of contemporary literary criticism, *modern* readers are a product of "formalism" and "structuralism";[2] they were formed principally by the work of Anglo and American New Critics and Saussurean structural linguists (the exponents of the latter being Russians, Czechs, French, and Spaniards). The *post-modern* reader is a product of post-structuralist (i.e. semiotic, deconstructive, psychoanalytic) inspired reading. Both these readers are students of contemporary criticism, which in turn has produced them. Their readings are relatively self-conscious and scientific. The *specialist*, on the other hand, has evolved from familiarity with the poet, his life, his work and the criticism it has generated. The *specialist* is a residual humanist in the reading strategy, the "ghost" in the reading machine.

1

Lyotard (*Postmodern Condition*) offers a helpful distinction between the terms "modern" and "postmodern." In his introduction, Lyotard distinguishes between "science" and "narrative." He says that while science considers narration to be a fable, it asserts that its own discourse leads to truth: the elucidation of meaning, the betterment of mankind. Hence, he adds:

> I will use the term *modern* to designate any science that legitimates itself with reference to a metadiscourse of this kind making an explicit appeal to some grand narrative, such as the dialectics of Spirit, the hermeneutics of meaning, the emancipation of the rational or working subject, or the creation of wealth. For example, the rule of consensus between the sender and the addressee of a statement with truth-value is deemed acceptable if it is cast in terms of a possible unanimity between rational minds: this is the Enlightenment narrative, in which the hero of knowledge works toward a good ethico-political end—universal peace. As can be seen from this example, if a metanarrative implying a philosophy of history is used to legitimate knowledge, questions are raised concerning the validity of the institutions governing the social bond: these must be legitimated as well. Thus justice is consigned to the grand narrative in the same way as truth.
>
> Simplifying to the extreme, I define *postmodern* as incredulity toward metanarratives. (xxiii–xxiv)

To use Lyotard's terms, I see *modern* readers as appealing to some grand design, some "great chain of being," Platonic Ideal, or transcendental signified; to Truth, to Presence, to Being. *Post-modern* readers, on the contrary, will be skeptical of all such teleological and evolutionary schemes; they believe that signification is circumscribed by the tricks and games the "prison-house" of language inexorably plays on its prisoners. The *post-modern* reader is the heir to Nietzsche, Marx, and Freud: "a triumvirate," writes de Man (*Allegories* 82), whose "work participates in the radical rejection of the genetic teleology associated with Romantic idealism."

Modern Reader

Two basic presuppositions distinguish my *modern* reader: the reification of the individual subject and the reification of the art-object created by that subject.

In a Modern world-view, the psychic autonomy of the creative artist remains paramount. The perceiving subject, the subjective ego, is considered to be an individual genius who has the capacity to transcend all dichotomies, to resolve all contradictions into a totality—Truth itself.[3] Modern artists—and readers—give their assent to the notion "that, deep down beneath all the texts, there is something which is not just one more text but that to which various texts are trying to be 'adequate.'" These are Rorty's words (*Consequences* xxxvii), although his context is different, and they bring into sharp focus the idealistic philosophical orientation of the Modern mind.

Such idealism also manifests itself in the methods *modern* readers employ to analyze a poem. A *modern* reader will search for ways in which all of a poem's elements cohere. For example, sounds will enforce theme; parts of speech will have been selected to focus thought; in the imagery there will be a pattern; all ambiguities (following Empson) will be ingeniously resolvable. Such coherence is discovered because *modern* readers conceive of the poem as a "well-wrought urn" (Brooks 17), a self-contained, autotelic, coherent artifact, whose value remains intrinsic.[4]

The *modern* reader believes that a poem's enigmas and paradoxes finally cohere in tense vitality. In fact, the notion that a work of art is complete in itself, an "organic whole," is so fundamental to a Modern point of view that it may be termed *the* "Modern" aesthetic ideal. Iser (*Act* 15) certainly implies this, when he writes: "in New Criticism . . . the value of the work is measured by the harmony of its elements; in modern terms this means that the more disparate those elements are at first, and the harder they are to relate to one another, the greater will be the aesthetic value of the work when, at the end, all its parts are joined together in a harmonious whole."

Various schools of criticism—Anglo and American, Russian, Czech, Spanish, French—have developed and refined these ideals, and they have provided the *modern* reader with an extensive repertoire for representing poems as holistic experiences.

T. S. Eliot's contribution to the self-sufficiency of the work of art was highly influential. In his essays "Tradition and the Individual Talent" and "The Metaphysical Poets," he suggested that poets separate their private pain and suffering from their public creations; indeed, he argued that poets erase themselves, their personalities, in creating the independent object which is the poem. The poet, Eliot claimed, fuses thought and sensation in the poem. The implication is that in this process both poets and their creations are made whole; "a self-translation which is a self-revelation," as Coke-Enguídanos (85) remarked on Jiménez's *Obra*.

In practical terms, in his essay "Hamlet," Eliot saw poets as searching out, from among their experience and the reality that surrounds them, images and symbols which can adequately embody their thoughts and feelings. He wrote (*Essays* 145) of "finding . . . a set of objects, a situation, a chain of events which shall be the formula of [a] *particular* emotion." He called this concept the "objective correlative"—a technique *modern* readers frequently find satisfactory in order to explain ways in which poems cohere.[5]

From the Russian and Czech formalists, *modern* readers acquired the concept of *ostranenie* ("making strange," "defamiliarization"). As presented by Shklovsky, in his essay "Art as Technique" (Lemon and Reiss, esp. 12, 22), habit (or "habitualization") kills a reader's sensations, feelings, perceptions. By making objects "unfamiliar," by de-automatizing a reader's perceptions, art recovers their life, gives them sensation, makes readers feel them. Tolstoy achieves this, for example, by having a horse as the narrator of one of his stories.[6]

Roman Jakobson's work proved particularly seminal in encouraging readers to be more linguistically rigorous in their *modern* reading strategy. In conjunction with the French anthropologist Claude Lévi-Strauss, Jakobson provided, for example, what has become a model for a detailed reading of ways in which sound and meaning, pattern and structure dovetail in a poem (Baudelaire's "Les chats"). In addition, Jakobson's description of the "poetic function" ("Linguistics" 358) was also fundamental: "The poetic function projects the principle of equivalence from the axis of selection into the axis of combination." Jakobson thereby postulated a vertical axis (of selection) and a horizontal axis (of combination); the former will generate metonymic, and the latter metaphoric signification. The notions of paradigmatic equivalences and syntagmatic combinations, which devolve from Jakobson's ideas, help explain a text's unique coherence.

The Spanish critics, for the present reader in particular, have also made specific contributions to *modern* reading strategies. For instance, Dámaso Alonso argued (*Poesía* 31–32) that whereas in ordinary language the relationship between the sign and its signified ("significante-significado," "signifiant-signifié") may, as Saussure insisted, be arbitrary, in the signs of a poetic text, however, the links between the signifiers and the signified are never "arbitrary" but always "motivated." The artificer, that is, ingeniously ties up signs and messages in the text; nothing is left to ambiguity and doubt.

Further research on poeticity by Alonso, and by another critic, Carlos Bousoño, has proved helpful in explaining a poem's coherence. Their studies reveal (*Seis calas* 47–71) how parallel repetition of words and phrases in a poem contributes to the concision of its message. Additional studies develop the notion of "correlation," which Bousoño applied to Juan Ramón (in Albornoz, *Jiménez* Escritor 299–306). Correlation reveals how, for example, similar syntactic elements (e.g. a noun) in like positions in consecutive lines or verses become features that condense meaning and theme. Parallelism and correlation, that is, both contribute to the density of the Modern text. Bousoño has extended this (*Teoría* 303–36) by demonstrating how a diversity of spatial locations and temporal moments can be fused together ("spatio-temporal superpositioning"), condensed into a single image in the Modern poem. This is another valuable element in accounting for ways poems foreground their messages and cohere.

Ricardo Gullón, in his work on modern poetry, has also stressed how poetic texts condense meaning. For Jiménez, Gullón's concern was polysemy (*Estudios* 161–73); he studies "símbolos múltiples" to reveal, for example, the polyvalence such symbols as "castillo" and "caja" can acquire in Jiménez's poems.[7] Claudio Guillén is another influential Spanish critic. In particular, his distinction (*Literature* 59–61) between "tradition" and "convention" helps explain the innovations of modernity. "Tradition," he writes, represents "authority and continuity"; "convention," on the other hand, is "the common air writers breathe."

The contribution of the French, which is extensive, was best refocused by Culler, whose account of French readings of poetry in *Structuralist Poetics* (161–88) was fundamental in the development of the *modern* reader. It sharply refocused basic rhetorical figures—metaphor, metonymy, and synecdoche—all of which are absolutely indispensable in explaining the concision of a Modern text.[8]

Culler also focused on the relationship between linguistics and literature (e.g. deixis). Indeed, the linguists' contribution to *modern* critical theories is profound. Chomsky's distinction between "surface" and "deep" structures is an important facet of *modern* mentalism, for it implies that beneath all surfaces there lie certain basic, kernel or deep, structures that regulate meaning. This lends support to the notion, or faith, that beyond all signs there is a stable signified.

Linguistic research (e.g. Benveniste's)[9] undoubtedly affected the way *modern* readers view texts. Recently, Traugott and Pratt cogently presented a practical account of this research, aimed at demonstrating how linguistics can illuminate poeticity. They describe nouns ($+/-$ concrete), verbs ($+/-$ action), speech-acts, and deictic features in full, clear, and cogent terms, and they offer models of how concise and condensed a Modern text can be.[10]

It should be apparent from the above discussion that the *modern* reader sees the poem as an artifact (a "well-wrought urn"), and Modern poets as geniuses skilled in selecting and combining *les mots justes* to express their truth, their beauty, and their selves. Modern poets are "artificers" who deliberately foreground their craftsmanship by constant rejection and selection of words, by ceaseless re-writing of the text, which Jiménez called "reviviendo."[11]

Accordingly, *modern* reading will attempt to elucidate the ingenious ways in which Modern artificers select the most apposite word and phrase to express their personalities and thoughts.

Post-modern Reader

Against this idealism (of artifact and artificer) post-structuralism has rebelled. In general, the *post-modern* reader is more inspired by semiotics, deconstruction, and psychoanalysis. For poetry, Culler (*Pursuit*), Riffaterre (*Semiotics*), and Scholes (37–56) have pioneered the field. For deconstruction, de Man and Hillis Miller are the models. For psychoanalysis, Lacan and Freud are the inspiration. There is also an indispensable anthology by Harari, which demonstrates how poststructural discourses have been appropriated by literary critics.

If Eliot fashioned the modern literary mind, it seems in retrospect that Barthes fashioned the post-modern. His studies were seminal, because they foregrounded two basic attitudes of the *post-modern* reader, both of which are utterly antithetical to a *modern* reader's world-view. These are that no "work" is complete unto itself; and that the "author" as human person—an originating, subjective consciousness—is a fallacy. Both these assertions systematically undermine the *modern* reader's faith in artifact and artificer.

Barthes expounded these ideas in such essays as "From Work to Text" (*Image* 155–64, and in Harari 73–81) and "The Death of the

Author" (*Image* 142–48), as well as in *S/Z*, a brilliantly exhaustive study of ways in which literature combines various systems of codes.

Barthes argued that a "work" has a specific author, that it contains a finite number of codes, and that it is destined for a specific audience. The "text," on the other hand, has a plurality of meanings and depends for its reception on an infinite set of "relations" between "writer, reader and observer (critic)" (*Image* 156). The "work" will give an objective type of "pleasure" (*plaisir*), whereas a "text" will provide a subjective "thrill" (*jouissance*), because it lends itself to being repossessed or rewritten by the reader/critic (see Heath, in *Image* 9).

A basic contrast, therefore, between *modern* and *post-modern* strategies is that whereas *modern* readers reduce a poem to its formal structures, which they treat as manifestations of a poet's psyche, the *post-modern* would situate a text within a plurality of semiotic systems, all of which are so impersonal and multifarious that no individual consciousness can be said to originate them. The *post-modern* reader would transform the artifact into a network of intersecting signs and experiences. Barthes describes this as a "multi-dimensional space in which a variety of writings, none of them original, blend and clash" (*Image* 146). In addition, in *post-modern* reading the artificer is displaced by language. Barthes asserts: "Linguistically, the author is never more than the instance writing" (*Image* 145). Barbara Johnson's phrasing is dramatic (*Critical* 58): "The poem is not generated naturally by the poet's subjective intentionality; it is, on the contrary, from the poet's mouth untimely ripped." All of which stems from Mallarmé, who remarked: "it is language which speaks" (*Image* 143).

In addition to dismantling Modernism's two sacred cows (artifact and artificer), such concepts substantiate Lyotard's belief that the post-modern mind makes no "explicit appeal to some grand narrative, such as . . . the hermeneutics of meaning" (xxiii). Post-modernity finds indeterminacies, focuses on that which is alogical and acoherent; it de-centers, or desacralizes, the subject.

The thrust of the post-modern is unlimited free play for the signifier, the total liberation of the text from tradition and authorial domination. Two contemporary discourses help in this liberation: deconstruction and psychoanalysis.

As for deconstruction, Derrida's philosophy is paramount. It has inspired *post-modern* readers to view the text as open, as well as to find their reading thrills in ingeniously unraveling whatever autotelic structure the Modern artifact was reputed to contain. Derrida's concept of *différance* is particularly important. It is a concept which denies priority to what I have called the artificer and the artifact, for in Derridean philosophy, neither can be known in themselves, only in their effects. "The signifier is an articulation in a chain, not an identifiable unit" (Johnson 139). "Nothing . . . is anywhere ever simply present or absent. There are only, everywhere, differences and traces of traces" (Derrida, *Positions* 26).[12]

Derrida's impact on criticism of poetry stems from ways in which his ideas have been domesticated and applied by de Man, Hillis Miller, and Culler. In his essays, which I cite in chapters 4 and 5, Hillis Miller often demonstrates ways in which traditional concepts (aletheia, logos) are subverted in modern poetic practice. But it was Paul de Man who in particular developed a deconstructive literary practice. He insisted on the figurality of all meaning.[13] Metaphor claims to unify, he remarked (*Allegories* 16), but it in fact depends "on the deceptive use of semi-automatic grammatical patterns." De Man's intention was always to illustrate "the priority of *lexis* over *logos*" in any structure (*Allegories* 45), and to demonstrate that language "does not designate the self-presence of a consciousness but the inevitable absence of a reliable referent" (*Allegories* 47). He argued that "narrative" is caught in a double bind. "As long as it treats a theme (the discourse of a subject, the vocation of a writer, the constitution of a consciousness), it will always lead to the confrontation of incompatible meanings between which it is necessary but impossible to decide in terms of truth and error. If one of the readings is declared true, it will always be possible to undo it by means of the other; if it is decreed false, it will always be possible to demonstrate that it states the truth of its aberration" (*Allegories* 76). As Johnson succinctly puts this dilemma: "Simultaneously asserting both the necessity and the undesirability of its own existence, the poem refers to its own referring and not directly to its referent" (63).

Psychoanalysis also plays a fundamental role in post-modern reading strategies. Freud's metapsychological theorizing (ego, id, superego) is basic; his belief that the dream "symbol" is a condensation and displacement of a complex set of neuroses is a continual source of inspiration. The Freudian symbol is "overdetermined," multilayered: it is thereby—in my opinion—better able to explain Modern poetic practice than the traditional literary symbol found in studies of nineteenth- and twentieth-century poetry. In addition, for the *post-modern* reader,

Freud's ideas on parapraxis ("Freudian slip") and his reflections on the "uncanny" are stimulating.[14] The uncanny ("unheimlich"), which I use throughout this study, represents "all that is terrible . . . that arouses dread and creeping horror" (*Collected* 368); it "is frightening precisely because it is *not* known and familiar" (370); it will "always be that in which one does not know where one is" (370). The "uncanny" is linked to "feelings of unpleasantness and repulsion," whereas "aesthetics," writes Freud, are associated "with feelings of a positive nature, with the circumstances and the objects that call them forth" (368–69).

Freud's distinction between positive feelings ("aesthetics") and negative feelings ("uncanny") is what I develop throughout this study. The Modern is positive ("aesthetics"); the pre- and post-Modern are negative ("uncanny").

Lacan's work has also had wide impact on literary studies, because of his eclectic combination of Freud and linguistics, especially Saussure and Jakobson (see Bowie, in Sturrock 123–32). Lacan too insists on the free play of the signifier, on the signifier's cleavage from the signified, and he emphasizes (in the following grapheme) that the signified [s] always slips beneath the signifier [S]:

$$\frac{S}{s}$$

No pure and true signified is attainable, insists Lacan. Lacan also views "the subject as 'merely' empty, mobile, and without a centre" (Sturrock 132). Selfhood (the subject, the ego) has no pure site where it sees itself, realizes itself, knows what it is. Self knows itself only as a lack, as that which it does not and cannot have but which it desires. To this gap, Lacan gives the name "the Other."

Like Barthes and Derrida, Lacan has therefore contributed to the undermining of the notion that individual human beings are in control of their psychic destinies. As Johnson has noted, Lacan rewrites "the Cartesian ego. Instead of 'I think therefore I am', we have: 'I think where I am not, therefore I am where I do not think. . . . I am wherever I am the plaything of my thought; I think of what I am where I do not think to think'" (70).

Lacan's distinction between the "Imaginary" and the "Symbolic" modes of psychic life has also proved fruitful. The Imaginary "is a seeking for identity and resemblance." The Symbolic "is characterized by difference, disjunction, and displacement" (Bowie, in Sturrock 133). The "Imaginary" is a state in which no distinction between subject and object is registered. It is the pre-Oedipal stage, in which a child recognizes no distinction between itself and its mother. The "Symbolic" is post-Oedipal, in which the child learns, to quote Eagleton (167), that "its identity as a subject . . . is constituted by its relations of difference and similarity to the other subjects around it." Whereas the "Imaginary" is plenitude, the "Symbolic," like language, is "an endless process of difference and absence."

The above traces produce a *post-modern* reader who will treat with suspicion any holistic claim a poet makes, who will ferret out a text's unresolvable indeterminacy and ambiguity, and who will draw on any extrinsic factors which seem relevant to a text in hand. This impulse in the *post-modern* reader is committed to the total liberation of the text, to the unlimited free play of the signifier.

The danger in such communication, in the meshing of such reading strategies, is that anything whatsoever could be justified. Against it, Eco's warning (*Role* 9) seems prudent: "You cannot use the text as you want, but only as the text wants you to use it. An open text, however 'open' it be, cannot afford whatever interpretation." This caveat is directed against the impulse in the *post-modern* reader which would grant infinite polysemy to the text.

Indeed, to tame and bridle the unlimited free play toward which psychoanalysis and deconstruction might lead, the *post-modern* reader in me resorted to semiotics, for, when semiotic critics analyze specific literary texts, they gravitate toward the description of stable and generalizable structural patterns. Barthes's codes in *S/Z* have this effect; so do Riffaterre's analyses and Greimas's theories.[15]

The Spanish critic Jenaro Talens (*Elementos* 23) hints at the above notion, that within a text there are self-regulatory systems at work, when he writes: "La lectura de un texto artístico consistiría, pues . . . en producir sentido a partir de una estructura articulada a dominante estética. [Esto] implica que debamos hablar, antes que de polivalencia, de restricción semántica como inherente al signo artístico en cuento tal." I take "semantic restriction" to be "overdetermination," as that phrase is used of "symbol" or image in the psychoanalytic process. I therefore propose that, in this particular instance, my task as a *post-modern* reader is to determine as many layers of the image's semantic field as possible (that is, as are actualized by the "Work" in hand). In specific terms, one of my concerns in the present study became to circumscribe and delimit the semantic field of a group of significant lexemes (nouns such as "sol"). I argue that semantic restriction is achieved as a noun moves through the "Work" in its totality. When the noun occurs in different contexts it acquires different connotations, but those connotations are not infinite, they are found to be restricted by the "Work" in its entirety.

Studies by Greimas and by Riffaterre have helped me to determine certain characteristics of a text's semantic field. Greimas foregrounds such terms as "actant," "lexeme," and "sememe." The term "actant" allows *post-modern* readers to describe the dynamics they detect in a text, and to denote that no individual, subjective ego consciously initiated those actions.[16] Greimas and Courtés (*Analytical Dictionary* 5) write that actant designates "a type of syntactic unit, properly formal in character, which precedes any semantic and/or ideological investment."

Likewise, the term "lexeme" is devoid of ideological presuppositions. Greimas and Courtés (*Analytical Dictionary* 279–80) explain that ". . . our lexeme [is] made up of a set of sememes." For example, the lexeme "table" has the sememe "flat surface with leg(s)," as well as the sememes "water table," "table of contents." In the present study, I have used the term "lexeme" because of its linguistic impersonality, and I have deliberately applied it in contradistinction to the term "symbol," because I believe the concept "symbol" to be a product of a highly subjective aesthetics. In most of nineteenth- and twentieth-century poetry, a symbol designates a fusion of the lower with the higher, the union of the finitude of mankind with the transcendent, eternal, and infinite Spirit beyond. A symbol confirms the belief that a "'correspondence' between the inwardness of the subject and the outside world" is possible. (The words are de Man's on Rilke [*Allegories* 35].) Symbol is, therefore, an idealistic concept; it cannot designate the a-teleological dynamics of a post-modern mind. I let the linguistic, and connotatively neutral, term "lexeme" denote that.

Hence, the terms "actant," "lexeme," "sememe" allow *post-modern* readers to signal impersonality as they describe a text's dynamics. Such objective terms indicate that poeticity is situated within broader sign systems, vaster, that is, than that of a single perceiving subject, or of a unique, originating consciousness.

Riffaterre's analyses of the poetic text are seminal for a *post-modern* reader. There is, in particular, the way his approach forces readers to focus on the "intertext" and on "intertextuality." Especially important is Riffaterre's insistence on the presence of a micro-text—an anomalous intertext, a cliché—which in highly condensed form manifests the macro-text's latent semantic content (*Semiotics* 39–42, 208).

The rigor of Riffaterre's method is admirable, although highly idealistic (based, it seems, on Chomsky's model for transformational grammar). I personally treat the micro-text and "intertext" much more freely than he does: for me, they are allusions within the text to any extrinsic discourse, written or non-written; allusions that is, to literature, philosophy, art, politics, or sociology.[17]

Modern versus Post-modern: Terminology

I have presented my *modern* and *post-modern* readers as two antithetical ideals. The *modern* reifies the subject (artificer) and the subject's property (artifact), both practices being inherent to capitalist society. The *post-modern* reifies the system, and minimalizes person and property, which are purportedly the practices of a communist society. But just as capitalism needs communism to legitimate its ideals (freedom), so Modernism needs post-Modernism in order that its world-view may be re-articulated for today. For poetry, this means that the "enfant terrible" of the *post-modern* reader can, by chipping away at Modernism's parts, give Modernism new life. The *post-modern* reader's role is to liberate and free by undermining the Modern *oeuvre*, otherwise the latter will stagnate, petrify, close itself off, and decay.

Given such sharp contrasts, a reader could employ contrasting terminology when describing Modern poems and post-Modern texts. For example, a *modern* reader can legitimately write and speak of a "poet" who addresses a "poetee."[18] A *modern* reader can say this in good faith because in Modern poems, poets are considered to be people who struggle to express their true, inner selves with their words; they are creative human beings whose goals are to speak with an authentic voice, to forge a harmonious integration of signifier with signified.

Unfortunately, there are really no consensual terms in post-modern discourse which contrast with poet/poetee. Addresser-addressee, sender-receiver, emitter-receptor do occur (inspired by Jakobson's model of communication ["Linguistics" 353, 357]). Such terms are apt because they background subjectivity. However, they are not widely used, perhaps because they are somewhat clumsy and inelegant.

The terms "implied poet" and "implied reader" are, however, frequently used. Iser writes: "The concept of the implied reader is . . . a textual structure anticipating the presence of a recipient without necessarily defining him;" and "the concept of the implied reader designates a network of response-inviting structures, which impel the reader to grasp the text" (34). Hence, "implied" is an epithet intended to objectify the process of communication; it certainly depersonalizes the process. Nevertheless, it retains the notion of a human person lurking somewhere in the wings: this renders it anomalous from a post-modern perspective.

A truly post-modern terminology would have to avoid the personal and the subjective, the individual and the human. To signify a *post-modern* reading strategy, a reader could choose to adapt Barthes (*Image* 145) and write of a "scriptor" that performs (utters performative speech-acts), and of a "scriptee" that engages the scriptor's performance. The implication here would be that scriptor and scriptee are constructs of language; they are "multi-dimensional space[s] in which a variety of writings"—bits of reading, fragments of knowledge and experience, remnants of biographies, autobiographies, criticism, and interpretations—"none of them original, blend and clash." The terms scriptor and scriptee might indicate, therefore, that in post-modern reading communication it is linguistic systems, not authors and readers, not persons and subjects, that meet.

These terms may not be acceptable (as they too are inelegant), but the contrast poet/scriptor, poetee/scriptee, does foreground the clash my *modern* and *post-modern* reading strategies are intended to generate before they can liberate a text.

Specialist Reader

Modern and *post-modern* readers are what critics and criticism over the last fifty years have educated them to be. Indeed, I shall argue that the discourses of criticism *produce* a type of reader.

Riffaterre objected (in Tompkins, *Reader* xiii, 26–40) that the insights attained by the Jakobson-Lévi-Strauss reading of "Les chats" could occur to hardly anyone. I find this not wholly tenable, because with their insights Jakobson and Lévi-Strauss inspire future readers; they "produce" *modern* readers, readers who attempt to deploy linguistic strategies in their analyses of poetic texts. By the same token, de Man and Hillis Miller have provided models for deconstructive readings of texts. Hence, *post-modern* readers can initially pattern a deconstructive *scripting* engagement on their body of work.

However, *specialist* readers, who filter these strategies through their reading practice, are not the product of the discourses of contemporary criticism. *Specialists* bring a traditional academic formation to the reading process.

First, a *specialist* is formed by a direct confrontation with the implied poet's complete work. In the case of a poet, this includes the poems and their variants; it must also encompass the poet's prose works (lectures, commentaries, translations, aphorisms, etc.). Autobiography, iconography, and any other art in which the poet dabbled (e.g. painting) will be included.

Second, a *specialist* is formed by reading the specialized criticism devoted to the poet's work, as well as by studying and reflecting on any literary, historical, and stylistic schools, movements, and writers who may have impinged on that work's genesis.

In the case of Juan Ramón Jiménez, a *specialist* is aware of the work that has been done on the *Obra*'s major themes. Sánchez-Barbudo gave a full account of the death wish. Basilio de Pablos studied time. In her writings, Nemes studies the love instinct. Numerous critics reflect on Jiménez's religious proclivities (Cole, Saz-Orozco, Santos-Escudero, Azam). Jiménez's poetics have received a full historical and critical study by Blasco Pascual.

The poet's standard and authorized biography, a careful balance of his life and his works, has appeared and is being revised (Nemes). There is even what might be termed a psychobiography, which indexes the poetry with the dominant neuroses (Paraíso de Leal).

Additional studies link Jiménez's thought and work to major literary movements: *modernismo* (Cardwell); Symbolism (Coke-Enguídanos, Gicovate); English poets (Young). There are monographs devoted to particular books of poetry: the *Diario* (Predmore); *Espacio* (Font, Albornoz); *Dios Deseado y Deseante* (Sánchez-Barbudo, Sánchez Romeralo). There are sufficient general introductions (e.g. Albornoz, González, Young). Jiménez's formalist-structuralist critics analyze major symbols in conjunction with his dominant concerns (Gullón, Ulibarrí, Olson).

The *specialist* in me assessed the above studies and opted to extend the latter approach to Jiménez's *Obra*. The present study concerns itself with less studied "symbols," and it describes in more detail than previous critical work the complex linguistic, rhetorical, and semantic patterns that occur in the Modern Jiménez poem.

Specialists are obligated to assess prior analyses; they must decide in advance if their contribution can be original. They do this because if they are to survive today, in what was once termed the "groves of academe," *specialists* should neither repeat, rephrase, nor platitudinize (see Culler, "Problems").

As a *specialist*, I believe with Harold Bloom that writers are blind to their real influences, but I have made every effort to recognize indebtedness in the appropriate place: I apologize in advance for my lapses. In general terms, this study swerves away from Paul Olson's *Circle of Paradox*. The latter employed a *modern* reading strategy to foreground Jiménez's Modern poeticity; this study uses both *modern* and *post-modern* reading strategies to foreground the post-modern impulse which occasionally threatens to undermine the Jiménez *Obra*.

Third, *specialists* have internalized their responses to the poet's work; they tend to consider their taste and judgment as "intuitive" rather than scientific. Intuition is not a nebulous concept for the *specialist*; it is a way of referring to the taste, the preferences, and the judgment a *specialist* reader acquires and develops over time. Intuition is a cultivated understanding of fundamental aspects of a poet's work, as well as of the time in which it evolved.

The issue of "norm" and "deviation" is, I think, relevant to this problem. Both Mukarovsky and Lotman suggest ways in which a *specialist* reader's intuition might be formed.

Mukarovsky distinguished between "the norm of the standard language and the traditional esthetic canon" (*Prague* 22). I suspect that for *specialist* readers of poetry the former is less important than the latter. In fact, I suggest that over a period of years *specialists* internalize their implied poet's "esthetic canon;" this eventually comes to constitute for them their poetic "norm" for that poet, with which "intuitively" they remain in touch.

In a diachronic reading of their poet's work, therefore, *specialists* can differentiate between the "traditional esthetic canon" they have internalized and all sudden deviations from it, which they register ("intuitively") as the poetic "Work" evolves.

Lotman's conception of the dynamic literary artifact helps explain this further. Eagleton (103) describes Lotman's theory of the structure of the artistic text as "a complex interplay of the regular and the random, norms and deviations, routinized patterns and dramatic defamiliarizations." Eagleton then shifts his focus from the artifact to the reader's perception of the text. He adds: "Lotman has learned the lessons of reception theory well. It is the reader who by virtue of certain 'receptive codes' at his or her disposal identifies an element in the work as a 'device'; the device is not simply an internal feature but one perceived through a particular code and against a definite textual background." I believe that this could amount to a technical description of the notion of "intuition," in so far as it describes the type of dynamics that exists between *specialist* readers and their poet's work. The intuition of a *specialist* is constituted by a complex set of internalized receptive codes, which are formed only by long and deep familiarity with a poet's work and epoch. *Specialist* readers have cultivated and developed these, and they deploy them automatically as part of their reading strategy.

Fourth, the *specialist* in the present study assesses the insights toward which his *modern* and *post-modern* readings impel him. If the *modern* is the ego, and the *post-modern* the id, then the *specialist* is the super-ego of this reading triad. In this triadic interplay, *specialists* must govern the insights achieved by "[ses] semblable[s]—[ses] frère[s]!" (Eliot, *Poems* 65)—the *modern* and *post-modern* readers within. This is to say that the *specialist* will govern and/or censor certain inappropriate *modern* and *post-modern* readings.

My triad of *modern*, *post-modern*, and *specialist* readers amounts to a formalization of a reading "competence." It is a way to delimit the "horizon of expectations" brought to the texts analyzed in this study. To use Culler's terms (*Pursuit* 5), this study, in its application of three reading strategies, makes an attempt "to advance [an] understanding of the conventions of . . . a mode of discourse." But, this *specialist* reader, in addition, will be advancing his own interpretation of the meaning and significance of the Jiménez *Obra*.[19]

That there is a reciprocity between texts and readers, that they create each other as they create (*script*) themselves, is surely apparent from the foregoing discussion. Readers emerge to satisfy interpretative demands of a text; they receive their insights from diverse linguistic, philosophical, and critical discourses. In so doing they "open" texts.

By playing these three reading strategies against each other, I offer new perceptions of the poet and his work and open up texts for future discussion. I hope that the texts included in this book will undergo further liberation by future readers who must emerge in due time from their particular critical discourses.

The *Obra*

Three Phases: Three Impulses

Sánchez Romeralo (*Poesías* 10–37) has described three phases ("tiempos") within the Jiménez *Obra*. For me, these three phases represent three aesthetic impulses, which I have called pre-Modern, Modern, and post-Modern. Each phase is dominated by a particular persona: the first pertains to that of a pre-Modern poet (or late-romantic, *modernista-simbolista*); the second is the domain of a Modern poet and "artificer"; the third reflects the indeterminacies of a post-modern mind.

Chronology is an important factor in periodization. Sánchez Romeralo's dates for these three phases are 1895–1913, 1914–30, 1931–56. In general I concur with this. I too find that Jiménez's pre-Modern impulse lasts until the end of 1912 (when Juan Ramón left Moguer for Madrid). His Modern impulse, that is the middle phase of his "Work," begins to emerge around 1914, but for me it reaches a peak in 1936 with the publication of *Canciones*. As the latter is an anthology containing much poetry that had already been written by 1930, I am again in general agreement with Sánchez Romeralo. However, for me, this middle phase, the Modern impulse, persists until the *Obra* ends. In addition, I detect a post-modern impulse in the late phase of the "Work," which I would date from 1936 to 1956. The post-Modern is articulated in a limited number of texts written after 1936, when the Jiménez exiled themselves from Spain to North America and the Caribbean ("el otro costado"); it peaks in 1954 with *Espacio*'s "Fragmento Tercero," and culminates with *Leyenda* in 1956.

Hence, though my "chronology" coincides with that of other critics for the first period of Jiménez's *Obra*, it is more *impulsive* for the second and third periods of his "Work." For me, the middle phase runs from 1913 to 1936; the late phase from 1936 to 1956.

Pre-Modern

Jiménez's early period began in 1900 with the publication of the *modernista* books, *Ninfeas* and *Almas de violeta*. Between then and 1913 Jiménez wrote and published an immense corpus of work: *Rimas*, *Arias tristes*, *Jardines lejanos*, *Elegías*, *Olvidanzas*, *Baladas de primavera*, *La soledad sonora*, *Pastorales*, *Poemas mágicos y dolientes*, *Melancolía*, *Laberinto*, to which must be added many more poems now published in the two volumes of *Libros inéditos de poesía*.

The poet resided principally in Moguer during these years. Nevertheless, in 1901 he spent a few months in a sanatorium in Bordeaux, from whence he moved to Madrid, living there until early 1905 under the watchful eye of his physician. From 1905 until 29 December 1912, Juan Ramón resided in Moguer.

The poems of these years are melancholy, nostalgic, world-weary. The work of this pre-Modern aesthete reflects a decadent personality, a languid "Mr. Hyde," whose prime concern is to remain withdrawn from the world and its contradictions, who prefers to concentrate on refining his emotions, his sensibility, and his impressions. This persona's dominant thought is that perfection can never be attained in present time and space.

Modern and High Modern

The middle phase of the *Obra*, which begins after 1912 and which culminates around 1936, is heralded with *Estío* (1916), an innovative collection, which was quickly followed in 1917 by *Diario de un poeta reciéncasado* and *Sonetos espirituales*. The latter were immediately followed by two important and often anthologized collections: *Eternidades* (1918) and *Piedra y cielo* (1919). After a lapse of four years, in 1923, selections from poetry written between 1918 and 1923 were published as *Poesía* (*en verso*) and *Belleza* (*en verso*). The second or middle phase of the *Obra* crystallizes and peaks with *Canciones* (1936).

It is in these years, 1916 to 1936, that what I call Jiménez's Modern voice, the "Dr. Jekyll" persona, reaches its maturity. During these years the poet is writing from the belief that his self is fully integrated; he has total faith in his ideals; he believes utterly in his goals and is supremely confident in his deployment of the language. This mastery expresses itself in symbols of perfection and unity: fountain, rose, circle, horizon (all studied by Olson), as well as tree, bird, and naked woman. "Dr.

Jekyll," the poetic persona of this stage, clearly believes that perfection and beauty are achieved in present time and space.

For me, this is the voice of a "solar" aesthete, and I will argue later that artifact and artificer are the dominant preoccupations of these years. In addition, the poet's basic concerns, the *Obra*'s "narrative topics"—love, work, death ("la mujer, la obra, la muerte" [*LP* 1343–44])—are manifest only in their most idealistic light during this, the Modern phase of the "Work."

In so far as I bracket or foreground this middle phase in the *Obra*, I differ from other readers of Jiménez's "Work." For me, the poetry from *Estío* to *Canciones*, 1914 to 1936, is prototypically Modern, in the European sense of this word—with connotations of beauty that is distinct and monumentality that is timeless.

Modern artificers foreground their craftsmanship. From Jiménez's perspective, the impulse of a Modern artificer is toward: "lo ardiente, lo claro, lo áureo, / lo definido, lo neto!" (*LP* 193); ". . . emoción y . . . gracia . . . fresca y fragante!" (*LP* 697). The Modern text is distinguished by its aura of perfection achieved, by its faith in idealism, by the taut control it retains on the intensity of its feeling. The impulse of the Modern poet and artificer is symbolized in the following stanza, with which *Canciones* concludes: "La mano con la luz / sobre el alma con forma. / Melodía del tacto, eternidad redonda" (*LP* 1228). This stanza recalls Yeats's definition of Modernism, given in the introduction to *The Oxford Book of Modern Verse*, cited by Perloff (156): "that 'form must be full, sphere-like, single', and that the poet's task is to get 'all the wine into the bowl.'"

These metaphors, one by a Spanish and the other by an Anglo-Irish High Modern, perfectly capture the Modern poet's preoccupation with the poem as a beautiful artifact that ingeniously contains the human spirit.

Jiménez's pure Modernity runs concurrently with the years of High Modernism in Western life and letters. The years from approximately 1910 to 1940 were different from prior and subsequent years for diverse reasons. In 1910, Halley's Comet was sighted, and Virginia Woolf is reputed (Howe 15) to have said: "On or about December 1910 human nature changed." Whether attributable to the comet or not, the fact remains that many signs of difference appeared over the next few years.

Manifestations of social and political change abounded. In Britain,

1912 was the year of the General Strike, and the suffragettes intensified their activity. In America, F. W. Woolworth founded his chain of stores, and Henry Ford initiated his assembly-line production of the automobile.

In science, Rutherford discovered the atomic nucleus (1911), and Niels Bohr first offered his theory of atomic structure (1913). Between 1912 and 1913, Freud moved beyond analysis of dreams and began demonstrating that his theories had a broader application (to art, morality, religion). Between 1911 and 1915, Frazer was compiling his eleven-volume *magnum opus*, *The Golden Bough*. In these years Saussure was dictating lectures that would become the *Course in General Linguistics* (1916). Bergson's theories also gained wider acceptance at this time, and Ortega was imbibing phenomenology in Germany. (Husserl's *Phenomenology* appeared in 1913.)

Nijinsky danced during these years (until 1917). In music, Elgar's violin concerto was first heard, in November 1910—it mourns the loss of an age. (Edward VII died in 1910.) Schönberg's atonal scores were heard, as were Berg's, and the first performances of Stravinsky's ballets "The Firebird" (1910), "Petroushka" (1911), and "Le sacre du printemps" (1913) were given. In art, the first Cubist canvases were seen, and Kandinsky originated his "nonobjective" style (1910). Apollinaire's *The Cubist Painters* appeared in 1913. Frank Lloyd Wright's fame extended throughout Europe, as did Charlie Chaplin's, whose first movies were made in 1913.

In literature, in 1911, Enrique González Martínez urged that the neck of the *modernista* swan be wrung. In France, Proust finished the first draft of *A la recherche du temps perdu*; Valéry recommended writing poetry and was at work on *La jeune parque*. In Russia between 1910 and 1913 the Symbolist school waned and Acmeism started up. In England, Eliot finished "Prufrock"; Yeats published *Responsibilities* (1914), signaling his entry into modernity. In Spain, *Campos de Castilla* (1912) was followed by *El sentimiento trágico de la vida* (1913), and by *Meditaciones del Quijote* (1914).

All these signs of change in various fields after 1910 initiated a period of High Modernism, which lasted until the 1930s.[20]

It is my opinion, therefore, that Jiménez's High-Modern impulse manifests itself during the years of High Modernism in Western culture. Jiménez's impulse begins to diminish around the end of the

1930s, which means that it is in control of the *Obra* for approximately twenty years: 1916–36. Hence, as Juan Ramón wrote from the 1890s to the 1950s, his truly Modern impulse is the dominant style for a little more than one-third of his creative life. After 1936, it begins to merge with what I have called a post-Modern style and mind (which runs concurrently with Modernism until the "Work" ends, circa 1956).

Post-Modern

Though the aesthetic idealism of the second phase of the *Obra* persists until the very end of the "Work," a less idealistic tone is present in certain texts written after 1936. I call this Jiménez's post-Modern voice, because—as I will demonstrate later—it calls into question the ideals of his Modern period. The texts I have in mind reflect the indeterminacies of a post-modern mind. They are found in *La estación total, Espacio, Animal de fondo,* and *Leyenda.*

This late impulse in the *Obra* is not clearly recognized by Jiménez's readers; when it is mentioned, it tends to be read as if the ideals of his Modern period persisted exclusively until the end. Briefly, in his third phase the poet first attempts to blend his lunar with his solar aesthetics; however, the bleaker, more pessimistic voice of the poet's "Mr. Hyde" finally has the last word.[21] In the context of the entire *Obra,* therefore, I see the Modern Jiménez—the "Dr. Jekyll," the magisterial optimist in style and mind—as one of the poet's three masks. The 'darker' shadows (pre- and post-Modern "Mr. Hydes") are the other two.

Jiménez as Jekyll and Hyde

To most of his "immense minority" of devotees, Juan Ramón Jiménez is a modern day seer whose consummate mastery of the Spanish poetic word remains unrivaled. For example, Sánchez-Barbudo's studies, which undeniably recognize Jiménez's struggle with the negative power of death, have as their primary focus the *Obra*'s supreme achievements (spiritual, aesthetic). Nemes's perspective is the poet's struggle against *modernista* excesses in order to achieve and maintain the resplendency of "la poesía desnuda" (which is a human, a divine, and an aesthetic love). Gullón's *Estudios* foreground spiritual, temporal, and aesthetic fulfillment, all of which are present in the "Work." Olson's frame of reference (*Circle*) is the poet's major symbols, which he shows to be resolutions of paradoxical states (of time and essence, being and nothingness). Young's argument (*Line*) is that in the 1950s Jiménez brought to a conclusion the tradition of the poet as visionary humanist which Blake initiated at the dawn of the nineteenth century. Coke-Enguídanos reads Jiménez as perfecting the ideals of the major French Symbolist poets, while Azam and others view the *Obra* as a major achievement for religious and spiritual instincts in the twentieth century.

Azam's study concludes with such phrases as "esa luz conquistada, esa plenitud, esa unidad" (638). Indeed, I find that critical studies of Jiménez's work dwell on the "light achieved"; that is, they either ignore or gloss over the darkness which had to be overcome in order to achieve that light. Such studies focus on what I see as Juan Ramón's "Dr. Jekyll" persona: the poet of light, assurance, eternity, beauty; the poet as seer, the consummate master who redeems the human soul through his art. But this is only one facet of Jiménez's poetic personae. This, his Dr. Jekyll personality, is what I see as his "High-Modern" poetic mask. It was monumentalized by the *Segunda antolojía poética*, first published in 1922, for which Jiménez made a selection from all of the poetry he had written between 1898 and 1918. This anthology was—and still is—widely divulged, and it was not superseded until 1957, just before the poet's death, when the *Tercera antolojía* was published. Thus it alone was responsible for creating and sustaining the image readers have of Jiménez as a poet.

For the *Segunda antolojía*, a *self*-anthology, poems for an implied first period (1900–1913) were specifically written (or rewritten, or "relived," or "recreated") between 1918 and 1920. In these poems, the "Modern" Jiménez chose to imply that he had received some celestial "Anunciación" (SA 31) for his poetic mission—"Anunciación" being the title he gave to the first selection of poetry in the *Segunda antolojía*. Such a divine mission, that of the modern day poetic seer, is undoubtedly a fundamental aspect of Jiménez's *Obra*. Indeed, the "Notas" that were appended to the *Segunda antolojía* stress the purity of the verse, its concern for eternal beauty, the poet's fastidious taste, as well as his desire to distill the essence from a moment. It is these— eminently "High-Modern"—ideals that subsequently passed into histories of literature and have been accepted by readers and critics alike.

I am in no way denying that such ideals are the mainstay of the *Obra*. I recognize, with Coke-Enguídanos, that Jiménez is the poet who appeals first to intelligence, in "¡Intelijencia, dame / el nombre exacto de las cosas!" (*Eternidades LP* 553), in order that his spirit ("mi alma") might discover *the* word that deciphers reality ("las cosas") once and for all and for all humankind. As Coke-Enguídanos concludes, in her analysis of this poem: "The liturgical repetition of 'Qué por mí vayan todos' suggests that having gained perfect mastery of reality through the Word, [the poet] will now be the instrument of universal salvation, offering the path to omniscience to all who would listen" (52). My one reservation with this judgment will be that it is only in the middle period of the *Obra* when such idealism is unequivocally embraced.

In addition, I recognize that Jiménez is also the poet who affirmed that once the artist creates nouns ("Creemos los nombres"), humanity ("los hombres"), reality ("las cosas"), and sentiment ("amor") are brought into existence. As man, life, and love are subsequent and subsidiary to the noun, the artist asserts his faith in the everlasting power of the latter:

> Del amor y las rosas,
> no ha de quedar sino los nombres.
> ¡Creemos los nombres!

Despite such a forceful affirmation of aesthetic idealism, the *post-modern* reader in me is intrigued by the fact that the poem itself appears only in the *antolojías* of the *Obra* (*SA* 128–29, *TA* 254). I see "Creemos los nombres," therefore, as an addendum, an afterthought: as an a posteriori attempt to crystallize, for the *antolojías*, the "Dr. Jekyll" persona. In the course of this study I shall be discussing additional tinkerings with the *Obra* (introjections, elisions, suppressions), which the "Dr. Jekyll" in Juan Ramón unceasingly performed, as well as studying poetry in which such idealistic faith is not the dominant norm.

As I earlier asserted, Juan Ramón's "Dr. Jekyll," Modern persona— the poet as seer, as redeemer of the human soul through his art—is purely articulated only in the second phase of the "Work." The poems this seer crafted are brilliant gems, "Vino, primero, pura" (*LP* 555) being a perfect example. "Vino, primero, pura / vestida de inocencia" is a prototypically Modern poem: it is an "organic whole;" it coheres; it is masterfully crafted; it is sufficient in itself. Also, as a text it implies that poets do in fact bring all to perfection; it subtends the myth of narrative closure, that happy endings are attained. This poem is a "well-wrought urn," and as such deserves a place on the mantelpiece of any self-respecting reader of twentieth-century Western poetry.

In the present study, I shall not be analyzing poems that are totally self-sufficient urns or gems. My reason is, quite simply, that I have found that this aspect of Jiménez's *Obra* has already received sufficient attention. I have selected Modern texts in which I detect indeterminacy, in which I find the Modern artist struggling with the "uncanny" power of negativity.

These are texts that represent different aspects of Juan Ramón Jiménez's "Mr. Hyde" persona: at times mournful, insecure, and nostalgic; at times doubtful of all his "Dr. Jekyll" achieved.

I now wish to demonstrate that the darkness of "Mr. Hyde" is present throughout the first or early, the pre-Modern phase of the "Work," despite the fact that the standard revised *antolojías* of the *Obra* succeed in either erasing or suppressing it. This dark persona is hardly manifest at all in the second or middle, the Modern phase of the *Obra*, when "Mr. Hyde" is suppressed, or makes only very brief appearances to express irony or doubt. However, a darker aspect of "Mr. Hyde" begins to reappear after 1936, "en el otro costado," and flourishes intermittently with the Modern persona from then until the poet's final years.

By comparing and contrasting these personae, my intention is to show Jiménez to be a poet whose vision is broader than the one traditionally attributed to him by students and critics. I also hope that my analyses of the texts provide additional evidence for the importance of the Jiménez *Obra* as a major High-Modern text.

Pre-Modern:
Lunar Aestheticism

2

A Beggarly Self:
"¿Soy yo . . . o soy el mendigo?"

By 1904 Juan Ramón Jiménez had published five important books of poetry: *Almas de violeta* and *Ninfeas* (1900), *Rimas* (1902), *Arias tristes* (1903), and *Jardines lejanos* (1904). These books established him as the master of an authentic voice within the *modernista-simbolista* tradition of Hispanic poetry.

Within the context of these early books however, the poem "¿Soy yo quien anda esta noche?" strikes the reader as being somewhat anomalous—a reaction Albornoz, I believe, wished to provoke by choosing to begin her *Nueva antolojía* of Juan Ramón's poetry with this poem.[1]

"¿Soy yo . . . ?," which appeared in *Jardines lejanos*, is the first text in the *Obra* in which Jiménez is confronted with the problematics of selfhood. As a poem, it has the mood of minor symbolist verse, notably Verlaine's *Fêtes galantes* which inspired the book to which it belongs, and it has the structure of much of Jiménez's early poetry. However, its philosphical implications mark it as *different*: "es lo mismo y no es lo mismo," as one of the lines from the poem itself sums up the experience that enthralls the speaker.

"¿Soy yo . . . ?" is a poem that has never ceased to intrigue Jiménez's readers, but its mysterious charm, its anomalous and innovative appeal, have remained veiled. In short, it needs a detailed analysis. Accordingly, in this chapter I will structurally describe the text and convey the unresolvable paradoxes it confronts. The reading presents two principal actants, one 'bright' ("Dr. Jekyll") and the other 'dark' ("Mr. Hyde"), in a dramatic struggle to define themselves in relation to a subsidiary actant (a beggar). Analysis of the function of these actants within the rest of the *Obra* can lead, I argue, to a reappraisal of Jiménez's work.

Here is one version of the poem:

I   1   Soy yo quien anda esta noche,
     2 por mi cuarto, o el mendigo
     3 que rondaba mi jardín,
     4 al caer la tarde?... Miro

II   5 en torno y hallo que todo
     6 es lo mismo y no es lo mismo...
     7 La ventana estaba abierta?
     8 Yo no me había dormido?

III 9   El jardín no estaba blanco
    10 de luna?... El cielo era limpio
    11 y azul... Y hay nubes y viento
    12 y el jardín está sombrío...

IV 13 Creo que mi barba era
    14 negra... Yo estaba vestido
    15 de gris... Y mi barba es blanca
    16 y estoy enlutado... ¿Es mío

V   17 este andar? Tiene esta voz
    18 que ahora suena en mí los ritmos
    19 de la voz que yo tenía?
    20   Soy yo, o soy el mendigo

VI 21 que rondaba mi jardín
    22 al caer la tarde?... Miro
    23 en torno... Hay nubes y viento...
    24 El jardín está sombrío...

VII 25   ...Y voy y vengo... Es que yo
    26 no me había ya dormido?
    27 Mi barba está blanca... Y todo
    28 es lo mismo y no es lo mismo...[2]

I   1   Is it I who walks this night,
    2 around my room, or the beggar

     3   who was prowling round my garden,
     4   as evening fell?... I look

II   5   around and find that all
     6   is the same and is not the same...
     7   Was the window open?
     8   Had I fallen asleep?

III   9   The garden wasn't white
    10 with moonlight?... The sky was clear
    11 and blue... And there are clouds and wind
    12 and the garden is dark...

IV 13 I think my beard was
    14 black... I was dressed
    15 in grey... And my beard is white
    16 and I'm in mourning... Is it mine

V   17 this gait? Has this voice
    18 that now resounds in me the rhythms
    19 of the voice I had?
    20   Am I myself, or am I the beggar

VI 21 who was prowling round my garden
    22 as evening fell?... I look
    23 around... There are clouds and wind...
    24 The garden is dark...

VII 25   ...And I go and come... But
    26 hadn't I fallen asleep?
    27 My beard is white... And all
    28 is the same and is not the same...

Conventional Story versus Innovative Plot

There is much that is conventional in the poem, and one source of its appeal must lie in its old-fashioned but enigmatic story line, a brief account of which will show immediately that the question posed in stanza 1 remains rhetorical.

The speaker, a "Dr. Jekyll," walks round his room at night as he reflects on "el mendigo" whom he had seen prowling round "*mi* jardín" as evening fell (ll. 1−4). The speaker looks around (ll. 4−6), but what he *now* finds (ll. 7−10) is very different from what he previously beheld (ll. 10−11): *then* there was a clear blue sky, but *now* the sky is filled with dark clouds (ll. 11−12) and white moonlight suffuses "*el jardín*" (ll. 9−10).

The different landscape makes the speaker aware of changes in himself: *then*, when he first saw the beggar, he *was* "Dr. Jekyll" with a black beard (ll. 13−14) and a grey suit (ll. 14−15); but *now* he finds he is "Mr. Hyde" with a white beard (l. 15) and a black suit (l. 16). *Now* he also finds that his present gait (l. 17) and voice (ll. 17−19) are different from those he had *then*, when he first saw the beggar. In the remainder of the poem (ll. 20−28) the speaker wonders whether he is himself, or if he has become the beggar. He reflects on his questions, and he doubts his own observations. His ruminations reduce him to a peripatetic condition of "...Y voy y vengo..." (l. 25), a state somewhere between sleeping and waking (ll. 25−26), which he does not comprehend.

Modern readers are immediately intrigued by past and present time modalities, and by the spatial contrasts the poem contains. They will want to know how these paradoxes are resolved, and they will want in their reading to specify what techniques are actualized to effect that resolution. *Post-modern* readers are captivated by the text's uncertainty, its lack of harmonious balance. They will expect no resolution; they will want in their reading to explain indeterminacy as part of the text's mysterious fascination.

Structure: Tradition versus Innovation

A poem of seven quatrains, with eight syllables per line and *asonancia* in /i—o/, a *romance* (ballad), is traditional enough. However, its frequent and deliberate use of *encabalgamiento* (enjambment) and *puntos suspensivos* (aposiopesis) render its structure unconventional and innovative. Weak or strong *enjambment* is in fact used in all except six lines (6+28, 7, 8+26, 19). Aposiopesis ("...") occurs 18 times in the seven stanzas (1-1-3-3-1-4-5); fully half (i.e. 9) occur in the last two stanzas. Such features of the poem's prosodic structure need to be explained in any satisfactory interpretation.

The rhythm is regular and conventional. All lines contain a rhythmic nucleus ($\cup\cup\prime\cup$) conjoined with two smaller units, which are either iambic ($\cup \prime$) or trochaic ($\prime \cup$).[3] The rhythm is uniformly smooth and rolling, even tending toward the monotonous. Line 17 breaks this uniform monotony by juxtaposing two primary stresses ($\cup \cup \prime \prime \cup \cup \prime$). By deviating from the rhythmic norm, line 17 foregrounds its content. This too requires interpretation.

Phonemic analysis encounters 280 consonants, 256 of which are smooth, quiet, mid and front sounds: /b m t d r l s n/. The latter constitute the poem's phonemic norm, from which the back sounds, (velars /k g x/), deviate. Of the 24 velars, 8.5 percent of the poem's consonants, one third are relative pronouns ("quien," "que"). A further third occur in words that are repeated twice (their frequency of occurrence is given in parentheses): "caer"(2×), "mendigo"(2×), "jardín"(5×). Most of the remaining velars occur in colors: "blanca"(2×), "negra," "gris". The association of colors with "mendigo," "jardín," and "caer" is another feature that requires interpretation.

As for the vowels: there are fewer far back /u/ and low central /a/ vowels than one might expect for an ominous, foreboding mood. The majority are front /i e/ and mid /e o/ vowels.[4]

The poem's diction is generally characteristic of this phase of Jiménez's poetry. Pronouns (subject and personal) designate the first person singular. Most nouns appear once or twice;[5] however, "jardín" appears five times and "barba" three. Nouns are selected from country, not city codes; they refer in the main to entities perceived by the human senses. In stanzas 1–4, the nouns have a vivid and concrete quality; they refer to objects ("cuarto," "ventana," "jardín," "luna," "barba") or to sights ("cielo," "nubes," "viento," "noche," "tarde") readily perceived by one or more of the human senses. With stanza 5, i.e. line 17, the imagery becomes more general and abstract ("voz," "ritmos," "voy y vengo").

The concrete noun pool contains unremarkable symbols from the late-romantic, symbolist lexicon. "Cuarto," "jardín," and "ventana" can symbolize the space the self inhabits; "luna," "cielo," "nubes y viento" are customary objective correlatives for the self's moods and feelings; "barba" symbolizes senescence and mortality, and "mendigo" is taken by *specialist* readers to represent the poet's fear of death.[6] Apart from "mendigo," all of these are conventional symbols whose meaning is extrinsic to their collocation in this particular text. The competent reader (of Western poetry) has little difficulty in understanding their significance. However, the abstract noun pool—"andar," "voz," "ritmos"—contains unusual images which purport to signify more than their literal meanings. Their significance must be intrinsic to this particular text and to the Jiménez *Obra* in general.

As for the adjectives: six are possessive ("mi"); three are demonstrative ("esta," "este"); four stem from past participles ("dormido"[2×], "vestido," "abierto"). The remaining nine adjectives are chromatic ("blanco," "azul," "negro," "gris"), or are used—at least on one level—with chromatic effect ("enlutado," "sombrío," "limpio"). There are an equal number of "light" and "dark" adjectives. Of the ten chromatic adjectives, five are bright ("blanco" [3×], "limpio," "azul") and five dark ("sombrío" [2×], "negro," "gris," "enlutado").

As for the verbs, the text employs twelve. Six of the twelve denote relatively static conditions (− action); the remaining six imply relatively dynamic states (+ action). Hence there is a balance, or paralysis, in the verbal patterning: − action verbs are equalized by + action verbs; neither predominates. However, the twelve infinitives the text employs are realized as thirty-five conjugations during the discourse: twenty-seven of which are static, and only eight of which are dynamic; the dominant mood is therefore one of stasis or inaction. Here is the usage: (− action)—"ser"(12×), "estar"(7×), "haber"(4×), "tener"(2×), "hallar"(1×), and "creer"(1×); (+ action)—"andar," "rondar"(2×), "mirar"(2×), "sonar," "ir," and "venir".

A *modern* reader, following the Russian Formalists, is now aware of what is "familiar" or normal, and of what is "strange," that is, what has been defamiliarized by, or deviates from, the poem's basic patterns (see chap. 1). In the case of the verbs, that which is static is semantically familiar, while that which is dynamic is unfamiliar. In the case of the consonants, the norm is soft and quiet, a standard from which the abrupt velars break. As for the rhythm, the norm is smooth, even monotonous, from which the tension and jerkiness of line 17 deviate. Added to this, there is lexical contrast: concrete imagery is the norm, from which the abstraction in the second half stands out.

A comparable opposition, between the familiar and the strange, is also a significant feature of the poem's syntax.

Syntax: Tradition versus Deviation

Syntactically, the poem begins in a conventional manner. The syntax in the first four stanzas is traditional, whereas in the last three it is distorted by a combination of enjambment, aposiopesis, and elision.

In stanza 1, there is a rationality and coherence to the syntax. A subject ("yo") followed by a verb ("soy") is modified by two noun clauses,

> a. [soy yo] quien anda
> b. [soy yo] el mendigo que rondaba

each one of which one is modified by determiners

	of time	and	of space
a.	esta noche		por mi cuarto
b.	al caer la tarde		mi jardín [.]

In addition, the initial syntax representing the landscape is traditional, linear, and sequential (N + V + Adj.):

> l. 7   la ventana estaba abierta
> l. 9   el jardín no estaba de luna
> l. 10 el cielo era limpio y azul[.]

The syntax representing the speaker is equally traditional (though complex, not simple):

> ll. 4–5   Miro / en torno y hallo
> l. 8   Yo no me había dormido
> ll. 13–14 Creo que mi barba era / negra
> ll. 14–15 Yo estaba vestido / de gris

The traditional patterning of the initial syntax suggests that the speaker believes at first that logic will be capable of solving the enigma posed, "¿Soy yo . . . o el mendigo?"

However, after an intense bout of self-questioning (ll. 16–22), the speaker never completes his utterances, he stammers and stutters. Instead of the rational coordination that is present at the start, elision and ellipsis predominate. What the speaker assumed would cohere is found to be incoherent, fragmented; instead of a confident outlook, a babbling tone: "Es que yo . . ." (the equivalent of "¡Qué sé yo!").

Added to this is the conjunction "y": a highly significant feature of the syntax. It occurs thirteen times in the 157 words that constitute this poem. With such frequency of use (8.28 percent), "y" is the poem's most marked part of speech. A chart of its appearance reveals it to be significantly foregrounded:

(A)	ll. 4–5	Miro / en torno	y hallo
(B)	ll. 5–6	todo / es lo mismo	y no es lo mismo
(C)	ll. 10–11	El cielo era limpio	y azul

Up to this point "y" is unremarkable because it does precisely what a reader expects it to do, it functions as a coordinating conjunction, hypotactically linking verb phrases (A, B) and adjectives (C). After this point, it acquires another dominant function:

(D)	ll. 11–12	Y hay nubes y viento	y el jardín está sombrío
(E)	ll. 15–16	Y mi barba es blanca	y estoy enlutado
(F)	l. 23	Hay nubes	y viento
(G)	l. 25	Y voy	y vengo[7]
(H)	ll. 27–28	Y todo / es lo mismo	y no es lo mismo

Although the integrating function of "y" continues, it now performs an additional task, that of introducing clauses (D, E, G, H,); it is now used anaphorically to insist on the difference and disparity the bewildered speaker registers around him. Whereas in (A) above, the speaker was able to subject all to logical coordination ("miro . . . y hallo"), in (G), the next occurrence in the text of a verb in the first person singular of the present indicative, such a controlling perspective is lacking. "Coming and going" makes all ("Y todo") more relative. "Y" has been defamiliarized, made strange; it is figuring coherence *and* dispersal.[8]

In addition, "y" is situated at the very center of this poem. There are one hundred and fifty-seven words, and "y" is the seventy-ninth (78–1–78). This occurs in line 15, "Y mi barba es blanca." Hence, for a *modern* reader "y" is the text's symbolic fulcrum; it indicates the moment at which the speaker became conscious of a change in his appearance, between a past and present actant. The past actant, "Dr. Jekyll," had a black beard and a grey suit, and lived under a clear blue sky. The present actant, "Mr. Hyde," has a white beard and is in a mourning suit (*enlutado*); his sky is either moonlit (ll. 9–10) or dark and stormy (ll. 11–12, 23–24), and he has a different walk, voice, and rhythm (ll. 17–18).

Structural analysis has shown, therefore, that a semantic shift occurs in the text between lines 15 and 17. Before this, the world view is formal and traditional. After it, the perspective is blurred, relative, disparate.

A *modern* reader infers from the syntax that the speaker initially hoped to coordinate vision, to make all cohere. A *post-modern* reader notes that the speaker ended up glimpsing merely disconnected fragments, for the second half of the poem is not a hypotactical sequence, nor a univocal vision; it is paratactical, a potpourri of multiple perspectives, of diverse and shocked reactions, which the speaker registers in a daze, but can no longer *subject* to a single point of view.

Structural analysis also revealed a preoccupation with past and present conceptions of time and space (which it attempts to harmonize in the conjunction "y"). As time and space have been shown to be fundamental concerns in modern Hispanic poetry (see chap. 1, n.7). analysis of their deployment in this particular text should offer further insights into its mysterious fascination.

Time and Space

At the beginning of the poem the syntax presents a simple opposition between past and present time *and* space. The first stanza consists of the following conceptual parallelism:

	Subject	Time	Space
(A)	yo ando	esta noche	por mi cuarto
(B)	el mendigo rondaba	al caer la tarde	[por] mi jardín[9]

The normality of the syntax here implies that there is a simple binary opposition between past (B) and present (A) time and space. Evening and garden are of the past; night and room are of the present. In addition, chromatic adjectives are used to sharpen this division. In the past, all was perceived as "limpio y azul" (ll. 10–11). In the present, there is white moonlight (ll. 9–10), clouds and darkness (ll. 11–12), which persist until the end of the poem (ll. 23–24). In the past, the speaker had a black beard and a grey suit (ll. 13–15); in the present, he has a white beard and is in a mourning (i.e. black) suit (ll. 15–16).

Time (Story versus Plot)

It certainly appears that there is a clear separation between past and present time modes. However, if the temporal sequencing in the poem is analyzed, if its "story" is distinguished from its "plot," no such exclusive opposition between past and present is found.[10]

The table below reconstructs in sequential order the actions that must have taken place before the discourses that constitute this text were effectively rearranged into a poem. The tabular account starts with (10), the most remote action, and works forward to (1), the most recent one:

(10) ll. 2–4   A "mendigo" is observed at dusk by a past-*yo*.

(9) ll. 8 & 26   The past-*yo* falls into a state of reverie.

(8) ll. 4–6   A present-*yo*, the speaker, in a dazed state, looks around him at night time.

(7) ll. 7 & 9–11 The speaker discovers that past setting (window, garden, sky) is not the same as:
ll. 11–12   present setting (clouds, winds, darkness).

(6) ll. 13–15   The speaker realizes that in the past he was "black" and "grey," which is not the same as:
ll. 15–16   his present condition ("white" and "enlutado").

(5) ll. 1–2   The speaker asks himself the question with which the poem begins: "¿Soy yo . . . o el mendigo?" At this point, the mid-point of the reverie, the question is not threatening, as an answer is considered possible (i.e. I am either one or the other).

(4) ll. 16–19   The speaker is surprised by his newly acquired voice and gait ("andar/voz/ritmos").

(3) ll. 20–22   He re-poses the question: "¿Soy yo . . . o *soy* el mendigo?" The repetition of "ser," first with "yo" and then with "el mendigo," unlike in ll. 1–2, foregrounds the speaker's fear that he has ceased to be a whole, integrated self, but has become split into two. The question has now turned into an enigma.

(2) ll. 22–24   The speaker repeats his former actions and checks on his former perceptions. He finds they lack the coordination they had at the beginning: "Miro . . . y hallo" (ll. 4–5) tapers off

into "Miro en torno..." (ll. 22–23). The speaker is now frightened by a painful dilemma: he is the pose(u)r of a question for which he can find no answer.

(1) ll. 25–27   Questions and impressions bombard the speaker, who reels around ("...Y voy y vengo..."), Oedipus-like before the sphinx, in a state of incomprehension ("Es que yo . . ."). He has a voice that can neither coordinate nor subordinate its responses; it rules him. He has a self that is unstable, fluent: "Mi barba *es* blanca," of line 15, becomes in line 27, "Mi barba *está* blanca."

It can be demonstrated therefore that the speaker's thoughts and re-actions are not presented to the reader in linear sequence.[11] In fact, they oscillate between present and past impressions, in a continual *vaivén* ("...voy y vengo...") of psychic tension.

Even the second half of the text, which is ostensibly in the present mode, turns out to be a temporal montage of past perfect, imperfect, and present tenses. It is a present that is involved in attempting to com-prehend and re-present a past. Hence, the temporal mode of the speaker in the closure is not a wholly present moment of integration, nor a completely past moment of idyllic escape. It is a compound of past and present experiences in which are encountered enigma and complexity, not transparent authenticity.

This complex and compound time mode is one of the text's original insights: with its multiple time layers it adumbrates that point of inte-gration between the human and the divine, which became one of Jimé-nez's major concerns in his mature work (and which will be discussed in chapters 4, 5, and 6).

Space (Inner versus Outer)

The text's spatial figures parallel its temporal sequencing. The speaker's territory is at first well defined: "mi cuarto . . . la ventana . . . mi jardín . . . el cielo." Two known and ordered spaces are clearly specified: the exterior landscape of "jardín/cielo" and the interior habitat of "cuarto/ventana." However, this sharp delineation between inner and outer space is lost the more the speaker attempts to come to grips with what is happening to him. In the latter half of the poem, the space is amorphous, unfamiliar, unknown. It is one the speaker cannot specify and over which he has no control.[12]

First, deictics indicate a change in the speaker's perception of exterior space. Reference to "jardín" shifts from "mi" in line 3 (repeated in line 21) to "el" when it appears as part of the ominous setting for the rest of the poem (lines 9, 12, 24). The speaker begins to perceive exterior space as impersonal ("el" not "mi"). In addition to "mi jardín," he also lost a sky that was "limpio y azul." The speaker feels disenfranchised from *his* space. The implication is that he was dispossessed of *his* territory—a space in which he was at ease—once the "mendigo" trespassed on it.

The significance of this is that, in the past, space for the speaker was an *hortus conclusus*, an idyllic bower in which, as "Dr. Jekyll," he lived out his private life, unperturbed by personal and social malaise. He contemplated this space in peace, and he enjoyed it somewhat like a pantheist in touch with nature. All of this "el mendigo" took away from him.

The speaker's inner space is represented by "cuarto" and "ventana." "Cuarto" is not mentioned after line 2, but *modern* readers will infer that it must be as dark and somber as the rest of the setting. "Ventana" is repeated (l. 7), but a *modern* reader will not know for sure the state in which the speaker found it.

The noun "ventana" is emphasized and enigmatized by the text. It occurs in a rhetorical question—"La ventana está abierta?" (l. 7)— which allows for two intonation patterns. Depending on intonation, this question can ask for confirmation of the fact that the window *was* open in the past (and is now closed), or it can register the speaker's surprise that the window, which he recalls as being closed, is now open.[13] In other words, the question about the window is ambiguous, and it signifies the speaker's ambiguous reactions to present space.

A *modern* reader will argue that this ambiguous space is neither fully exterior nor fully interior but a compound of both. One reason for this is that the speaker is walking around in contemplation and observation ("miro y hallo"), as if he were outside; he even acquires the idiosyncrasies of a beggar in the street (i.e. "rondar"), that is, he looks like a ruminative prowler. The speaker is therefore walking as if in exterior space ("este andar" [l. 17], "voy y vengo" [l. 25]), but he struggles with the *vaivén* of senses, of mind and feelings, as though he were walking around his own mind.

The speaker's persistent question "Am I dreaming?" (ll. 8 and 26) foregrounds the interiority of the struggle. His space is comparable to that of the dark ("sombrío") night ("noche" [l. 1]) of the soul, although it is more nightmarish than the mystic's journey.[14]

A further reason for interpreting this space as a compound of inner and outer spaces is that the room is figurally transformed into a road, along which the ruminator comes and goes ("...Y voy y vengo..." [l. 25]). As he prowls round this road-room, he is concerned with his inner psychic life ("esta voz / que ahora suena *en* mi"), and is simultaneously aware of what goes on outside ("Miro / en torno," "Hay nubes y viento . . . / El jardín está sombrío . . ." [ll. 23–24]).

This compound space of interior and exterior landscapes, which the speaker now inhabits, parallels the enigmatic compound of present with past time modalities. It also adumbrates the compound space, which is a condensing of multiple spatial planes or perspectives ("en los espacios del tiempo" [*TA* 958]), which is another distinctive feature of Jiménez's mature vision.

This space is as yet undefinable because it represents a strange, new poetic imagination into which the speaker has been projected (introjected) by his fearful reaction to "el mendigo." This space becomes not the exclusively inner space of total self-absorption (closed room or garden), nor the exclusively outer space of pantheistic union with nature (sky or garden); it is a compound of both, from which the speaker intuits what is the same yet not the same—the inner, yet not the inner; the outer, yet not the outer.

The foregoing *modern* reader's analysis of time and space has described a resolution for the poem's spatial and temporal paradoxes. The actants which occupy these spatio-temporal modes must now be described and interpreted.

Semantics

In *Leyenda* this poem bears the title "Mi posible," a sign of the fact that Jiménez was aware that different actantial others existed inside him. There are two principal actants: a 'bright' actant ("Dr. Jekyll") who existed in the light of day; a 'dark' actant ("Mr. Hyde") who exists in the somber light of night. There is also a subsidiary actant, a beggar, which affects both. The beggar functions as a catalyst: it makes the speaker aware of 'brighter' and 'darker' others inside himself. Hence, its significance will be discussed first.

"Mendigo"

Despite infrequent reference, the beggar looms large in the text. "El mendigo" is the only human actant in the poem to attain the full status of a noun [+ male, human]. The fact that it is the only noun in the poem to designate a human subject foregrounds it automatically and implies that it, a substantive, has more substance than the speaker, whose pronominal status, "yo," leaves him in a less clearly defined and more tenuous ontological space.

In addition, the beggar's verb, "ronda[r]" (l. 3), acquires semantic and phonological emphasis, in comparison with the "anda[r]" of the "yo" (l. 1). Whereas the latter is simple, clear, prosaic, the former acquires a darker, an ominous, threatening connotation, aided by the initial trilled "r" (/r̃/). These sounds imply that the beggar menaces and besieges the speaker. Also, the beggar is associated with velar sounds, which phonosymbolically are back and deep; this reinforces the beggar's dark, foreboding influence as he trespasses on "*j*ardín" and "*c*uarto," transforming what was peaceful and bright into "ne*g*ra" and "*g*ris." [15]

The power of attraction the beggar exercises over the speaker is figured in line 20. As noted earlier, when the question "¿Soy el mendigo?" was first posed, in line 2, the verb "ser" designated the speaker; but when re-posed in line 20, it designates both the beggar and the speaker.

The beggar's powerful influence is also foregrounded in the imagery. The speaker comes to imagine himself dressed in the dull attire and possessing the idiosyncratic (near psychotic) mannerisms a beggar often has in the popular mind: white beard, black suit (ll. 15–16), strange voice, walk, rhythm (ll. 17–19).

In addition, the *modern* reader notes, the dynamics of the beggar ("rondar") set up a dynamic reaction in the speaker: "andar," "mirar," "ir y venir". In fact, six out of eight possible (+ action) conjugated verbs represent the speaker's dynamism; so the text clearly foregrounds the speaker's active attempts to dispel (suppress and displace) what the beggar symbolically figures.

Thus, the "mendigo" is pushed into the background; in fact, "el mendigo" remains a predicate of the main verb; it never becomes the autonomous subject of a main verb, a subject capable of utterly dominating the speaker (in the manner that death obliterates an individual). A *modern* reader also notes that "el mendigo" is located not in "el jardín" (l. 9) but in "mi jardín" (ll. 2–3). Beggar is part of self: a figurative emanation, an ominous and threatening double, of which the self stands in antithetical thrall. As a projection of the speaker's fear, it will remain in menacing but subservient opposition to him.

At this point in the interpretation, *modern* reading comes to an impasse, for there is not sufficient evidence in this text to fully understand the significance of "mendigo." Hence, the reader assumes a *post-modern* mantle and resorts to psychoanalytical and semiotic readings to hypothesize the significance of this "dark" and threatening figure.

A post-modernist will suggest, in general terms, that the beggar represents libidinal drives that need to be curtailed if the artist is to pursue his art. In particular, however, it can be argued that the appearance of the beggar in the garden of innocence aggravates social, spiritual, and aesthetic neuroses.

Social anxieties might include fear of "[e]l caer" (ll. 4 and 22), of falling from that station in life one has already attained; fear of becoming a social outcast, a pariah, a misfit; fear of being economically deprived, of being placed at the mercy of others for one's sustenance. In addition, the beggar, as a representative of the proletarian class, threatens the leisure and wealth of the bourgeoisie. Such psychoanalytical hypothesizing, although somewhat fanciful, may be justified by the fact that in 1900 Jiménez's father died and the family's fortune suffered a considerable decline.

Spiritual (i.e. religious, metaphysical, existential) anxieties stem from the beggar as a symbol not of the evil self but of the antithetical self; it represents the unknown *other* the speaker must embrace if he is to develop fully. This constitutes a positive psychological interpretation.

In this respect, the beggar is taken as a symbol for a spirit that is carefree, one unfettered by societal norms.[16] The speaker's failure to embrace the beggar indicates his reluctance to allow his spirit to embark on something new, to permit his inner psyche to develop, to respond to whatever creative potential the beggar stirred up within him. He is loathe to project himself into a different condition simply because that condition is different from the one with which he is familiar.

A *modern* reader would opt for that reading. However, a *post-modern* reader will be inclined to follow Lacan and Derrida, and to encounter a negative psychoanalytical reading. In this reading, the beggar represents the state of "the Other"; it is the amorphous gap between 'brightness' and 'darkness,' and it is as close as the speaker will ever come to knowing himself. The beggar also represents the condition of *différance*, that state of amorphous coming and going, peripeteia (motion/reversal), rumination, which, again, is as close as the speaker will ever come to knowing himself.

Aesthetic anxieties concern the speaker's fear of losing control of his "palabra," "poema," *Obra*. Such a neurosis is discerned by interpreting "mendigo" as a parapraxis, as a combination of the two words "menos" and "digo" = "men[os]digo." Although the pun might seem ridiculous, it can be justified in Freudian theory as an example of the type of displacing and condensing that characterizes all dreams.[17] The beggar sparks off the poet's fear of being forced into a nightmarish condition in which the skills he has successfully mastered, and the perceptions he has so keenly developed, will fail him, a condition in which he might be able to say and write less than he is able.

Semiotics might extend this insight, arguing that the 'bright' actant is the poet who considers himself to be in control of what is traditionally called a "poem"—"limpio y azul." The fact that the actant is afraid of becoming "negro [y] blanco" indicates his fear of being transformed into the "white" paper and "black" ink of text and discourse: a different, 'dark' and beggarly state. The speaker would mourn ("enlutado") if the creative impulse could no longer be attributed to his own self's individual and unique consciousness; he would mourn if his self became a mere participator in the production of a message, a vessel interpenetrated by an *other*.

These speculations on the significance of the beggar can now be tested—developed and clarified—by analyzing the text's dominant actants. These two, I shall argue, are a 'bright' actant, the aesthete "Dr. Jekyll," who perishes but is reborn in this text; and a 'dark' actant, the aesthete's opposite ("Mr. Hyde"), a post-modern consciousness, who will challenge the aesthete's Modern ideals.

'Bright' Actant

The 'bright' actant—"Dr. Jekyll"—is an aesthete with two aesthetic impulses. One of those impulses is figured in the persona with the grey suit and elegant black beard (stanza 4). The sky that persona contemplated was clear and blue ("limpio y azul" [ll. 10–11]); the garden it observed, through the window, was bathed in the light of the sun. Selfhood and azure clarity are essentials of this scene. This is the persona of the young poet, the naive idealist who believes that poetic inspiration springs from the contemplation of natural beauty. This is the pre-Modern poet.

A further aesthetic actant is represented with a white beard and a dark suit, and, in lines 16–19, as having acquired a new walk, new voice, new rhythms. This is the regenerated 'bright' actant, the prefiguration of the Modern poet.

'Bright' Actant as Pre-Modern Poet

Grey suit, black beard, clear blue sky are pieces of a jig saw puzzle dispersed throughout the discourses that constitute "¿Soy yo . . . ?" Intrinsic analysis, as practised by exemplary *modern* readers, would not wish to assemble a picture from such pieces. However, *postmodern* readers will claim to form one, by resorting to extrinsic factors.

To begin with, a *specialist* reader knows that in 1903, the year this poem in all probability was written, Joaquín Sorolla painted a portrait of Juan Ramón Jiménez.[18] In the portrait, the poet is dressed in a white suit and is seated in front of an open window that overlooks a pleasant, sunny garden. The window looks onto an ordered natural world.

The figure that sits in thoughtful contemplation, musing, displays pulchritude, formality, elegance, reticence. Sartorially and socially, that figure is as distanced from a "mendigo" as anyone can be. It is the figure of the "caballero" to whom the "jardinero" in a contemporary poem (*PLP* 420; cited in full in chap. 3) makes obeisance. It is the figure of a subject whose particular talents have been recognized and rewarded, of a person who has a valued place in society, both social and literary; of one who doubts neither his purpose nor his direction.

Such pieces are brush strokes on an impressionist canvas; they emblematize the *simbolista-modernista*, who savors sensual impressions in quietude, whose pleasures are vivid but reserved, intense but tasteful. The association of window and sunlight with an ordered reality, a clear perspective, is a particularly suggestive topos for the artist who lives a harmonious existence, who is attuned to nature's cyclical round, and who meditates on life from the security and comfort of his own room.[19]

This is the figure of the aesthete, who rescued Spanish *modernismo* from its decadence. A *post-modern* reader will argue that this early manifestation of the 'bright' aesthete is a remnant of nineteenth-century poetic idealism (late-romantic, French symbolist). He is a pre-Modern poet with late-romantic tendencies; he has pantheistic yearnings in so far as he believes that the ideal self should remain attuned to nature.

The beggar challenges the idealized vision of man and world reified in such aesthetics: that the artist uncovers a harmony ("la correspondance") between outer and inner reality; that there is a natural, unmediated correspondance between man and nature, that there is a spiritual link between inner and outer, a mysterious connection between self and other, a divine bond between body and soul. The beggar initiates the undermining, or de-construction, of these notions.

"¿Soy yo . . . o soy el mendigo?" encodes the deliquescence of that pre-Modern poet.

'Bright' Actant as Modern Poet

However, the beggar-actant does not kill the 'bright' aesthete: it stimulates the genesis of a new, 'bright' actant. The beggar does not oblige the pre-Modern aesthete to reject aesthetic values, he jolts him into questioning them, transforming and reconstituting them. This regeneration of the aesthete—the foreshadowing of Modern poetic values—is figured in "¿Soy yo . . . ?"

The *modern* reader noted that line 17 is rhythmically deviant (∪∪ ⁄ ∪∪ ⁄). That rhythm is attained as the speaker realizes his difference from the aesthete of the past.

The *modern* reader also noted that in stanza 3 the hypotactic function of the conjunction "y" is modified; it begins registering disparity *and* integrity. The regeneration of the aesthete is figured in the defamiliarization of this conjunction. Such a basic part of speech begins to figure the impulses of the Modern aesthete: one whose latent desire is to conjoin all experience—no matter how diffuse—into a center, which, as the *specialist* reader knows, is what the poet achieves in 1949 in *Animal de fondo.*

The reconstituted aesthete strives to create a syntax in which such conjoining will be articulated. In fact, the regenerated aesthete begins discovering such a syntax at the very center point of this text, when it encounters "este andar/esta voz/los ritmos" (ll. 17–18), which both delight and disturb it.

Deictics emphasize the contemporaneity of this discovery. It is "esta noche" (l. 1) on which the actant experiences "este andar" (l. 17) and hears the sound of "esta voz" (l. 17), which "ahora" resounds within it. The demonstratives insist on a dramatic intensity, a sense of wonder (*aletheia*),[20] and surprise, which is mixed with a dread that emerges as the actant ruminates on its condition and becomes more and more conscious of physical change and physiological difference: "Es mío / este andar . . . esta voz / que ahora suena en mí[?]"

"Este andar" and "esta voz" are linked to "los ritmos" in lines 17–19. Unlike previous imagery, these are abstract images, mental not visual perceptions (prefiguring the more abstract "poesía desnuda" of the *Obra*'s second phase). To interpret the "andar/voz/ritmo" isotopy, a *post-modern* reader takes the nouns not as synecdoches (i.e. standing for an implicit whole) but as metonyms, existing contiguously without any manifest syntagmatic connections. The metonyms do have a latent connection, which can be traced to the occult lexicon, to clichés that claim that during a séance mediums enter a trance in which they acquire a new voice, one which sounds different from their own and which can imitate that of the *other*. This is a motif of late-nineteenth-century literature (Mallarmé, Yeats); it stems in part from Mme. Blavatsky's renown, and occurs elsewhere in the Jiménez *Obra*.[21]

"Andar/voz/ritmo," therefore, alludes to an aesthetic, of which the re-formed aesthete is somewhat afraid; it is reluctant to deliver the autonomous self, in a trance or séance-like activity, to an unknown and different creative rapture.[22] But what is this aesthetic?

A "voz," in Modern aesthetics, is what poets must discover for themselves, if they are to be original. "Ritmo," Jiménez later came to believe, is what distinguishes poetic writing (poetry and prose) from prosaic writing.[23] "Ritmo" certainly supersedes "rima" as a distinguishing feature of the poetry of the second phase of the work and, as I argue in chapter 4, becomes an important element in the aesthetic of *la poesía desnuda*. Hence, "voz [con] ritmos" is synonymous with an original poetic voice.

"Este andar" phonologically alludes to "anda" (l. 1), which describes the speaker, as well as to "rondaba" (l. 3), which describes the beggar's gait (a*nda*-ro*nd*aba); it hints thereby at a state that is an amalgam of both. In addition, "ritmo" associates with "andar"; "andar [con] ritmo" or "[con voz rítmica]" is the equivalent of dancing. "Baile/bailarín" become symbols in the work's second phase for its aesthetic ideals. That symbol was also used by Yeats, a fact known to Juan Ramón, and suggests aesthetic perfection, as well as the enigma of modernity.[24]

Hence, the "andar/voz/ritmo" syntagmatic chain prefigures a *different* aesthetic, one which springs from within the self, while the actant struggles to confront inner and outer experiences. It is an aesthetic which is "the same and yet not the same," for it will transform and modify many of the pre-Modern ideals.

'Dark' Actant

The main manifestation of the 'dark' actant, "Mr. Hyde," in the early Jiménez *Obra* is that of the poet who is enthralled by the moon ("El jardín . . . blanco / de luna" [ll. 9–10]). This persona is not developed in "¿Soy yo . . . ?" It is, however, the persona Jiménez projects throughout the first phase of his *Obra*, and it will be studied in the next chapter.

In "¿Soy yo . . . ?" it is a 'darker' facet of the 'dark' persona which begins to emerge. It is figured in the syntagma "el jardín está sombrío" (ll. 12 and 24). The 'dark' actant of "¿Soy yo . . . ?" exists only in traces, in the ruminations the "mendigo" provokes by calling into question the social, literary, and philosophical ideals to which the 'bright' actant adheres. It flourishes inside a room at night, from which is observed a threatening exterior. Darkness, moonlight, clouds emblematize the state of occlusion, the limited vision and anxiety that pertain to this actant.

Although the text provides no easily accessible symbol or image to characterize its 'dark' actant, a *modern* reader will find in the defamiliarized syntax a major figure for its thoughts; a *post-modern* reader, on the other hand, will see in the speaker's abstract ruminations a kernel for understanding the indeterminacy of its anxious state.

The constant use of *encabalgamiento* and of *puntos suspensivos* figures its condition. In general, they symbolize the disquiet, the amazement and marvel, the disturbance, which beset this actant in the final stanza.

Encabalgamiento helps foreground the fragmented vision and confused state which typify this actant. Enjambment's first occurrence, in line 2, associates it with the impact the "mendigo" has on the speaker. Its next occurrence, in line 4, links it to fragmentation of vision: the perceiver ("Miro /") is disassociated from what is perceived ("/ en torno y hallo"). Throughout stanzas 3 and 4 strong enjambment splits perceptions ("blanco / de luna?" [ll. 9–10], "vestido / de gris..." [ll. 14–15]). Between lines 16 and 22, enjambment runs all thoughts together and figures the speaker's confused state. In stanzas 6 and 7, it both fragments perception and runs confused thoughts together in quick succession. Enjambment thereby figures the 'dark' actant's enigmatic uncertainty, that its responses to reality (exterior and interior) have ceased to be ordered and objective but have been rolled together in a rapid, simultaneous, successive manner.

Puntos suspensivos, although used throughout, are a marked feature of the last stanzas, where "..." occurs 9 times, and where inability to uncover words that can coordinate experience is paramount. Aposiopesis figures the actant's loss of words, and it also figures the failing of its vision. Vision is now incomplete, incoherent; instead of "miro y hallo" (ll. 4–5), "miro / en torno..." (ll. 22–23). The actant's mental acuity peters out; its confidence and aplomb dissipate. It is either unable to complete its utterances ("Es que yo . . . ," which is equivalent to "I know nothing"); or, it sees all in flux, in process and change ("...Y voy y vengo..." [l. 25]). At the beginning of the poem, the speaker claimed he was walking; by the end, he paces around in a state of utter agitation and disturbance. His vision is no longer bright, empyrean, magisterial.

Together these syntactic features figure the actant's "coming and going," the peripatetic condition that prevails in the final stanza. They are figures not of logic and coherence, but of dispersal and relativity, of what "is the same and is not the same."

"¿Soy yo . . . ?" began with logical syntactic structures whose rationality implied that any enigma the speaker confronted would be resolved. However, by the end of this text the speaker is confronted with a series of uncanny premonitions whose paradoxes are unresolvable. The supposition of the rationalist mind, that enigmas can be traced back to their origins and dispelled, has proved fallacious. No original cause, locus, or logos is encountered.

Hence, the state of indeterminacy encountered in the 'dark' actant of this text is analogous to what Derrida describes as *différance*: "[a] principle [that] compels us . . . not to privilege one substance . . . but . . . to consider every process of signification as a formal play of differences" (*Positions* 26). He continues, in this interview with Kristeva: "The play of differences supposes, in effect, syntheses and referrals which forbid at any moment, or in any sense, that a simple element be *present* in and of itself, referring only to itself. . . . Nothing, neither among the elements nor within the system, is anywhere ever simply present or absent. There are only, everywhere, differences and traces of traces" (*Positions* 26). Later, Derrida adds: "there is no presence before and outside semiological *différance*, . . . Nothing—no present and in-*different* being—thus precedes *différance* and spacing. There is no subject who is agent, author, and master of *différance*" (*Positions* 28). In addition, Derrida explains that "intuition, perception, consummation—in a word, the relationship to the present, the reference to a present reality, to a *being*—are always *deferred*. Deferred by virtue of the very principle of difference which holds that an element functions and signifies, takes on or conveys meaning, only by referring to another past or future element in an economy of traces. . . ." Derrida concludes that this "confirms that the subject, and first of all the conscious and speaking subject, depends upon the system of differences and the movement of *différance*, that the subject is not present, nor above all present to itself before *différance*, that the subject is constituted only in being divided from itself, in becoming space, in temporizing, in deferral" (*Positions* 29).

Derrida's contention that such traditional ideals as integrated being, complete truth, total reality, can never be fully present but are always deferred in "an endless process of difference and absence" (Eagleton 167), can therefore be appreciated by a *post-modern* reader of "¿Soy yo . . . ?" It is an analogous condition that confronts the 'dark' actant by the end of this text.[25]

In the first place, the 'dark' actant perceives its condition as different from sameness. The text we have says: "[y] todo es lo mismo y no es lo mismo" (ll. 5–6, 27–28). In the final lines of the version of "¿Soy yo . . . ?" in *Leyenda* (114), the play of differences itself is foregrounded: "Y todo no es lo mismo y es lo mismo." The play of differences ("no es lo mismo") here predominates over the constant sameness ("lo mismo"), but the one is not known without the other; neither one is perceived as a discrete phenomenon, but only in contrast with numerous other and conflicting perspectives.

This lack of a single perspective is foregrounded in the last stanza, where the 'dark' actant is staggering in its own perceptions, neither dominating nor being dominated by one particular all-embracing view. The voice in the text had first attempted to describe a beggar; it then attempted to describe the 'bright' actant; it next attempted to view and present the 'bright' actant contemplating the beggar; it then went on to attempt to comprehend and to re-present the 'dark' actant in its efforts to understand the 'bright' actant contemplating the beggar. These perspectives make one reel, which is precisely the condition of the speaker in the final stanza, by which time the 'dark' actant has sensed that no overarching perspective will be attainable; that there will be no perspective to satisfy all stimuli and points of view.

The text is more specific than this, for it alludes to the 'dark' actant's hazy intuitions regarding truth and selfhood. One major characteristic of the 'dark' actant's state is lack of form or structure; that is, lack of clearly defined contours in which to describe truth and reality. For example, the 'dark' actant is able to articulate no parameters in which experience and perceptions may be assessed. No framework is provided or known in which to contrast "este andar" with "ese andar" or "aquel andar"; nor are there any specifications of what characterized "la voz que yo tenía" (l. 19). Speaker and reader know only of an "andar/voz" phenomenon that is different from whatever preceded it. The true specifics of this phenomenon therefore remain amorphous; they can be described only as not having quite the same form as their predecessors. The 'dark' actant's uncanny condition is that it has attained no inherently particular form or vision, no reality that is coherent and distinct from other realities. Like Derrida's *différance*, the 'dark' actant's reality is one that is never present; it is one that is always and only something that is different from every other reality.

Another aspect of the 'dark' actant's condition in this text is constant motion: coming and going, peripeteia (motion and reversal). In the last stanzas, the quietude and stasis of "miro . . . y hallo" is replaced by the disturbing dynamics of "... Y voy y vengo ..." This is not passive contemplation or self-absorption, but struggle with multiple perceptions, in body ("voy y vengo") and in imagination, approaching an enigma that remains a captivating enigma, whose resolution is desired but elusive. The 'dark' actant's uncanny condition is a restless, indeterminate state—which will prevent the articulation, the en*vision*ing, of distinctly personal truths.

As for selfhood, that 'dark' actant in this text does not know whether it is asleep or awake (ll. 8 and 25–26). The implication in the last stanza is that selfhood, if it exists, is momentary. The "es" of line 15 becomes "está" by line 25, to imply a continual state of becoming, of change and process. Hence, the 'dark' actant's condition is one that is without an individual essence or inherent particularity; it is one in which self cannot be isolated as a whole and clearly grasped. This is the condition that negative, Lacanian psychoanalysis would refer to as "the Other"—the state in which Self is always and only in some other place. Indeed, a *post-modern* reader might claim that this confrontation with the negative *other* and different self is figured rhetorically in the text: the grey (suit) and black (beard) of the 'bright' actant are transformed, as in a photographic negative, into a black (mourning suit) and white (beard) of the 'dark' actant.[26]

From the point of view of aesthetics, what the 'dark' actant has sensed is that: when self reflects on the actions of an earlier self, self-reflection ensues; when self struggles with a text to find itself, the self to emerge is a self-reflexive textual reality. The 'dark' actant suspects that self might be no more than a textual Narcissus, a "beggar" to a text. It suspects that self might be incapable of representing in words an experience, might fail to create a signified (an *Obra*) that adequately contains all signifiers. This nightmarish condition of poly-perspectival textuality, in which self can never be known to itself because it is always deferred, is again analogous to Derrida's play of *différance*.

The 'dark' actant has dimly intuited much that would unnerve the Modern poet Juan Ramón Jiménez: that there will be no lasting coordination for selfhood; that there will be no single moment in which self will be totally present to itself, unaffected by the lures of the past; that there will be no ideal, authentic voice discovered in the absoluteness of a present moment and fully articulating aesthetic ideals.

Hence, the last stanza, which seems utterly inconclusive, is rhetorically fundamental, for what the 'bright' actant comes up against is a 'dark', amorphous actant, which comes and goes like a beggar; it has no identity of its own, but is dependent for its existence on its difference from both. This constitutes a totally different view of life, art, self—one the 'bright' actant will need to combat in order to attain the glorious vision of the *Obra*'s second phase.

A *specialist* reader knows, after Olson's studies, the impact such negative insights would have had on Jiménez, for he more than most Modern poets placed prime importance on the present moment, on controlling it, defining it, and on rescuing it from passing time. In addition, in his analysis of essence and existence, Olson showed how Jiménez sought to resolve into coherent wholes the enigmas and paradoxes of multiple points of view.

That Jiménez suppressed the uncanny insights of the 'dark' actant of "¿Soy yo . . . ?" is therefore not surprising.

Conclusion

I have been arguing that the actantial drama in "¿Soy yo . . . ?" is more than just a representation of Juan Ramón's neurasthenic paranoia with regard to dying and death (although the emblems for such a reading are clearly apparent [see n. 6]). The text evolves into a struggle between two actants: a 'bright' "Dr. Jekyll" and a 'dark' "Mr. Hyde." The 'bright' actant is first an innocent pantheist, but is then reconstituted and envisions, in "andar/voz/ritmo," a psychic state, through which eventually all will cohere at a central point. The 'dark' actant comes up against a condition of *différance*; its destablizing views will undermine the spiritual optimism of its 'bright' other.

The 'bright' actant will evolve into a Modern poet. The 'dark' actant, with its post-modern orientation, will have the potential to ravage the perfection and beauty of the Modern poet's *Obra*.

In fact, the 'bright' Modern aesthete throughout the *Obra* resists randomness, chaos, lack of control. This actant labors to construct a world of sunlight, a world in which all will cohere at a central point. Also, the 'bright' actant will reaffirm the onto-metaphysical postulates on which its formation and civilization's depend. The Modern poet resists the notion that vision, image, representation, self, are constituted by the play of differences.

On the other hand, as I argue in chapters 4 and 6, the 'dark' persona will urge the 'bright' actant to recognize that the dynamic play between that which is the same and that which is different is constitutive of reality. "Mr. Hyde" will urge "Dr. Jekyll" to accept that that which is established, recognized, secure, and traditional ("mismo") exists and emerges as part of a web or network of that which has not yet been formulated or canonized ("no es lo mismo").

Sorolla caught the anguished struggle between the poet's "Dr. Jekyll" and "Mr. Hyde" in 1916, in another portrait of Juan Ramón, which now hangs in the Hispanic Society in New York. In 1916 Jiménez wrote his most famous Modern book, *Diario de un poeta reciéncasado*, alternately given its symbolic title, *Diario de poeta y mar*. By that time the poet had embarked on the onto-metaphysical journey his different others had destined for him.[27] The face in Sorolla's painting is very white, gaunt, drawn, severe; the suit is black, totally black, but elegant; so is the beard. The poet sits, as he did in 1903, under a window that looks onto a garden: but now it is a painting of a window overlooking a garden, not a garden proper. What Sorolla captures is the Modern artificer confined within the spatio-temporal dimensions of the Modern mind.

The Modern artificer in Jiménez—great High-Modern that he was—welcomed this Herculean task—to impose light on darkness—and managed to suppress for most of his creative life the knowledge that such tasks are doomed, as Sisyphus was doomed. His *Obra* can therefore be characterized in terms of a struggle between 'bright' and 'dark' actants, "Dr. Jekyll" and "Mr. Hyde," which is what I now wish to do.

The texts I analyze are similar to "¿Soy yo . . . ?" That is, they attract the attention of the *post-modern* reader who sees in them the seeds of later disintegration and doubt. I shall argue that the first phase of the *Obra* is written under the enthrallment of the 'dark' other; I refer to this as lunar aestheticism (chapter 3). The second phase, however, is inspired by the 'bright' actant; I refer to this as solar aestheticism (chapters 4 and 5). The *Obra*'s third phase is post-Modern. It first attempts to blend lunar and solar aesthetics, but the 'darkest' voice of the 'dark' actant finally has its say in the third and final fragment of *Espacio* (1954), where it faces up to the thought that there will never be one absolute, all-embracing reality that resolves all enigmas and dilemmas and reassures all subjects; that there will never be one single Self, pristine and transparent, one pure and authentic voice that penetrates enigmas back to origins and illuminates all.

3

An Uncanny Self: Negative Lexemes

In "¿Soy yo quien anda esta noche?" Jiménez confronted his possible regeneration ("Mi posible") as a "brighter" aesthete, but he was unable to envision a path through the "road-room" of the imagination which would lead him toward the light. Hence he remained in thrall to his "dark," somber, and uncanny other.

In effect, throughout the first phase of the *Obra*, Jiménez is dominated by the 'dark' actant, his "Mr. Hyde," and this chapter is a study of its various manifestations.

I want first to dispel the notion that there is much "bright" light and joy in the *Obra*'s first phase. Lines 10 and 11 of "¿Soy yo . . . ?"—"El cielo era limpio / y azul,"—stand out in retrospect as one of the few 'bright' syntagmas in the early poetry. In *Arias tristes* there is another: "Cuando yo era un niño, un tiempo / de sol, de flores y risas" (*PLP* 238). Azure clarity, purity, bright sunlight, and flowers allude metaphorically to a spatio-temporal realm of perfection. As images, they also imply that the speaker vividly recalls such a state of bliss.

In the second section of *Pastorales*, "El valle," a reader finds the undeniably joyous "Mediodía; sol y rosas" (*PLP* 585), as well as the euphoric:

> ¡Granados en cielo azul!,
> ¡calle de los marineros!,
> ¡qué verdes están tus árboles!,
> ¡qué alegre tienes el cielo! (*PLP* 587)

Then, in *Baladas de primavera*, a generally mournful book, is found the now renowned affirmation:

Dios está azul. La flauta y el tambor
anuncian ya la cruz de primavera.
¡Vivan las rosas, las rosas del amor
entre el verdor con sol de la pradera!

Vámonos, vámonos al campo por romero,
vámonos, vámonos
por romero y por amor... (*PLP* 739)

The combination of "azul, rosas, sol" is, however, most infrequent in
the first phase of the work. The syntagmas in which these words occur
are more like nostalgic cries for a lost Arcadia or *hortus conclusus*.[1]

Specialist readers know, of course, that further expressions of clarity
and joy are to be found in the *Obra*. However, they occur in the
Segunda antolojía poética (1898–1918), which was *not* compiled
during the *Obra*'s first phase. The often cited "Verde verderol, / ¡en-
dulza la puesta del sol!," for instance, from *Baladas de primavera*, appears only in the 1922 anthology and not in the original *Baladas*
(1910). In addition, the first section of the *Segunda antolojía*, "Pri-
meras Poesías 1. Anunciación 1 y 2" (*SA* 31–34), contains poems
written (or "relived") around 1920. A reader who examines these
texts finds the self-anthologizer, Jiménez, implying that there was an
"abrazo tan blanco y tan puro" ("Alba") between the poet and nature.
The initial poems allude to a state of innocence ("Azucena y sol"), to
"lirios blancos" ("Blanco y violeta"), in which were heard "estribillos
alegres / por los campos tempranos" ("El idilio").

The *Segunda antolojía* thereby promotes the fiction of an Eden, an
idyllic and blissful time and place. That fiction is repeated in the *Tercera antolojía* (but not, I shall argue, in *Leyenda*). The point is that in
the selections and rejections that constitute the major anthologies of
the *Obra*, which contain the poems that created Jiménez's reputation,
the poet attenuated much of the pervasive darkness that characterizes
the first phase of his work. The *Segunda* and *Tercera antolojías* manifest a latent desire to rewrite the script, to recreate the self, to represent the poetic persona. Accordingly, they should be read as public
script, which the *Obra* in its entirety, a more private because less accessible script (especially in Spain), on many points contravenes.[2]

I propose to begin this re-reading of the first phase of the *Obra* with
a study of "negative" symbols. I have selected certain "dark" nouns
and will describe the polysemic connotations they acquire as they re-

cur in the first phase of the work. The words selected are related by metonomy to the dynamics manifested by "el mendigo" of "¿Soy yo quien anda . . . ?" They constitute a "dark" or "lunar" cluster of imagery. They form a cosmology ("sol," "luna") and a bestiary ("perro," "pájaro agorero," "cuervo," "corneja," "sapo"); they include nature ("troncos") and possess corporeality ("hombre enlutado," "fantasma," "sombra," "mendigo"). These nouns were selected, also, because they reappear with their negativity in the third phase of the "Work" in *Espacio*. However, in the *Obra*'s second phase, they are either positive or totally missing.

Apart from "luna," the above are not prototypical symbols from the first phase of Jiménez's work. In fact, as I argued in chapter 1, I do not refer to them as symbols, because by that term I understand an object—such as a rose—that links the inferior to the superior, the inchoate to the luminous.[3] The words I have selected for study connote a negative power that makes them utterly inapt for symbolizing "fusion" or Baudelairean *correspondance*—the Platonic ideal of Symbolist poetics.[4] They are words, on the contrary, that signify what had to be defused; they represent the negative thoughts and feelings the poet had to keep suppressing in order to keep writing. In addition to this, and like "mendigo" in "¿Soy yo quien anda . . . ?," they signify a state of uncanny indeterminacy (unspecifiable either by writer or reader). They are acoustic images that bring to mind visual signifieds, but their particular significations remain imprecise.

Because I am dealing with such uncanny words, I choose to refer to them as *lexemes*. They are lexemes that have a number of connotations; that is, they are polysemic. I refer to their multiple connotations as their *sememes*.[5] A lexeme, therefore, consists of a number of sememes, and my task is to determine a particular lexeme's sememic components. My method is to describe diachronically the lexeme's various contexts; this description limits the lexeme's connotative range, restricts its semantic field.

These lexemes are not "symbols" in the manner in which that term is understood in the Symbolist and Post-Symbolist traditions of poetry. However, they are "symbols" as psychoanalysis understands that term. In Freudian metapsychology a symbol functions through association, displacement, and condensation to reveal complex psychic states. I shall argue that lexemes function in a comparable manner.

Further discussion of the lexeme is postponed until the conclusion of this chapter. However, another Freudian metaphor helps indicate ways in which the lexeme functions: it floats freely between a number of 'dark' states of mind and feeling, but is not "bound" to any one particular state.[6] "Free-floating" was opposed by Freud, in remarks related to the "uncanny," to "bound." Most phobias manifest themselves, he explained, by floating freely from one object to another. But once an anxiety affixes itself to a single object (symbol, image), Freud considered it "bound" (*Complete Psychological*, vol. 16, 398–401). The negative lexemes studied here float freely between a varying cluster of psychic states; they are *not* bound to a single, dominant phobia.

Although the lexemes do represent a desire to repress certain states of mind and feeling from conscious awareness, they do not just manifest Juan Ramón Jiménez's well documented fear of death. They manifest a need to repress various neurotic impulses which, I shall argue, are of four kinds: spiritual (i.e. metaphysical, existential, religious, pyscho-spiritual anguish); aesthetic (i.e. poetic and artistic concerns); erotic (i.e. sensual and sexual drives); and ethical (i.e. a social concern for humankind).

Context

Specialists have already noted that dark phantom figures are a manifestation of Jiménez's poetic selves. For instance, Young observed that Jiménez would have been intrigued by "the malevolent figure [of] the poet himself," which Eliot includes in "Ash Wednesday," because he "frequently had recourse to this device, called *desdoblamiento* in Spanish."[7] Young cites as an example the strange figure in the following poem from *Arias tristes*:

> Los perros están aullando;
> yo tengo miedo a los perros
> cuando lloran a la luna
> en estas noches de invierno.
>
> No sé si verán fantasmas
> por el jardín, y yo pienso
> en blancas apariciones
> y en lejanos cementerios.
>
> Algunas noches de luna,
> mirando hacia atrás, he abierto

un poco el balcón; y he visto
que alguien se ha escondido. Y tiemblo,

y detrás de las maderas,
sin atreverme a abrir, veo
ese siniestro fantasma
que me hace ronda en silencio. (*PLP* 268)

"Ese siniestro fantasma" is the poet's double: a sign of the negative powers against which he had to struggle. In addition, there are
several negative lexemes in the above poem ("perro," "luna," "fantasma") whose contexts I propose to describe. Similarities between it
and "¿Soy yo quien anda?" are also obvious: "blancas apariciones,"
"noches de luna," "detrás de las maderas," and "me hace ronda."
Moreover, both poems are set in moonlight and the speaker is con-
cealed behind a window, while a "mendigo" or "fantasma" prowls
"por el jardín."
    Another important text in this vein, a companion piece to "¿Soy
yo . . . ?" in *Jardines lejanos*, contains more diffuse negative lexemes.
It is better known as a "relived" poem ("—No era nadie. El agua.
—¿Nadie?" TA 75), but here is its original version:

> Quién anda por el camino
> esta noche, jardinero?
> —No hay nadie por el camino...
> —Será un pájaro agorero.
>
> Un mochuelo, una corneja,
> dos ojos de campanario...
> —Es el agua que se aleja
> por el campo solitario...
>
> —No es el agua, jardinero,
> no es el agua... —Por mi suerte,
> que es el agua, caballero.
> —Será el agua de la muerte.
>
> Jardinero. ¿no has oído
> cómo llaman al balcón?
> —Caballero, es el latido
> que da vuestra corazón.

—¡Cuándo abrirá la mañana
sus rosadas alegrías!
¡Cuándo dirá la campana
buenos días, buenos días!

...Es un arrastrar de hierros,
es una voz hueca, es una...
—Caballero, son los perros
que están ladrando a la luna... (*PLP* 420)

This poem, like "¿Soy yo . . . ?," dramatizes the psyche's dark night. The sounds of footsteps, owls, crows, voices, chains are signs of its fears. The speaker is again behind a window ("balcón") in moonlight ("a la luna"). The condition of the "caballero" is analogous to that of the aesthete "Dr. Jekyll" in "¿Soy yo . . . ?" He has been frightened out of the security of his sunlit garden, and his fears for the future aesthetic can no longer be assuaged. The dash (—) in the text indicates the separation of past from present realities; no coordination between them is achieved. The text is restless; it never settles on any particular image for the negative power sensed by its sensitive speaker.

Both of the above poems contain phantom figures, who are the poet's doubles, explicitly mentioned in the former, implicitly in the latter. In both poems the double's 'dark,' uncanny powers occur in free association with "perros" and "luna," and, in the latter, with ominous birds.

It is clear, therefore, that the negative double, this 'dark' otherness, is part of a much broader context: the somber, phantom figure occurs not by itself but in context with other ominous lexemes. It is this fuller context I want to examine.

Cosmology: "Sol" versus "Luna"

The moon traditionally symbolizes late-romantic dreaming, while the sun, in turn-of-the-century verse, is often associated with the waning of time. The sun will set on the poet's failure in love; the lovelorn artist will retire to his "novia la luna."[8] As opposites, "sol" and "luna" might connote, in general terms, a Jungian antithesis between light and dark, health and madness. However, once a diachronic account of the lexemes "sol" and "luna" is provided, their connotative range in

Jiménez's work can be more precisely delimited. Their meaning can be assigned to three sememic groups.[9]

"Sol"

I choose to begin with the sun, because in subsequent phases of Jiménez's *Obra* it is transformed into a symbol of magnificence. In *Animal de fondo* (pub. 1949) it signifies total and utter fulfillment.[10] "Al centro rayeante," for instance, concludes with these lines:

> Todo está dirijido
>
> . . . .
>
>   a este rayeado movimiento
>   de entraña abierta (en su alma) con el sol
>   del día, que te va pasando en éstasis,
>   a la noche, en el trueque más gustoso
>   conocido, de amor y de infinito. (*LP* 1303)

This strong, resplendent, ecstastic sun never once shines in the first phase of Jiménez's work. At the dawn of the *Obra*, *Ninfeas* and *Almas de violeta*, both 1900, the sun has already set. In *modernista* excess, it is "dead": "el Sol . . . en frío sudario" (*PLP* 1479, and see 1538); "el Sol muerto" (*PLP* 1482). In 1902 it is linked with death and dying (*PLP* 173); in 1903 it is autumnal: "sol amigo / del otoño de mi vida" (*PLP* 237; 229). Between 1908 and 1911, it reflects sadness (*PLP* 798, 918), indolence (*PLP* 1199), nostalgia (*PLP* 1237); it connotes what Kermode termed "The Sense of An Ending," life's crepuscularity (*PLP* 819, 894, 1446). The sun therefore evolves into a symbol of pervasive spiritual desuetude.

The sun also acquires an aesthetic sememe. *Melancolía* refers to "el sol interno que me dora . . . me hace de hierro fuerte" (*PLP* 1428), a metaphor that acquires an explanation in the poem "Poeta," from *Bonanza* (1911–12). In "Poeta," a poet picks up a book of poems and declares: "Cuando cojo este libro . . . Me da luz en mi espíritu . . . sin ver yo sol alguno." The closure to "Poeta" also clinches what the sun is to symbolize: ". . . el sol: gloria, / aurora, amor, domingo" (*LIP II*, 127). The inner sun is one of aesthetic regeneration, and in "El corazón roto," of *Sonetos espirituales*, that connection is firmly established when poetry—"la lira" and "el canto"—becomes equivalent to "la luz del sol" (*LP* 30).

In addition, in the *Sonetos espirituales* the sun becomes firmly associated with love and the beloved. In "Hastío" the speaker, addressing his beloved, notes that: "Tu sol discreto que desgarra un punto / el cielo gris de enero, . . . dulce, dora / mi pena" (*LP* 25). Henceforth in the *Obra* the sun will always on some level be an allusion to love and the beloved (see also *LP* 29, 67).

This brief diachronic study of the lexeme "sol" in the first phase of the *Obra* demonstrates that it is constituted by three sememes: spiritual, aesthetic, amatorial. When "sol" is referred to in subsequent phases of the "Work," the reader may need to draw on either one or more of these three sememes in order to appreciate its full significance. For instance, they are present, on some level, in the following jubilant lines from "Soy animal de fondo":

> "En el fondo de aire" (dije) "estoy",
> (dije) "soy animal de fondo de aire" (sobre tierra),
> ahora sobre mar; pasado, como el aire, por un sol
> que es carbón allá arriba, mi fuera, y me ilumina
> con su carbón el ámbito segundo destinado. (*LP* 1339) [11]

The sun in this poem signifies more than religious perfection. It is a fusion of all the speaker held dear: an aesthetic, a spiritual, and a vitalistic evolution of mind, of body, and of spirit.

"Luna"

Although the sun's semantic range is complex, it is by no means a dominant lexeme in the first phase of the work. "La luna" is far more important, as Rubén Darío prophetically noted in his 1904 review of *Arias tristes*. He saw the poet-ephebe Jiménez as enchanted by the moon, and he evoked the mournful penumbra that was settling on the work of his Andalusian heir. [12]

In the first phase of the *Obra*, the moon certainly gathers about it prototypically 'dark' passions and sentiments. Voluptuousness is one of these. In *Ninfeas* the moon presides over the lascivious pleasures of "desnudas, radiantes y blancas, / hermosas bacantes" ("La canción de la carne" *PLP* 1484); it later shines on Francina's naked body (*PLP* 1115, 1117; and see 1022), as well as on the shoulders and surging bosom of a woman the speaker desires (*PLP* 1178). The moon is both apostrophized (*PLP* 718–20) and anthropomorphized as a naked woman ("redondo seno enhiesto y crudo de alabastro" [*PLP* 1245]), and it eventually comes to personify for the lovesick poet the ideal feminine beauty he would possess: "Toda desnuda, surge, bañándose en su lago; . . . es una rosa blanca en el fondo de un pozo" (*PLP* 1238; and see 1046−47).[13]

Another of the moon's sememes is grief. "Pesares" (PLP 1487), "tristeza" (*PLP* 258−59; 452, 1014, 1030), "penas" (*PLP* 264, 1031, 1366), "desilusión . . . desencanto" (*PLP* 700−701) are the nouns selected to describe the feeling it evokes in the poet. In *Leyenda* (27 no. 42) the speaker asks himself if the moon stays "para darme demencia."

In fact, a demented grief, inspired by love, that is, a lovesick poetics, is another of the moon's sememes (apart from being the stimulus of much of the early poetry). "El alma de la luna," from *Ninfeas*, proclaims such a mingling of grief, love, and poetry:

> El pöeta que sueña Amores imposibles,
> mujeres de almas de oro y carnes intangibles;
>
> en la escala celeste del alma de la Luna
> sube a los áureos reinos en donde la Fortuna
>
> lo estrechará en su pecho...; (*PLP* 1489)

Added to a lovesick poetics is a poetics of suffering in general ("algolagnia").[14] In *Pastorales* artistic suffering is proclaimed as the essence of art: "El que tiene el corazón / bien rimado con la luna / sabe llorar estas penas / recónditas . . ." (*PLP* 630). "A la luna del arte" makes this aspect of the poetics explicit; it presents the poet as having given his best art to the moon every night: "me has concedido, reina, la divina costumbre / de tener, / como tú, el alma desvelada" (*LIP* I, 279).

The moon's sememes are comparable to the sun's but in comparison the spiritual suffering it connotes is more profound; the love with which it is at times associated is more sexual; and the aesthetic is more painful. Clearly, however, it is much more than a sign of a late-romantic, lovestruck poet; it evolves to a level where it connotes a complex existential, aesthetic, and erotic anguish.

Bestiary: "Perro" and "Pájaro"

These lexemes have provoked little commentary. Dog, in fact, is rarely mentioned in studies of Jiménez's work. An account of the use of "perro," however, would allow the reader to appreciate its uncanny significance in such subsequent poems as "Convalecencia" from *Estío*: "Solo tú me acompañas, sol amigo. / Como un perro de luz, lames mi lecho blanco" (*LP* 195). "Pájaro" receives more commentary, especially for the *Obra*'s second phase, where it symbolizes the spirit's desire to ascend. However, the only bird traditionally mentioned in the work's first phase is the "ruiseñor," because it symbolizes the poet and his melancholy poetics.

"Perro"

Frequently in the early poetry, as in "Los perros están aullando" (from *Arias tristes*) cited earlier, a dog is found barking in the shadows of the moon. Dog always occurs in the first phase of the work in free association with the negative lexemes that interest me here.[15] Its significance, therefore, is basic.

A later poem from *Arias tristes* begins with two self-pitying introductory stanzas—"Los gusanos de la muerte / harán su nido en mi pecho" (*PLP* 291)—after which the speaker embarks on a long deliberation on the futility of life. He apostrophizes his somber heart ("corazón mío, / que en la sombra estás latiendo") and warns it:

> La tierra será tu gloria,
> y allá en las noches de enero,
> cuando se cubran de nieve
> las cruces del cementerio,
>
> y la luna amarillenta
> alumbre el dormido pueblo
> y llore el aullido largo
> de los desvelados perros,
>
> tú, triste corazón mío,
> flotarás solo en el sueño
> de mi padre, que llorando
> se incorporá en su lecho; (*PLP* 292)

Rather than an outright fear of death, "el aullido largo de los desvelados perros" becomes a metaphorical lament on the separation of soul from body.[16] "Sombra" and "luna" combine with it to express a general metaphysical dread, occasioned by a sense of the futility of living in a world without hope for the future.

In *La soledad sonora*, "perro" is combined with "luna" and "sombra" ("Llora un clarín agudo y la luna está triste . . . ," [*PLP* 1012]), a combination that results in the bald assertion that life is pointless:

> ladra un perro a las sombras, y todo lo que existe
> se hunde en el abismo sin nombre de la nada... (*PLP* 1012)

Such pessimism is found in other books. In *Elegías* the speaker compares his situation to that of "un can sin destino" (*PLP* 842), and elsewhere implies that his existential condition is comparable to a dogfight, "no importa que los perros, en un encono hirviente / de alfaro, nos asalten en las encrucijadas" (*LIP II*, 81). Hence, the anguish and dread associated with dog is profoundly spiritual (both metaphysical and existential).

"Perro" also occurs in an erotic context. The dejected poet, aware of "l'amour bleu," which he calls "fantasmas / de amor azul," laments:

> Estar ya preparado
> para lo más altivo, para lo más sereno,
> y seguir, como un perro—enfermo—encadendado
> en las calles de pasión y en charcos de veneno. (*LIP II*, 92) [17]

The poem, which appears only in the *Libros inéditos*, does make the connection between "dog" and excessive sexual urges. But dog also acquires an amatorial (as distinct from sexual) sememe in other early poems. In "Sin ti nada es la vida," from *Monumento de amor*, the lover tells the beloved:

> Tranquilo,
> sobre tu corazón, yo dejaría
> el mío
> y hoy, que no estás aquí,
> jadea, ardiente y triste, como un perro,
> perdido... (*LIP II*, 432)

The pathos of this poem yields to recrimination in *Estío*, when the lover reproaches the beloved with: "Tú no oistes el aullido de mi pena" (*LP* 149).[18]

"Perro" also acquires an aesthetic sememe. In *Melancolía* the following strange juxtaposition is found:

Triste palabrería que embota y que marea,
perros y polvo, una interjección, un grito.
...¡Un grito acanallado, que le quita a la idea
su ocaso abierto, embelesado e infinito! (*PLP* 1431)

"Perros" and "acanallado" occur here in free association with both the poetic word ("palabrería") and poetic idealism (referred to metaphorically in the last line). Elsewhere, "belleza" is imagined as lost: "por la gavía roja y apestosa / de perros muertos y de almejas malas" (*LIP II*, 135). The selection of "dog" in these lines foregrounds the notion of aesthetic contamination, denoting one that is impure, lost to excesses.

Like sun and moon, the lexeme "dog" comprises three sememes. Its spiritual anguish is broadly metaphysical; the love it connotes is both platonic and sexual; the aesthetic it figures is impure. Hence, in *Estío*, in "Convalecencia" ("Solo tú me acompañas, sol amigo" [*LP* 195]), the speaker is "convalescing" from an illness suffered by his art, his love, and his spirit.

"Pájaro"

The ominous bird is another figure found in the bestiary of negativity in the first phase of the work. "Pájaro agorero," mentioned in several poems (*PLP* 420, 1025, 1457), always has a negative connotation. It also occurs with "una corneja" (*PLP* 420), which elsewhere is a death omen (*PLP* 120; *Leyenda* 29 no. 45). The crow haunts trees (*PLP* 563): as "esa vieja fea y loca" (*PLP* 775), it intensifies a lugubrious atmosphere. The dark bird in these poems is associated with dread, with a fear of life. When the dark bird is a "cuervo," it acquires additional connotations. "Cuervo" signifies pervasive sadness and nostalgia (*PLP* 839) and has a generally pessimistic and ominous foreboding attached to it (*PLP* 551; *Leyenda* 135 no. 200). "Cuervo" is also associated with a cloying, lugubrious, and decadent sensuality, both in "La canción de la carne" (*PLP* 1487 and 1453) and in *Rimas* (where masochistic flocks of crows pick out men's eyes [*PLP* 155]). Hence, the dark bird's sememic content is existential and sensual, as well as being thanatotic.

Nature: "Tronco" and "Arbol"

From among numerous nature symbols I have selected trunk and tree primarily because they are such important symbols of positivity in the second phase of the work. In the first phase, however, they can be negative; and in the third phase, with *Espacio*, they reacquire that negative tag. The transformation to which they are subjected will be better understood once their gestation in the *Obra* is described.

"Tronco"

Although they are by no means exclusively negative lexemes, trees and trunks often figure an uncanny force in the first phase of the *Obra*.[19] A basic sememe of "troncos" is pervasive sadness, especially with respect to death: "troncos secos" (*PLP* 287), "viejo tronco, caído" (*PLP* 941), "hoy desgajados y negros" (*PLP* 602). A "relived" poem ("Ya están ahí las carretas") refers pathetically to "los troncos muertos" (*SA* 57).

In addition, tree trunks figure the decadent self. In *Ninfeas* ("Quimérica") the connection between self and tree trunks is firmly established: "mi tronco" is continually subjected to the axe-blows of "penas y desdichas" (*PLP* 1508–1509). *La soledad sonora* compares "mi corazón" to a "tronco abierto y desnudo" (*PLP* 926).

This existential sememe, linked with other negative lexemes, is clearly apparent in the following little-known poem:

> ¡Enmedio de la vida, igual que un árbol seco
> que, desde su ruina, mira pasar los años;
> igual que un árbol seco que vive seco siempre
> entre el prodijio de los fríos campos.
>
> Mi corazón, alerta, doliente, sin temores
> perdura en el misterio de su propio cansancio,
> perdida ya la idea de lo que son abriles
> sin memoria siquiera de su antiguo entusiasmo.
>
> Y siempre es inminente el hacha del destino
> y siempre pasa sin herir su desencanto...
> ¡...y hasta parece negro, cual pájaro de muerte,
> el pájaro que viene a su tronco engañado! (*LIP II*, 121)

A withered tree, a black bird, a dried-out trunk metaphorically figure the existential negativity experienced by the speaker. They are supported in other poems (e.g. *PLP* 212) by the moon, grey skies, and stagnant water to express a comparable message.

Trunk and tree, therefore, have a broadly spiritual sememe (connoting existential and metaphysical angst). They are the least developed of the lexemes studied here, and only by association do they also connote aesthetic and erotic anxieties. For instance, the poet might sit in an "arboleda" reading his own verses in compensation for thwarted love; or, they become associated with a suppurating sexuality in so far as toads ("sapo") croak from not so distant bushes at lovers out taking a stroll in the country.[20]

In the second phase of the *Obra*, however, trunk and tree are transformed into dominant symbols of the fulfillment of "amor y poesía"— love and aesthetics. But, in *Espacio*, as we shall see, they reacquire their initial negativity.

Corporeality: "Enlutado," "Fantasma," "Sombra," "Mendigo," "Poeta melancólico"

"Hombre enlutado," "siniestro fantasma," "sombra," and, as I shall argue, "poeta melancólico" are metonymic counterparts of the "mendigo" figure of "¿Soy yo quien anda esta noche?" As individual lexemes, they belong to the same paradigmatic class of dark, ominous figures whose sememic content is extended by association with other members of the class. Indeed, I would argue that "enlutado," "fantasma," "sombra," "mendigo," and "poeta melancólico" become interchangeable; that the significance generated by any single one will be contained, through accrued intertextual association, in the significance of any other.

"Enlutado"

"Enlutado," associated with "mendigo" through metonymy in "¿Soy yo quien anda . . . ?," frequently appears as an adjective describing a person, or as a verb representing a condition.

As an adjective, its sememic content pertains to existential angst. In nightmares the speaker imagines: "que del fondo de las sendas / unos hombres enlutados van saliendo..." (*Rimas*, *PLP* 103); or, "un hombre enlutado / que no deja de mirarme" (*Arias tristes*, *PLP* 280).[21] When the speaker reflects on his life's sad state of disillusionment, he observes: "en cada encrucijada / un enlutado mudo me parte el corazón / con una espada o con una carcajada" (*Elegías, PLP* 829).

As a verb, "enlutar" is used to imply metaphorically the death of a once idyllic state. The sememic content becomes spiritual and aesthetic in such syntagmas as: "la nube del dolor enluta mi armonía" (*Elegías, PLP* 836; also 853, 893), and "Mi aurora siempre surgirá enlutada?" (*Laberinto, PLP* 1292). In *El corazón en la mano* the speaker inquires: "por qué destino, existe / esa idea sombría que me enluta" (*LIP II*, 98).[22] With the *Sonetos* the sememe is also erotic. The thwarted lover exclaims: "hoy, un negror tenaz . . . me enlutece / el sagrario inmortal del pensamiento" (*LP* 21). Here the shroud that envelops him is apparently amatorial, aesthetic, and existential.

"Fantasma" and "Sombra"

"Fantasma" is another negative lexeme. In *Arias tristes*, as noted earlier, the speaker behind his shutters sees "ese siniestro fantasma / que me hace ronda en silencio" (*PLP* 268). In *La soledad sonora* he states: "torna el fantasma antiguo a sentarse a mi lado" (*PLP* 1006). "Fantasma" therefore alludes to existential angst (and in the latter example it may also be erotic).

"Sombra" occurs in a well-known poem from *Rimas*:

> Me da terror cuando miro
> mi imagen en un espejo;
> me parece que es la sombra
> de alguien que me va siguiendo.
>
> Mis ojos clavo en mis ojos
> y hay un influjo magnético
> que me espanta, recordándome
> la fijeza de los muertos.
>
> Siento miedo de mí mismo,
> de mi imagen siento miedo,
> y queriendo desarmarla
> me doy a mí mismo un beso. (*PLP* 162)

As in "¿Soy yo . . . ?," the speaker ("miro," "clavo," "siento," "doy") is afraid of a phantom figure, which is death-like and even séance-like ("un influjo magnético"). He attempts to deal with this negative double ("mi imagen") by loving it. "Sombra" is therefore existential and sensual.[23]

"Mendigo"

"Mendigo" is the most important of these negative lexemes of corporeality because it is the most polyvalent. However, the word "mendigo" itself is rarely mentioned in the poetry. Apart from its importance in "¿Soy yo quien anda . . . ?" its only other occurrence is in an earlier poem, "Las amantes del miserable" (*PLP* 1491), from *Ninfeas* (1900). The latter, a powerful and distasteful poem, is important because it clearly establishes that "mendigo" has more sememes than any of the other negative lexemes studied here.

Briefly, "Las amantes del miserable" dramatizes the plight of a hungry beggar in the final hours before his horrendous death. The beggar has two companions. They are called his "amantes" and are personified as two prostitutes. They lure him back to the hovel where he lives ("su tugurio"), where they embrace him to death. Sensuality and sexuality are therefore sememic elements in this, the earliest "mendigo."

These two companions are called Loneliness ("la negra Soledad") and Death ("una Sombra . . . la Muerte"). Death and solitariness are clear existential sememes. They are present in this, the earliest manifestation of the phantom figure in the "Work," and, as we have already noted, they frequently occur in its subsequent manifestations.

In addition, the existential sememe in "Las amantes del miserable" acquires a metaphysical dimension, in so far as the poem's rhetoric describes a battle between flesh and spirit. The snowflakes that are falling are the spiritual "tears"—"de algún alma que no quiere desligarse de la Tierra"; the beggar's body is described as fighting furiously against the departure of its soul ("da señales de un combate furibundo . . ."). "Las amantes del miserable" may therefore be read as an allegory, in which the beggar represents the body, and "las amantes" represent the soul or spirit. The latter are vulgarized (prostituted) by contact with earth, but prefer to suffer every form of deprivation and abuse rather than give up their terrestrial habitat.

"Las amantes del miserable" also contains an aesthetic sememe. Cardwell (161, 175) writes that the beggar in this poem is the poet. Also, the poem's last line, which describes the dead beggar's face, hints at an aesthetic element: "como presa de un Ensueño de dulcísimos deleites..." (*PLP* 1493). "Ensueño" in *Ninfeas* is a metaphor for the poetic imagination (see "Ofertorio" PLP 1465).

We have to add to this a fourth sememe—social or ethical conscience—because Jiménez's first readers, Blasco reports, found Jiménez empathetic with the poor and the outcast. Blasco (76) cites the reviewer in *Vida Nueva* who wrote that Jiménez "llora las tristezas de los menesterosos, de los explotados, de los perseguidos y los humildes, no con lamentos femeninos, sino con el impulso de arrebatada ira, cerrando el puño y alzando amenazador al cielo, de donde no nos ha venido ni vendrá nunca la justicia."

I cite this to show that Jiménez's early readers, who knew his interest in Ibsen, were left with the impression that "el mendigo" was a reflection of the young poet's concern for his fellow men. Cardwell (172) is of course right to argue that Jiménez is not a socialist poet, and that "Las amantes . . ." is "not a rational argument for change and improvement." A *modern* reader accepts this argument, because Jiménez's social awareness was never realized politically, but a *post-modern* reader must insist that the early selection of the noun "mendigo" is a clear indication of Jiménez's latent social awareness (which transforms itself later into "la ética estética").

Hence, "mendigo" has four sememic levels: spiritual, erotic, aesthetic, and social. It is therefore the most plurivalent of all negative lexemes studied in the *Obra*. In this respect, the fact that it is never mentioned, that it is repressed from subsequent phases of the "Work," is surely significant and worthy of deliberation.

"Poeta melancólico"

The beggar is an outcast; he is cursed and aimless; he represents, I argued in the last chapter, all that the 'bright' aesthete is afraid of becoming. In this respect it is curious to find that the lexemes studied in this chapter consistently associate themselves throughout the first phase of the work with a negative, twentieth-century poetic persona, as it attempts to adjust to different poetic realities. In other words, the "poeta" himself is presented as metonymically part of "hombre enlutado," "fantasma," "sombra"—in short, as a "mendigo." In his negative persona the "poeta" is a dissipated, decadent soul, one whose imaginative impulse has failed, and whose only talent is for killing artistic inspiration.

This is clearly figured in *Melancolía*, where the artist is "una diosa mendiga":

> ¡Ah, mi vida! ¡Lo mismo que una diosa
> mendiga, por sus rotos andrajos muestra el cielo! (*PLP* 1433)

The poem prefigures "la reina fastuosa de tesoros" (of "Vino, primero, pura" [*LP* 555]), and glosses Baudelaire, as Jiménez acknowledges (*PLP* 1433). It presents the artist as a beggarly goddess in her attempts to bring light ("el cielo") into darkness.

A comparable figure persists throughout the first phase of the work. The second poem of *Arias tristes* concludes:

> A la puerta del jardín
> se ha parado un pobre ciego
> llorando con su organillo
> un aire dormido y viejo.
>
> Y no sé cómo ha dejado
> mi jardín el soñoliento
> organillo con sus notas
> falsas y sus ritornellos. (*PLP* 208–209)

The "pobre ciego" relates metonymically to "mendigo," the "organillo" represents his art. Both art and artist are "enfermos," says the poem (*PLP* 208), "con sus notas falsas."

At the very end of *Elegías*, in "Hombres en flor—corbatas, variadas, primores / de domingo—" (*PLP* 898), the implication is that the artist ("este humilde ruiseñor de paisaje") is the sick man, the outcast, in the modern world. He is a "huérfano"—a figure pushed to life's sidelines, like the beggar. He lacks the purpose of his civilized contemporaries ("corbatas"), so he resolves to shut himself off from life for beauty's sake: "sé igual que un muerto, y dile, llorando, a la belleza / que has sido como un huérfano en medio de la vida!" (*PLP* 898).

The artistic self as alienated figure persists throughout this phase of the work. "Espectral" in *La soledad sonora* (*PLP* 1001), it dies for its pale beauty ("muerto por los rosales pálidos del olvido..."). "Poeta mudo" in *Melancolía* (*PLP* 1451), its imagination—"un sueño malo de harapos y de cuervos"—has led it into "el abismo" (*PLP* 1453).

Hence, poetry ("un sueño malo") is a beggar ("harapos"), a dark bird ("cuervo"), and, by association, a "sombra," a "fantasma." The poet and his creation are beggars.

Conclusion

Lexeme versus Symbol

The foregoing discussion demonstrates that negative lexemes are present throughout the early work. Those that are used more frequently are seen to attain various sememic levels of meaning: spiritual, sensual, aesthetic. Less frequently used lexemes, such as "tronco" and "sapo," have a more limited sememic range, but to a certain extent they acquire polyvalent resonance through intra- and intertextual association with those that accompany them. In addition, the phantom figure lexemes can be read as consisting of interchangeable sememes.

I am therefore arguing that the lexeme has no inherent or natural meaning prior to its introduction into and evolution within the *Obra* itself. Like a phoneme, its significance must be determined by its contexts. In this respect, I distinguish it from a "symbol," which has already acquired a general meaning and brings its positivity to all contexts. The lexeme is indeterminate until its significations are specified by a diachronic analysis of its manifestations in the work.[24]

The lexeme "perro" can further exemplify linguistic characteristics of the lexeme. In the poems cited at the beginning of this chapter, "Los perros están aullando" and "¿Quién anda por el camino / esta noche, jardinero?", the speaker is hidden; therefore "los perros" are not seen, they are merely heard. "Perro" is, patently, a sound-image; it is present to the speaker's imagination but refers to no specific reality in the outside world. It *is* a sign divorced from its signified. When a sign does not fuse with its signified, slippage occurs and signification takes place along numerous channels. This is what has happened to the negative lexemes studied here. Hence, a lexeme does not signify one particular object, state, or condition; it evolves into a plurivalent sign, which can signify various modes of dread.

The poem "¿Quién anda por el camino esta noche, jardinero?," by subtly combining so many negative lexemes, is a highly condensed expression of such pervasive angst. It combines "perro" with a host of uncanny lexemes that generate cacophonous sounds ("pájaro agorero," "corneja"). Together, these lexemes manifest a general spiritual disquiet, which they would be incapable of generating if they had to function individually. As a group, they become the latent expression of an anxiety the speaker feels toward all things important to him—life, death, art, love.

A poem from the final section of *La soledad sonora*, "Rosas de cada día," combines numerous prototypical negative lexemes, which it conjoins with ominous figures as well as with a "dark" sensuality. I quote the poem in full, because I do not wish to leave the impression that negativity utterly overwhelms the "Work" in its first phase; it does not. In the following poem, the subtle and tenuous manner in which negative sentiments are incorporated into the sublunar atmosphere of much of the early verse is clearly depicted:

> El árbol juega, hoja por hoja, con el brillo
> de una luna desnuda—hoguera verde y viva—,
> y bajo el cielo gris, velado de amarillo,
> entona una monótona romanza pensativa.
>
> Entre los troncos hay claridades distantes,
> pasa un voluble olor de rosas cristalinas,
> los grandes surtidores, cargados de diamantes,
> irisan sus rasgadas y frescas muselinas...
>
> Viene el mar en el sueño; de oro es la verdura;
> los horizontes tienen claridad de bengalas;
> y cien pájaros raros vuelan por la espesura
> en un silencio blanco de picos y de alas... (*PLP* 1005)

In the first stanza, the moon is sensual (l. 2), and the aesthetic (the music of the tree) is mournful ("gris") and melancholy (l. 4). "Los troncos" of the second stanza together with the "pájaros raros" of the third stanza are ominous. However, such negativity is counterbalanced by the flickering brilliance of what little light remains. The light is in the distance, as if it were at the end of a tunnel. The poet makes the power of these negative forces apparent, but he incorporates them into a scene of mournful, heady beauty to indicate that negativity is not total. This exemplifies the manner in which Jiménez struggles with negative impulses in the first phase of the "Work": the uncanny negativity predominates but the poet strains to mitigate it with mournful beauty.

Antolojía versus *Obra*

The *antolojías'* view of the poet Juan Ramón Jiménez is at best biased, and at worst erroneous. The *Segunda* and *Tercera antolojías* were compiled in the *Obra*'s second phase and reveal, I proposed, a self-anthologizer who is intent on purifying his work of the negative powers, the dark otherness, the somber doubles, which have been studied in this chapter. The *antolojías* rewrite and recreate the *Obra*. They even include poems from its second phase as parts of its first phase. In fact, I would argue that not only do they manifest a desire to purify, strip, or denude the work of its darker broodings, they also sustain and advance another fiction: that as a poet Jiménez began in blissful innocence. As such, they run the risk of presenting him as another high-romantic who, like Wordsworth, in his youth began in gladness. This is not so. Jiménez began in mournful sadness, as Darío so rightly noted and as we too have seen in this chapter.

In this respect, it is curious that *Leyenda* (1896–1956), the most recent anthology of the *Obra*, and the only one compiled from the "Work" in its entirety, deconstructs the Edenic fiction of "un tiempo de sol y flores" found in the initial poems of the *antolojías*.

In *Leyenda*'s first poems, this fiction is transformed into metapoetical text. That is, the new text deliberately refers back to what had been previously written. Indeed, a *post-modern* reader will argue that in these texts a critical, self-reflective, mature poetic mind alludes, with very subtle irony, to the distance it now perceives between itself and the illusion (the "legend") it had earlier spun.

A *post-modern* reader will become conscious of this in the closure to certain poems, which gain in significance once the prior utterances to which the speaker is alluding are identified.[25] For example, the first three stanzas of "Un despertar de Moguer," *Leyenda*'s second poem, depict the "casa de campo," the poet's retreat, where, it is claimed, Platero lay buried:

> Bajo mi sol, mi mañana ¡qué alegre mi viña fresca,
> con mi río amoratado entre mi marisma y Huelva!
>
> A la sombra de los pinos, por mi honda carretera,
> mi jente se entra despacio, aquí y allá, por mis tierras.
>
> Y en mi colina dorada de mi sol, mi primavera,
> entre mi humo, Moguer, mi Moguer blanco despierta.

After this loving and utterly subjective re-presentation of the "casa de campo," the speaker concludes by apostrophizing *his* fictive scene:

Pero tengo un tú sin mí, una sílaba desierta
como mis cuatro horizontes: mar, colina, pino, sierra.

(*Leyenda* 8 no. 2)

The fictional scene ("un tú"), or the conscious awareness of that scene, the speaker notes dispassionately, is no longer part of his present consciousness ("sin mí"). It is a poetic scene ("sílaba") now as deserted, as abandoned by his consciousness, as whatever natural elements (such as the sea) constituted that scene, when he in reality was a part of it (between 1905 and 1912).

And again, in the seventh poem, the speaker recalls "mi casa en mi campo" symbolically emblazoned in vivifying sunlight: "un sol de fuego la anida . . . el sol que me hizo sentir grana el grana, labio el labio, / el sol que me hizo reír de fe." The closure again recognizes that "fe," "casa," and "sol" were imaginative constructs, idealized images, valid for their time and place:

¡Mi fe parece hoy tan cerca del pasado tan lejano,
tan lejano, casa mía, casa cerrada en mi campo!

(*Leyenda* 10 no. 7)

The mature poetic "conciencia" recognizes that a literal time of "sol y rosas," "limpio y azul" was never a reality, either for the speaker or for the *Obra*. The mature "conciencia" deconstructs its 'bright' actantial other.[26]

From "ruiseñor" to "alondra"

The metaphor is Rubén Darío's, who concluded his 1904 review of *Arias tristes* with the following prophetic sentence: "Y al ruiseñor que canta por la noche al hechizo de la luna, sucederá una alondra matutina que se embriague del sol" (Albornoz, *Jiménez* Escritor 32).

The question therefore arises: why did it take Jiménez almost another decade to discover his "lark"? For he does discover it, as "Canción de despacho" from *Estío* proclaims:

¡Qué buen hijo me dio a luz
aquella sombra! Lo que era

luna en mutilada cruz,
es sol en rosa primera.

Allí queda, en un montón
teatral, el romanticismo;
fuerte, ahora, el corazón
está mejor y es el mismo.

¿Recordar? ¿Soñar? ¡Querer!
¡Bien por la *alondra* de oriente!
¡No hay más que mirar y ver
la verdad resplandeciente! (*LP* 105, [my italic])

The syntagma "el corazón / está mejor y es el mismo" (ll. 7–8) re-calls "¿Soy yo quien anda esta noche?" where "todo es lo mismo y no es lo mismo." The reference to "¿Soñar?" (l. 9) alludes to the "¿yo no me había dormido?" syntagma of that poem. The significantly titled "Canción de despacho" is dismissing the *Obra*'s first phase as well as the dominance of the 'dark' actant, the "Mr. Hyde."

The negative lexemes studied here indicate that Jiménez remained enthralled by the 'dark' actant in the first phase of his work. These lexemes are signs of an inner darkness of an *other* which the poet could never confront, could never bring fully to consciousness. These lexemes are a sub-text embedded in the poet's pre-conscious thoughts.

Jiménez's enthrallment by his 'dark' *other* is also to be noted in the titles of the books, *Melancolía* and *Laberinto*, which conclude the *Obra*'s first phase.

In the last poems of *Melancolía* (as noted earlier), the speaker presents himself as a "poeta mudo" lost in "el abismo." Another poem, but from *Leyenda* (218 no. 325), from what used to be the *Poemas mágicos*, concludes with: "El cielo, el mar, la tierra, todo es único abismo." The "abysmal silence" in which the speaker finds him-self is that of the *modernista* cum *simbolista* aesthetic, which, together with the poet's desire to cater to his audience's appetite for mournful beauty, drained him, reduced him to a "men[os]digo." By 1912, that is, Jiménez's poetic explorations had encountered more 'darkness' than light.

However, the *Sonetos espirituales* (1914–15, pub. 1917)—the tran-sitional volume between the first and second phases—shows a considerable decrease in darkness; somber lexemes are attenuated by the first rays of light from what *Eternidades* recognizes as "Amor y Poesía Cada Día" (*LP* 549). By *Estío* (1915, pub. 1916), all darkness has been banished from the work. It is again the "Canción de despacho" (*LP* 105) which spells this out: "¡No hay más que mirar y ver / la verdad resplandeciente!"

To achieve this brightness Jiménez had to alienate himself from Moguer and Andalucía. He had to cut himself off from all he sensuously and dearly loved. He had to put a "gulf" between his art and the immediacy of life in that garden in Moguer (to which "¿Soy yo . . . ?" alludes). This accords with Harold Bloom's belief that the artist in this belated Modern age has a profound need to orphan himself, alienate himself, in order to find his unique poetic voice.[27]

By another ironic twist, in the second phase of his "Work," Jiménez had frequently to ostracize himself, in a padded study, from the literary and social milieu of Madrid. He did this, and he found his "alondra." He transformed himself into a High-Modern, who created the fiction of "la poesía desnuda."

In the second phase of his *Obra*, the "Dr. Jekyll" in Jiménez forges a terse and laconic Modern aesthetic of clarity, light, and intelligence. He has at his command a powerful, poetic imagination, which creates the "tiempo de sol y rosas" which had heretofore eluded it:

Otoño

Quememos las hojas secas
y solamente dejemos
el diamante puro, para
incorporarlo al recuerdo,
al sol de hoy, al tesoro
de los mirtos venideros...

¡Solo a la guirnalda sola
de nuestro infinito ensueño,
lo ardiente, lo claro, lo áureo,
lo definido, lo neto! (*LP* 193)

Modern:
Solar Aestheticism

4

A Sunless Self:
"Golfo"

Jiménez's intention in the second phase of his *Obra* is to banish the uncanny, lunar aestheticism that dominated its first phase. The "lark" (Darío's "alondra") is to ascend, and the sun is to shine resplendently on the poet's endeavors: "¡No hay más que mirar y ver / la verdad resplandeciente!" (*LP* 105). In place of the negative, lunar aestheticism, its antithesis, an affirmative, solar aestheticism, is the ideal for the *Obra* in its second phase.

A brief survey of the fate that befalls the negative lexemes in the second phase of the *Obra* can demonstrate this point.

Negative Lexemes

The phantom figure is hardly in evidence. If it hints at an appearance, as it does in "Yo no soy yo. / Soy este / que va a mi lado sin yo verlo," it lacks the ominous uncanniness it had in the first phase; the poem even continues with such lines as, "[Soy] el que perdona, dulce, cuando odio, / el que pasea por donde no estoy" (*Eternidades*, *LP* 676).

One poem, "Mendigos," turns out to be concerned with the beauty of an ephemeral sensation: "—¡El aroma que una rosa / deja en unos ojos suaves... !" (*LP* 603). The lexeme "enlutado" does not appear after the *Sonetos*,[1] and the lexeme "sombra" is made positive. "Ante la sombra virjen" begins: "¡Siempre yo penetrándote, / pero tú siempre virjen, / sombra[!]" (*LP* 871).

The cosmography "sol" and "luna" are similarly transformed. The "sol," from "Obra y sol" (*Belleza*), symbolizes the maximum attainment of the "Work":

> ¡Cerrado libro mío,
> cielo estrellado de la siesta!
>
> ¡Libro mío entreabierto,
> cielo estrellado de la tarde!
>
> ¡Abierto libro mío,
> cielo estrellado de la noche! (*LP* 1079)

"Luna" is affirmative: "La luna blanca . . . / . . . / hace que la verdad ya no lo sea, / y que sea verdad eterna y sola / lo que no lo era" (*Diario*, IV, *LP* 446). In *La estación total*, in the important poem "Sitio perpetuo," the moon is the complete opposite of effete melancholia:

> "Este mar plano frente a la pared
> blanca al sur neto de la noche ébana,
> *con la luna acercada en inminencia*
> *de alegre eternidad.*" (*LP* 1137, my italics)

"Sol" and "luna" appear together in *Animal de fondo*, in "En amoroso llenar," to express rapturous fulfillment:

> ...Y yo, dios deseante, deseando;
> yo que te estoy llenando, en amoroso
> llenar, en última conciencia mía,
> como el sol o la luna, dios,
> de un mundo todo uno para todos. (*LP* 1318)

The bestiary "perro" and "pájaro" is also transformed. Again in *Animal de fondo*, in "En igualdad segura de espresión," the dog expresses the speaker's sense of harmony with existence:

> ¿El perro está ladrando a mi conciencia,
> a mi dios en conciencia,
> como a una luna de inminencia hermosa?
>
> . . . .
>
> El perro viene, y lo acaricio;
> me acaricia, y me mira como un hombre,
> con la hermandad completa
> de la noche serena y señalada.
>
> El siente (yo lo siento) que le hago
> la caricia que espera un perro desde siempre,

la caricia tranquila del callado
en igualdad segura de espresión. (*LP* 1314–15)[2]

The barking dog, negativity, is caressed, made positive, by the speaker's well-being. Similarly, "pájaro" symbolizes spiritual fulfillment:

¡Esta es mi vida, la de arriba,
la de la pura brisa,
la del pájaro último,
la de las cimas de oro de lo oscuro! (*Poesía*, *LP* 904)[3]

Similar to the other classes of lexemes, the bestiary expresses the sense of harmony the speaker has attained.

"Tronco" is also made positive. Two poems, both well known, are significant because they combine several of the transformed lexemes. From *Eternidades*:

Sé bien que soy tronco
del árbol de lo eterno.
Sé bien que las estrellas
con mi sangre alimento.
Que son pájaros míos
todos los claros sueños...
Sé bien que cuando el hacha
de la muerte me tale,
se vendrá abajo el firmamento. (*LP* 673)

There is negativity in the last lines, but it in no way undermines the speaker's positive stance. A negative power is also apparent in "Cuesta Arriba" from *Piedra y cielo*:

¡Inmenso almendro en flor,
blanca la copa en el silencio pleno de la luna,
el tronco negro en la quietud total de la sombra;
cómo, subiendo por la roca agria a ti,
me parece que hundes tu troncón
en las entrañas de mi carne,
que estrellas con mi alma todo el cielo! (*LP* 721)

The negative is backgrounded by the positive in this poem.

These very brief comments on the treatment of negative lexemes demonstrate that in the *Obra*'s second phase negativity is either suppressed, or transformed, or balanced with positivity. Such positive transformations typify the "Obra con sol."

From Negativity to Positivity

Such positive transformations were undoubtedly due in part to a change in the poet's life which occurred between 1913 and 1914. At the very end of 1912, Jiménez moved to Madrid; in 1913 he first met Zenobia, whom he wooed, "in the old high way of love,"[4] until she agreed to their marriage, which took place in New York on 2 March 1916.

As for the "Work," the transformation of the negative into the positive begins around 1913 and is completed by 1916. It is partially manifested in the *Sonetos espirituales*, where, for example, the final tercet of "El jardín" alludes to the symbolic sun of love, work, and life:

> Es abril porque abril está pasando,
> ¡mas no lo es, porque en su verde aurora
> no se levanta el sol de mi esperanza! (*LP* 67)

In *Estío*, the next book of poetry, the speaker affirms his intuition that the symbolic sun ("sol de la inmortalidad") is about to rise in all its glory:

> La oscura alegría fuerte
> que bajo la tierra áspera
> tendrán las vivas semillas
> la tengo dentro del alma.
> ¡Sol de la inmortalidad,
> ya verás la verde vara,
> con su flor carmín y oro,
> pura, fiel, llena de gracia!
>
> Estoy triste de hoy, pero
> contento para mañana. (*LP* 104)

When he set out for New York from Madrid in January 1916 Jiménez started to keep a diary of his impressions and reactions, which were eventually extended into six sections that constitute *Diario de un poeta reciéncasado* (1917). Section 1 consists of poems written from Madrid to Cádiz, where Jiménez embarked for New York. Section 2,

"El amor en el mar," contains poems of euphoric expectation on the imminence of love interspersed with poems that express a nadir of spiritual depression. In "Sol en el camarote," from Section 2, the poet's symbolic sun and symbolic rose are fused in joy, as he proclaims all he believes the future has in store:

> Amor, rosa encendida,
> ¡bien tardaste en abrirte!
> La lucha te sanó,
> y ya eres invencible.
>
> Sol y agua anduvieron
> luchando en ti, en un triste
> trastorno de colores...
>
> .   .   .   .
>
> Hoy, amor, frente a frente
> del sol, con él compites,
> y no hay fulgor que copie
> tu lucimiento virjen.
> ¡Amor, juventud sola!
> ¡Amor, fuerza en su orijen!
> ¡Amor, mano dispuesta
> a todo alzar difícil!
> ¡Amor, mirar abierto,
> voluntad indecible! (*LP* 256) [5]

"Sol en el camarote," of which these lines are the beginning and end, represents in its entirety the speaker's desire that a strong positivity, in the second phase of the *Obra*, subjugate the negativity that pervaded its first phase.

Section 3 of the *Diario*, "América del este," deals with the poet's social and spiritual reactions at this crucial time and place in his life. This section of poetic texts (poems and poetic prose) so clearly presents a new, a unique, an innovative, Modern Jiménez to the Hispanic world that I want to analyze in detail another text—titled "Golfo"—in which the speaker is again involved in a serious meditation on selfhood.

The Text

In "Golfo" the speaker finds an objective correlative for his emotional, spiritual, and aesthetic predicament in the image of a symbolic sun hidden behind clouds. The resplendent sun envisioned in certain texts does not appear. Hence, this text prefigures the problems that will beset the self in its desire to attain a solar vitality.

Here is the poem:

New York
29 de febrero,

GOLFO

I 1   La nube—blanco cúmulo—recoje
    2 el sol que no se ve, blanca.

II 3   Abajo, en sombra, acariciando
    4 el pie desnudo de las rocas,
    5 el mar, remanso añil.
    6   Y yo.

III 7   Es el fin visto,
    8 y es el nada de antes.
    9 Estoy en todo, y nada es todavía
   10 sino el puerto del sueño.

IV 11   La nube—blanco cúmulo—recoje
   12 el sol que no se ve, rosa.
   13   A donde quiera
   14 que llegue, desde aquí, será a aquí mismo.

V 15   Estoy ya en el centro
   16 en donde lo que viene y lo que va
   17 unen desilusiones
   18 de llegada y partida.

VI 19   La nube—blanco cúmulo—recoje
   20 el sol que no se ve, roja... (*LP* 287)

GULF

I 1   The cloud—white cumulus—gathers in
    2 the sun that cannot be seen, white.

II 3   Below, in shade, caressing
   4   the naked foot of the rocks,
   5   the sea, an indigo quiet-water.
   6   And I.

III 7   It's the end foreseen,
   8   and it's the nothingness of before.
   9   I'm in all, and it's still nothing
  10 but the port for dreams.

IV 11   The cloud—white cumulus—gathers in
  12 the sun that cannot be seen, pink.
  13   Wherever
  14 I get to, from here, will be a return to this very place.

V 15   I'm now in the center
  16 wherein whatever comes and whatever goes
  17 will merge the disillusions
  18 of arriving and departing.

VI 19   The cloud—white cumulus—gathers in
  20 the sun that cannot be seen, red...

The speaker stands at the water's edge (stanza 2) and watches the sun behind the cumulus clouds (stanza 1, ll. 11–12; stanza 6). He reflects (stanza 3, ll. 13–14; stanza 5) on what the clouded sun means to him at that moment, "desde aquí" (l. 14). His responses fluctuate from high ("el fin visto" [l. 7], "en todo" [l. 9], "el centro" [l. 15]) to low ("el nada" [l. 8], "sino el puerto del sueño" [l.10], "desilusiones" [l. 17]).

Innovation versus Tradition

Poem into Text

Compared with the *romance* "¿Soy yo quien anda esta noche?" this is structurally an innovative poem. Indeed, rather than a poem, it is a "text"[6] which clearly displays its differences from the poetry written in the first phase of the work. As a text it consists basically of: (a) the time and place these lines were entered in the poet's diary; (b) a title; (c) 20 lines of varying length.

Time and Place

The time: the twenty-ninth of February occurs once every four years. The text was composed, therefore, on a day that is a metaphorical "gulf" in time.

Nineteen-sixteen was a leap year, and the *Diario de un poeta recién-casado* was—in retrospective judgment—a "leap" in Jiménez's maturation as a poet. The previous leap year (1912) had found him ensconced in Moguer with a solid reputation which, however, was limited to the Spanish-speaking world. The subsequent leap year (1920) would find him well and truly established as an international figure, as well as the undisputed "maestro" of Modern Hispanic poetry. The "Notas" to the *Segunda antolojía poética*, the figurative seal on his reputation as a master, were signed "Madrid, enero, 1920" (*SA* 261–64).

In addition, "Golfo" appears in the *Diario* two days before the poet married, on March 2. That is, it was written during a personal "gulf" in the poet's life.

The place: in New York Jiménez for the first time confronted the English language. The poem that follows "Golfo" in the *Diario* has the English word "Sky" as its title. While in New York and the northeastern United States, the poet, with his wife's constant help, developed an interest in English and American literatures.[7] These factors were instrumental in transforming him from a minor *simbolista-modernista* into a major European Modern.

"Sky," as I said, follows "Golfo" in the *Diario*, and following "Sky" is Juan Ramón's elegy to Rubén Darío, written the day before he married Zenobia. The elegy begins: "No hay que decirlo más. Todos lo saben / sin decirlo más ya. / ¡Silencio!" (*LP* 290). Although it commemorates Darío, Jiménez's strong precursor poet, this poem is a recognition of the critical position he himself must now occupy in Hispanic poetry, for, he writes, the chief Hispanic "ruiseñor" has finally been called home: "Sí. Se le ha entrado / a América en el pecho / su propio corazón" (*LP* 291).

In retrospect, those lines are ominous, for they descriptively prefigure the re-entry into America of Jiménez and his wife in September 1936, where they would die (Zenobia in 1956, Juan Ramón in 1958), and where their hearts would reside until (in the elegy's own words) "el definitivo cariño de la muerte" (*LP* 291) reinterred them in Moguer.

Hence, numerous extrinsic reasons can be adduced for treating

"Golfo" as a potentially significant text. That the poet later chose the title "Enigma" for the poem is some indication of his sense that it is a network of converging but unresolved tensions.[8]

The Title

"Golfo" in the vernacular means "pilluelo." An urchin or raga-muffin is a "mendigo" in the early stages of development—a connotation which delights a *post-modern* reader. Other meanings of "golfo" are immediately apposite.[9] As "estar en el golfo de la cosecha," it means to be at the heart of something, at the most difficult moment of a task. Two further meanings—one literal, the other figurative—are indispensable. Literally, a "golfo" is a place where the immense extension of the sea enters the land. Maritime imagery is sufficiently evident in the text to warrant pursuing such a reading ("nube," "cúmulo" [l. 1]; "rocas" [l. 4]; "el mar, remanso" [l. 5]; "el puerto" [l. 10]; "llegada y partida" [l. 18]).

Figuratively, "golfo" is an existential gulf, an abyss, one associated with the condition of twentieth-century man, who doubts the metaphysical tenets of the past and who feels a hollow in his being. There are sufficient existential lexemes and syntagmas to justify pursuing such an interpretation ("el nada" [ll. 8 and 9]; "será a aquí mismo" [l. 14]; "desilusiones" [l. 17]).

The title "Golfo," then, has negative and positive, concrete and abstract connotations. Also, as it is modified neither by a definite nor an indefinite article, it permits both specific and general interpretations. In this sense, the title prefigures an indeterminacy, which a *post-modern* reader finds also in the rest of the text.

Stanzaic Form

Although the text is twenty lines in length, six of those lines are repetitions with slight, but highly significant, differences: the beginning (ll. 1–2), the middle (ll. 11–12), and the end (ll. 19–20). These lines form an *estribillo* of two lines (*endecasílabo* plus *octasílabo*). The *estribillo* is, intertextually, a recognition of the flourishing historical tradition (Encina, Quevedo, Lope), which the text is appropriating for its own ends.

The *estribillo* takes up six lines; six from twenty leaves fourteen—the number of lines in a sonnet. Admittedly, this is no conventional sonnet. However, the Modern artificer did choose to present the material in four distinct groupings: lines 3–6 (stanza 2), 7–10 (stanza 3), 13 and 14, 15–18 (stanza 5). In point of fact, the poet inverts the sonnet's form: two quartets (stanzas 2 and 3) are followed by the sextet (ll. 13–18). In addition, there is a *volta*, a twist in the thought, which as readers we have learned to expect from a sonnet.

In the present context, the sonnet form is an allusion to Dante and Petrarch, who made of it a hallowed expression of their love. It is also an allusion to the *Sonetos espirituales*, in which Juan Ramón himself wrestled with his reactions to Zenobia during their courtship.[10]

The basic structure of this text, therefore, an *estribillo* interspersed within a sonnetic form, is innovative but alludes to the historical tradition to which it is indebted.

The varying line-length in the text provides further intertextual allusions. Twelve of the twenty lines are either *endecasílabos* (ll. 1, 3, 9, 11, 14, 16, 19), or *octasílabos* (ll. 2, 8, 12, 18, 20). One is an *eneasílabo* (l. 4). Four are *heptasílabos* (ll.5, 10, 15, 17). The text therefore combines traditional lines of verse in no fixed combination. These are lines Jiménez frequently used in the first phase of his work.[11] This free combination of traditional lines signifies that the second phase of the *Obra* responds to the first by developing it dialectically.

There are, of course, three lines which are utterly innovative. They foreground themselves by containing so few syllables in comparison with the others. Line 6 has two syllables, lines 7 and 13 have five. Line 6 defamiliarizes, i.e. foregrounds, the speaker; lines 7 and 13 foreground his thought clusters.

The text's structure can therefore be seen as reflecting Jiménez's predicament at the beginning of 1916, after his first Atlantic crossing. A sophisticated, Modern, twentieth-century artificer is conscious of the rich Hispanic poetic tradition that fostered him, and of which he is to become the head. This competes with a passionate, individual human being, who is aware that newly found love and interests are transforming his capacity to live and his inspiration to write. Jiménez, that is, hesitates; he is pulled in two directions, which are to be observed in the text's rhythmic structure.

Ritmo

It is appropriate to study, at the beginning of the second phase of the "Work," the impact rhythm has in foregrounding semantic difference. The reasons for this are: that rhythm is one of the distinctive features of Jiménez's new style ("desnudo"); that Jiménez thought of *ritmo* as a fundamental characteristic of his Modern poetry; and that he believed *ritmo* rather than *rima* distinguished the poetic from the prosaic.[12]

In fact, if rhyme is considered to be the "tradition" in Hispanic poetry in 1915, then rhythm (and other suprasegmentals) can be seen as that which is innovative, that which undermines but liberates the tradition.

Rhythm, therefore, should be thought of as another textual actant: that, at least, will be one level of my reading of "Golfo." As my reading moves slowly, let me first signal its broad outlines.

The text is initiated by a trochaic actant (gól-fŏ), which it then opposes with an iambic actant (ў yó; ĕl már). The former is a 'bright' actant (blán-cŏ); the latter is a 'dark' actant (ă-ñíl). Hence, the actantial struggle between the 'bright' "Dr. Jekyll" and the 'dark' "Mr. Hyde" is manifest in this text as a pull between trochees and iambs.

I demonstrate that neither of these actantial rhythms controls the text. Instead, it is controlled by a softer, more lilting, rocking rhythm (one stressed surrounded by two or more unstressed syllables). The text moves therefore toward a melding and fusing of the contrary rhythms, the 'bright' and 'dark' actants. This is a pattern which persists, I demonstrate, in the text's sounds (phonemes), parts of speech (adjectives, nouns), spatial figures, and lexematic contrasts.

The emphatic trochaic rhythm foregrounds itself in the title:

$$\overset{\prime\quad\smile}{\text{gol fo.}}$$

The same rhythm, a stressed followed by an unstressed syllable, is found in isolation—either in a syntactic unit, or in a breath group—in four significant places in the rest of the text. It occurs in syntactic isolation in the adjectives that terminate the *estribillo*: *blanca* (l. 2), *rosa* (l. 12), *roja* (l. 20). These adjectives receive additional emphasis, a *modern* reader notes, because they are placed at the end of a line, from which they are separated by a preceding comma. The fact that the adjectives have the same rhythm as the title, and are foregrounded by their position, should be accounted for by any satisfying Modern reading of the poem.

At the opposite end of the rhythmic scale from the trochee lies the iamb: unstressed followed by stressed syllable. The emphatic iambic rhythm functions independently in this text in line 5, in both a noun and an adjective:

$$\overset{\cup\quad\;\prime}{\text{el mar}}\qquad\overset{\cup\;\;\prime}{\text{a ñil.}}$$

This places "el mar" in rhythmic opposition to "golfo"; it also places "añil" in rhythmic opposition to all other colors. Such oppositions must also be semantic, a *modern* reader assumes.

A basic semantic difference between *golfo* and *mar* is, of course, one between water near land versus water out at sea: inner and outer. It is a contrast between the extensive sea versus the circumscribed gulf; extensive versus intensive sensations. "Añil," an indigo blue color, is a mix of colors; it is also one of four adjectives of color selected for use in this poem and like the others is positioned for emphasis at the end of the line. Colors, clearly, are semantically invested and linked to "golfo." Why this "golfo" is associated with both 'dark' and 'bright' colors is an ironical contradiction any satisfying reading of the text will need to confront.

Modern readers, noting the rhythmic distinction between "golfo" and "el mar," detect a semantic opposition in the polarity. They will draw a distinction between 'dark' iambs ("Abajo, en sombra, / . . . / el mar . . . añil") and 'bright' trochees ("golfo, blanca, rosa, roja") thus:

trochaic		*iambic*
{light}		{dark}
{positive}		{negative}
$\overset{\prime\;\;\cup}{\text{golfo}}$	versus	$\overset{\cup\;\;\prime}{\text{el mar}}$
blanco }		
rosa }	versus	añil
roja }		

Despite this polarity, line 5, *el mar re man soa ñil*, has three iambs ($\cup/\cup/\cup/$), which thereby distinguish it emphatically from "golfo" ($/\cup$). Line 5 also introduces the lexeme "remanso," which is semantically related to both "mar" and "golfo," but which has, in addition to a different connotation, a different rhythm ($\cup/\cup$): one that oscillates between an emphatic trochee (gól-fŏ) and emphatic iamb (ĕl-már). "Remanso" thereby begins to emerge as a possible conciliating point between these oppositions.

As for the rhythm in the rest of the text, there are very few additional rhythmical units that function independently of each other (that is, in their own syntactic unit or breath group). All further rhythmical units are modified by or integrated into whatever rhythmical unit precedes or follows them.

Although there are a few units which either begin with a stress, as does a trochee, or end with a stress, as does an iamb, and which are therefore as potentially emphatic as they, the position of these units in the line results in their being pronounced as part of contiguous breath groups. For example, the dactyl *cu mu lo* (/∪∪, [ll. 1, 11, 19]), is integrated with "blanco," and the potentially emphatic anapest, *e sel fin* (∪∪/ [l. 7]), is compounded with "visto." (The latter juxtaposes two primary stresses: *fin vis.*)

Related to the anapest, but with an additional unstressed syllable, there is *y lo que va*, (∪∪∪/ [l. 16]), which is attenuated by enjambment with "unen." There is also *que no se ve* (∪∪∪/ [l. 2, 17, 20]), which is emphatic, but which is compounded in pronunciation, after a slight pause, with the following adjectives ("blanca, rosa, roja"). (This too brings together two primary stresses: *ve ro*—which associate with *fin vis.*)

Every other unit of rhythm in this text veers away from the emphatic extremes of initial or terminal stress. These are the units that sustain the impression of a lilting, rocking, wavy motion, which occurs, for example, in the amphibrach *re man so* (∪/∪). In English, the amphibrach is hypocoristically called "rocking rhythm,"[13] and there are ten amphibrachs in the text, such as *la nu be*. Related to the amphibrach, but with additional unstressed syllables, there are seven units of: *lo que vie ne* (∪∪/∪); and two of *a ca ri cian do* (∪∪∪/∪).

Hence, by far the majority of the rhythmical units in this text veer away from the extremes of emphatic stress, they rock or oscillate toward a central, balancing, middle position.

The dominant rhythm of this text, therefore, is lilting, meditative, slow. It is a pulsating movement, which the *estribillo* consistently brings to the fore. A comparable pattern is discernible in other features of this text's structure.

Phonemes

Rhythm is sustained by vocalic stress, therefore the alternation of stressed and unstressed vowels in the text needs to be analyzed.

In the title, "Golfo," the /o/ is foregrounded. This is curious, because analysis of the text's vocalic structure reveals that there are more /o/'s than the norm in its sound system. Nearly 11 % (10.6%) of the sounds are /o/, as opposed to the norm, which is 9.8%.[14]

In addition to this, there are 17 stressed /o/'s in the text, which is more than any other stressed vowel. There are 15 stressed /a/'s, 14 /e/'s, 11 /i/'s, and 8 /u/'s. These are phonemic facts which need interpreting. Is /o/ a circle of paradox, as Olson interprets that symbol, or is it a gulf?

In addition, /o/ is a mid vowel, and by far the majority of the vowels in this poem are articulated in the mid position. There are 104 of /e/ and /o/, as opposed to 37 of the high vowels /i/ and /u/, and 40 of the low vowel /a/. So, the text concentrates a plurality of its vocalic activity in the mid range.

This is also true of the text's consonantal activity. The title contains three consonants, in significant order: [g l f]. The significance is that these consonants occur in "golfo" in accordance with their point of articulation in the mouth:

l

g

f

The above represents the point of articulation of the three consonants. Velar /g/ is articulated near the back of the mouth; labiodental /f/ near the front; and alveolar /l/ mediates, rocks, oscillates between the back and the front, between the relatively higher and lower sounds, between the inner and the outer.

In fact, when the text's consonants are classified by a *modern* reader according to their point of articulation, it is found that medial sounds, the alveolars [s l n r r̄], far outnumber the back sounds (velars, palatals), or front sounds (bilabials, dentals): there are 98 alveolars; 33 velars and palatals; and 58 bilabials and dentals.

Hence again, a pattern is observed of movement away from extremities toward a mid area. Curiously, the "centro" referred to in the text (l. 15) is embodied in the text's phonemic and rhythmical structure.

Parts of Speech

Adjectives

As noted, adjectives are chromatic. "Blanco[a]" occurs four times; "añil," "rosa" and "roja" once each. "Blanco" is the color of the cumulus cloud. It is the color that veils the sun, and all the sun symbolizes, from the speaker's eyes. As Hillis Miller remarks in another context: "the sun is the figure par excellence . . . in Western tradition generally . . . [of] that which cannot be looked at directly but is the source of all seeing."[15] Hence, the speaker is not to experience the wonder (the *aletheia*) of the sun's appearance. Chromatics thereby introduce a spiritual code into the text.

"Blanca" in the progression "blanca—rosa—roja" can suggest the development from innocence and purity ("white") to passionate emotion ("red"). The selection of "rosa" is significant. There are other ways of referring to pink in Spanish, but *rosa* connotes both the color "pink" and the flower "rose"—a symbol in Juan Ramón for perfect love and beauty (Olson 67–110). Chromatics thereby incorporate an amatorial code into the text.

Intertextually, "rosa" (as noun) signifies "obra"; the latter is also present in "sol" (see *LP* 1079, "Obra y sol"), as the colors designate the sun's change of color. Hence, an aesthetic code is present in the text, though backgrounded.

The chromatic adjectives have the same rhythm as the title, one that is not absorbed by a preceding or subsequent rhythmic unit; also like the title, they are syntactically independent. For these reasons, the process they symbolize affects a *modern* reader's understanding of "Golfo." The gulf is one in which the goals for spirit, love, and work are veiled, unclear, indeterminate, "the same, and yet not the same."

"Añil" (l. 5) is indigo blue, the color of the becalmed sea. Indigo blue is blue with a dark admixture of black or red or grey. Blueness is, of course, a traditional color symbol for transcendent idealism. With its darker admixture, it can symbolize evil. Other sources say it has deep red (i.e. passion) in it.[16] It can therefore be interpreted as the poet-painter's chromatic attempt at blending opposing colors and codes.

Nouns

The nouns are concrete up to line 5 and, apart from the *estribillo*, abstract from line 6 to line 20.

The maritime nouns range from most (+) to least (−) concrete: (+) concrete are "pie" and "roca" (they are tactile and visual); (−) concrete are "sol," "nube," "cúmulo," "sombra," "mar" (they are visual).

The abstract nouns are spiritual ("sueño," "centro"), existential ("fin," "desilusión," "[el] aquí"), and metaphysical ("nada" "todo"). The abstract maritime nouns ("remanso," "puerto *del sueño*," "llegada," "partida") suggest that the speaker is reflecting in calm ("remanso") on the effects of sea-travel.

As "sol," "nube," "cúmulo" are each repeated three times, there is a balance beween concrete and abstract nouns (thirteen each). (When the style becomes more "desnudo," the abstract will predominate.) Again, a *modern* reader notes, the text opts for neither extreme.

A comparable pattern is found in the verbal structure.

Verbs

There are in this text eight comparatively passive ("el sol que no se ve") and eight comparatively active states ("recoje").

Dynamic activity is associated with the cloud ("recoger") and the becalmed sea ("acariciar"). Static activity is associated with the speaker ("ver" [3×], "ser" [4×], "estar" [2×]) and his thoughts ("llegar," "ir," "venir," "unir"). However, some of these static conditions are comparatively dynamic—"ir," "venir," "unir," verbs which represent the speaker's thoughts. Indeed, the speaker's mind and perceptions are at work and *estar* can be perceived as expressing both active and passive states. The clauses "estoy en todo" (l. 9) and "estoy ya en el centro" (l. 15) signify conditions that are subject to change, or a subject conditioned by change. *Estar* therefore fluctuates between active and passive, static and dynamic states. It represents outer and inner, expansive ("todo") and intensive ("centro") moods. "Estoy" figures the speaker's desire (not his success) to bring polarities together.

Conjunction

"Y" occurs 5 times. Apart from the definite article "el" (which occurs 10 times), it is the most frequently used part of speech in the text. Here is a chart of its occurrence:

(A) l. 6	el mar remanso añil.	Y	yo	
(B) l. 8	es el fin visto,	y	es el nada de antes	
(C) l. 9	estoy en todo,	y	nada es todavía	
(D) l. 16	lo que viene	y	lo que va	
(E) l. 18	llegada	y	partida	

In (A), "mar" is conjoined with "yo" (ll. 5–6), but after a period. In (B), "fin" is conjoined with "nada" (l. 7–8), but after a comma. In (C), "todo" is conjoined with "nada" (l. 9), but again after a comma. Up to this point the text is placing a figurative gulf, in the form of punctuation, between any coalescence.

Contrasted with this, textual punctuation does not interfere with subsequent conjoinings. In (D), "coming" is conjoined with "going" (l. 16), as it was in "¿Soy yo . . . ?" However, this turns out to be a "disillusioning" activity, associated, in (E), with "arrivals" and "departures" (ll. 17–18). Hence, the conjoining ("unen" [l. 17]) is a disillusionment ("desilusiones" [l. 17]). No gulf has really been bridged or filled, no balance or mediating center has really been discovered, even though this "union" occurs at that point in a traditional sonnet, the *volta*, where readers would expect a resolution.

Adverbs and Prepositions

All such deictics focus on the here and now. The adverbs are "antes," "todavía," "aquí mismo," "desde aquí," "ya." The prepositions are "abajo" and "en" (4×). This implies that the fulfillment desired and symbolized in the sun was not attained at that moment, in that place ("New York, 29 de febrero, 1916").

Spatial Figures

The analysis so far has hinted at the presence of spatial figures, and indeed, the text separates itself into distinct spatial groups. One of these is the *estribillo* which, with its nouns "nube" and "sol," represents a celestial space. Stanza 2—"Abajo . . . pie . . . rocas . . . mar"— is terrestrial space. Stanza 3 and the sextet of lines 13–18 represent mental, interior space.

The activity perceived and described in the *estribillo* takes place in the sky: "La nube—blanco cúmulo—recoje / el sol que no se ve, blanca." The impression that this space is distant from the other two spaces is reinforced by phonology: there are many velar sounds /n, ku, x, ke/, and back vowels /u, o, a/; internal rhymes suggest echoes /ú e/ "nube," /ó e/ "sol que." That is, sounds emphasize that there is a distance between the speaker and the clouded sun. The speaker perceives that the ideals represented by the sun have distanced themselves from his purview of reality.

The second spatial plane is earthbound, lower down ("Abajo, en sombra,"), at the feet of the speaker ("acariciando / el pie desnudo de las rocas"), and under his very eyes ("el mar, remanso añil"). This place is in the shadows; however, it is sensual ("acariciando / el pie desnudo"), and it is solid ("las rocas"): all of which suggest that it has an appealing vitality.

The third space begins with "Y yo" (l. 6), which from a spatial perspective is symbolically located: it straddles the second and third spheres, the terrestrial and the imaginative. Indeed, as there is an *espacio en blanco* after line 6, textual topography displays the "Y yo" out in its own space, on a limb; in its own gulf. The speaker is therefore situated on the earth ("el pie desnudo de las rocas"), and distanced from celestial ideals. He wrestles with this condition ("estoy" [ll. 9, 15]), as he begins to *engulf* the inner spaces of mental and spiritual enigmas. In addition, the imaginative space the "yo" occupies is abstract. Phrases such as "el fin visto," "el nada de antes," "estar en todo . . . en el centro," "lo que viene y lo que va," "desilusiones" all develop and sustain this abstract, philosophical ("nada") and spiritual ("desilusiones") space.

As the speaker is once more between outer and inner spaces, his situation is comparable to what it was in 1904 in "¿Soy yo . . . ?"

Semantics

In each of the above spaces there are lexematic oppositions which generate meaning in the text. "Nube" is in opposition with "sol," "roca" with "mar," "nada" with "todo," and "viene" with "va." Analysis of these basic oppositions uncovers their tripartite sememic content— spiritual, erotic, aesthetic. The speaker's struggle represents a desire to balance all, to adjust these ideals to the reality of "New York, 29 de febrero, 1916."

"Nube"-"Sol"

Lines 1 and 2 signify that "dark" will be melded with "light," negativity with positivity.

"Nube" is defined by apposition with "blanco cúmulo." A self-conscious Modern artificer chose to foreground the latter by placing it between dashes, as opposed to separating it with commas.[17] This device delimits "nube"'s connotations. "Cúmulo" implies white heaps of cumulus clouds, which suggest mild, pleasant weather; they are not the threatening clouds that precede severe thunderstorms. Hence, the initial lexeme the speaker chose as an objective correlative for his mood is neither dark nor bright, but an amalgam of both. It will not be adequate for signifying either deep depression or intense elation.[18]

In addition, "nube" suggests that the speaker is on the point of reappraising life, love, and art. His existential condition, his thoughts and goals, are clouded (Unamuno's *Niebla*). His amatorial situation is veiled: white cumulus clouds are veils, but when he marries he will symbolically lift them. In addition, as "blanco" signifies "la obra," his aesthetic condition is hopeful: one of the poems titled "La obra" begins, "Día tras día, mi ala, / . . . / me entierra en el papel blanco . . ." (*LP* 1125). The white particles of the clouds hint at his prolific, future creativity.

The next link in the syntagma is "recoje" ("la nube . . . recoje . . . el sol"). "Recoger" is not a verb with negative connotations. On one level, it contains the idea of harvesting. A cloud harvesting the sun suggests the blending of contraries (negative + positive). The cold cloud garners heat from the sun. In addition, the action *recoger* is affectionate, protective, almost maternal; as though the cloud provides the sun, and all the sun symbolizes, with a shield behind which it may recollect, recuperate. "Cloud/sun" therefore suggests spiritual regeneration.[19]

"Nube"-"sol" is therefore a lexematic contrast which signifies not total depression or negativity, but a mingling of negative and positive stimuli.

Lines 1 and 2 foreground the philosophical change of mind the speaker is undergoing. He is meditating on "el sol que no se ve," which is behind "la nube . . . blanca." Indeed, the sun is never visible in this text, nor does its particular rhythmical unit, *el sol que no se ve* (∪ ′ ∪ ∪ ∪ ′), occur elsewhere. The speaker is perceiving a fusion of cloud and sun. This implies that he is meditating on the notion that reality for him is now being glimpsed through a cloud. This is a paraphrase of St. Paul's Platonism, which it stands on its end: to perceive things through a cloud (darkly) is to perceive reality as it is. The implication is that perfection may be, or will be, glimpsed or envisioned through a haze, or in a mist.

Indeed, the lexematic contrast "nube"-"sol" changes color as the *estribillo* is repeated (ll. 11–12, 19–20). Sun and cloud become "rosa," and by the end of text, "roja." The "nube"-"sol," therefore, is transformed by new stimuli; it remains comparatively amorphous, but it is changed by new experiences, which it ac*cumul*ates.

The lexeme "nube"-"sol" thus hints at an anti-Platonizing belief that perfection will be experienced even though the sun—and all it symbolizes—remain in haze.

In addition to this, the color progression, "blanca—rosa—roja," implies either the setting or the rising of the sun.[20] If the sun is setting, a reader can assume that it becomes redder in the clearing that exists between the horizon and the clouds. If it is rising, it gets redder as it appears above the cumulus clouds. A *post-modern* reader will prefer to keep both these possibilities, for the speaker is at a stage in his development where both alternatives —progress and regress—are possible. If he succeeds in his love and work, the sun symbolically rises; if he is rejected in love, if he fails to resolve his aesthetic and metaphysical enigmas, the sun will symbolically set. In this reading, the lexematic contrast "nube"-"sol" is indeterminate; it reflects the speaker's enigma (the poem's alternate title), his ambivalent response to this situation.

Such an enigmatic lexeme will also affect a reader's understanding of the spatio-temporal "golfo" in which the speaker is situated. The "gulf" he is in could be one that is a vacuum, sterile, empty, unproductive, but it could also be one in which the processes of transformation work themselves through, to a flaming and passionate intensity ("roja"), to a profound depth (*a fondo*). The gulf, filled with cloud and sun, represents a potential for growth or dearth, for change or stagnation.

In its initial stage, therefore, the text enigmatizes the speaker's condition.

"Roca"-"Mar"

The next spatial enclave is the land and sea: "Abajo, en sombra" (l. 3). Again, a potentially negative phrase, "en sombra," is immediately modified by a positive, sensual phrase, "acariciando / el pie desnudo."

The "mar" had acquired a negative connotation by the end of the second section of the *Diario*. As a lexeme, it signified radical spiritual insecurity (religious, existential, metaphysical, ontological), for on his first Atlantic crossing the poet experienced "la nada" both within and without. "El mar" became "un inmenso, negro, duro y frío / ¡no!" (*LP* 263, also see *LP* 254); he saw it as "¡azogue sin cristal; / mar, espejo picado de la nada!" (*LP* 268).

As the sea has now entered a gulf, it no longer lashes the boat in fury, nor does it terrify the speaker with its monstrous power or its nothingness. It is now part of a "remanso," a quiet place where it laps against the rocks and soothes the shore. In this "golfo," the poet can meditate on the trauma of nothingness "el mar" represents. He can reflect with some security ("rocas") on the existential, aesthetic, and amatorial insecurity of this phase of his life. Hence the lexematic contrast "roca"-"mar" implies that within the parameters of a "remanso," the sea's negativity combines with the land's positivity to produce an initial sense of security, a tentative balance between opposing forces.[21]

The existential code is accompanied by an erotic one, for stroking a naked foot is a sensual image (more provocative in 1916 than now). However, the dominant meaning of this metaphor lies elsewhere. The notion that the sea "caresses the naked foot of the rocks," is so strange for a *modern* reader that it must mean other than what it says. As a metaphor it draws attention to itself, because in comparison with the rest of the text's imagery it seems forced. It is an anomaly in the "naked" style ("la poesía desnuda") of the second phase of the "Work," and even hints at being a hold over from *modernista* euphemism. It is so anomalous that it has the ring of a cliché. As such, for *post-modern* readers, who follow Riffaterre (*Semiotics* 39–42), it is a clue to the fact that the text is developing its semantic content.

A *post-modern* reader, more prone to accept extrinsic evidence, will find here allusions to beauty and to poetics. The interminable and laborious process of waves washing against stone results in the natural sculpting of a beautiful object: "el pie desnudo." Walter Pater believed that maturation of beauty was a distinctive feature of the Mona Lisa's smile. He evoked her as "the presence that rose beside the waters" and later claimed that "she is older than the rocks among which she sits." These words are from the essay on Leonardo in *The Renaissance*, a volume Juan Ramón purchased in New York in May 1916, and they may have inspired in him comparable thoughts on aesthetic beauty, that true beauty blends positive and negative, pure and impure attributes, and that, in addition, it must develop slowly over a period of time.[22]

However, "el pie" is not just a part of the human body. It is, in another connotation, part of a line of verse. It is "el pie desnudo" of "la poesía desnuda." Although this seems farfetched, it is lent some credence by the fact that it is embedded in a *modernista* type of image— as if to imply with shock that "la poesía desnuda" emerges from "la poesía fastuosa de tesoros."[23]

In addition, "remanso" (l. 5) is no ordinary backwater, for within the *Obra* it has intertextual depth. "Remanso" was the quiet-water of the imagination to which, in the first phase of the "Work," the lonely and melancholy poet withdrew to concentrate on his art. In, for example, "El cielo rosa muy pálido" (*Arias tristes*), the speaker reflects that:

> Los árboles son de cobre,
> el cielo de rosa mate,
> y es tan dulce esta armonía
> en la quietud de la tarde,
>
> que el paisaje se refleja
> en el remanso del valle
> del corazón, como un sueño
> de bosques primaverales (*PLP* 241)

Hence, the strange metaphor "mar . . . acariciando . . . el pie desnudo" combines metaphysical ("mar"), sensual ("acaricia"), and aesthetic sememes ("pie") to suggest the manner in which the new aesthetic, "la poesía desnuda," will be strong and clear of contour, though long in gestation ("roca"); intense with feeling ("roja") but profound of thought ("mar").

"Añil" is also significant. The rhythmical opposition between it and the text's other chromatic adjectives ("blanca," "rosa," "roja") has already been noted. Further remarks on the semantic opposition are pertinent, because indigo blue is a blend of "bright" (blue) and "dark" (grey, black, red) colors (see n. 16). Indigo therefore alludes to the blending of positivity (blue) and negativity (grey, black) found elsewhere in the text. It may also allude to a change from frigidity (grey) to passion (red), as well as to a desire to incorporate celestial (blue) with terrestrial (grey) ideals, the there with the here, *el más allá* with *el más acá*.

The fact that indigo may have red in it is most significant, because one of the deep red seas in Jiménez's *Obra* occurs in the *Sonetos espirituales*, in "Nada": "A tu abandono opongo la elevada / torre de mi divino pensamiento" (*LP* 19). In this sonnet, "la mar empurpurada" alludes to the young lover's fear of rejection; it also signifies his anguish at having to make sense of a meaningless existence by himself, without the companionship of the beloved ("buscaré en mis entrañas mi sustento"). In addition, indigo as purple sea, in "Nada," alludes to the power of the poet's imagination, mind, and spirit ("¡y soy yo sólo el pensamiento mío!"), as they combat the senselessness they discover around them. Indigo is therefore a further development of the text's spiritual, amatorial, and aesthetic codes.

Hence, whereas the lexematic opposition "roca"-"mar" first foregrounds an unresolvable contrast (solid rock versus unstable sea), once it is synthesized into the compound "remanso añil" it foregrounds a desire to harmonize all spiritual, amatorial and aesthetic polarities, to transform a "gulf" into a "remanso" in which such fusion may be effected.

"Nada"-"todo"

The speaker of these utterances is introduced in line 6, "Y yo." He by himself, as in "Nada," desires to resolve these enigmas, to meld negative and positive polarities.

"Y yo" is foregrounded by being the shortest line in the poem. In the context of the struggle, the speaker is a David and his task a Goliath (but he will recognize this only in the third fragment of *Espacio* [see chap. 6]). The speaker implicitly questions his potential. However, the line's typographical setting suggests that the speaker has his feet on the rocks while he searches the spiritual, erotic, and aesthetic "gulfs" of mind and feelings.

The rhythm (‿ ′) of the line "Y yo" is interesting. It is an iamb and contrasts with the text's significant trochees: "golfo", "blanca", "rosa", "roja." A *modern* interpreter will place the "yo" in opposition to "golfo," on the opposing rhythmical parameter to the sun-cloud that is changing color. "Y yo" hopes that its rhythm can bring to an end the rhythm "golfo" initiates, thus:

$$\acute{\text{gol}} \; \breve{\text{fo}} \qquad\qquad \breve{\text{Y}} \; \acute{\text{yo}}$$

The speaker wonders if he can impose parameters and boundaries, so that a mediating rhythm (the amphibrach) may rise, so that a space for positive transformations (the rising sun) may be established. The speaker as hero desires to create a structure in which a rhythmical and semantic balance between the extremes of "dark" and "light" may be secured.

The wide gulf between lines 6 and 7 is bridged by assonance: "Y yo" - "visto." The same assonance in /i - o/ occurs in line 14 and points to the fact that all these thoughts pertain to the speaker.

Once across the gulf between lines 6 and 7, the rhythm changes. Instead of a gentle rocking rhythm (∪′∪), *la nu be* (l. 1), of waves lapping against the shore, *a ba jo* (l. 3), there is a more staccato rhythm: *e sel fin vis to* (∪∪′′∪ [l. 6]), which brings two stressed syllables together (*fin vis-*). Another coincidence of stressed syllables in this text is at the end of the *estribillo*: *ve / blan, ve / ros, ve / roj*. A *modern* reader draws a semantic connection from this rhythmical coincidence: the "fin visto," the goal that was foreseen, was to effect the positive transformation of "white" into "red." But by juxtaposing two primary stresses, the text emphasizes that the "fin visto" in the sun-cloud will remain distanced, unseen, at this time.

The first contrast in this sequence of the text is between "nada" and "fin" (ll. 7–8). The speaker contrasts his life's elusive goal ("fin visto") with the nothingness ("nada") that engulfed him in the past, on the Atlantic. The speaker therefore presents his self as a gulf between past emptiness and future unrealized fulfillment. He is caught in a gulf which could lead to imminent joy or profound sorrow. He feels himself on the verge of achieving a long desired goal ("es el fin visto"), but is conscious of the fact that all may still come to naught ("y es el nada de antes"). Indeterminacy best epitomizes him, for he does not know whether his sun will rise or set.

Lines 9 and 10, "Estoy en todo, y nada es todavía / sino el puerto del sueño," seem to repeat the "fin" / "nada" opposition of lines 7 and 8. But in fact, they do what apposition did earlier in the text: they present the negative from a positive perspective. There is, to begin with, a contrast in sound. The sounds in these lines are softer. All the consonants are articulated toward the front of the mouth; there are several clusters of alveolars and fricatives [st bs ds]. The rhythmic units are not from the extremes of the scale, but from the middle, predominantly; the rhythm also undulates, as more unstressed syllables are used (e.g. *si noel puér to del sué ño* [ᴗᴗ╱ᴗᴗ╱ᴗ]). These functions, plus the enjambment, create a billowy sensation symbolic of "being in all" ("estoy en todo" [l.9]). The speaker intuits imminent plenitude for the self, but he now quite clearly recognizes what he had been totally unaware of a month previously, in the harbor ("puerto") at Cádiz, when he was about to set off to meet his beloved. He now knows that "nada es todavía," which apart from meaning that he has not yet achieved anything, also implies that nothingness still exists, that it was not left behind on the sea, that it is now, and will be henceforth, a reality he must confront.

The speaker in "Golfo" is therefore metaphorically still "in port" as far as the fundamental (spiritual, amatorial, aesthetic) ideals and desires of his life and work are concerned. That port is a gulf: a self ("estoy") which is "todo" and "nada," in different places, at different times. He can foresee "all" and is elated; he is at the same time aware of "nothingness" and is deflated.

The next sequence of thoughts begins with line 13 (the first line of a sextet). Another typographical "gulf" separates it from the process symbolized in the *estribillo*. The rhythm of *A don de quie ra* (ᴗ╱ᴗ╱ᴗ) is the same as the initial rhythm of the *estribillo*; the syntagma thereby alludes to the notion that the speaker is beginning to appropriate these transformations for himself. The revelation is somber, not grandiloquent. The /i - o/ assonance, "mismo" (l. 4), recalls "Y yo"; this implies that the gulf is an aspect of self, that selfhood is an indeterminate "golfo," a battle between positive and negative impulses. It is from such a gulf that all effective transformations must emerge. That this is a painful recognition is echoed in line 14 in the harsh, grating sounds "e-a" of "desde aquí," and in the "a-a-a" of "será a aquí." The rhythm of "desde aquí, será a aquí mismo" (╱ᴗ╱ᴗ╱ᴗ╱ᴗ) is also particularly abrupt.

In fact, the "aquí mismo" (l. 15) is the third (and final) rhythmic group which is emphasized by the juxtaposition of two primary stresses (*a ki mis mo* [∪ ′ ′ ∪]). This rhythmical feature associates "aquí mismo" with *fin vis* and *ve blan- ros- roj*. This suggests that the speaker must now perceive the "aquí" for all that it is, potentially. He must imagine his goals and ideals from here; he must envision for himself the desired transformations ("blanca - rosa - roja"). In fact, although it seems that nothing has been achieved, the expression the Modern artificer selects is "a donde quiera que llegue," not "que vaya." The implication in "llegue" is that *something* has been and in future will be reached in this process of returning to the gulf of the self to meld the positive with the negative.

The speaker is coming toward the realization that all that the sun symbolizes (perfection in art, love, and life) must be envisioned "desde aquí . . . mismo"; the speaker senses that he must return to where he is to re-orient his life's goals.

These ruminations, returning to where one is for one's idealistic orientation, initiate an implicit deconstructing of Jiménez's prior ideals. His idealism was, in broad terms, Platonic. From the French Symbolists, for example, he learned that the artist forever approximates the perfect "correspondance," the Ideal Form. In addition, there is Pauline Platonism, which insists that truth and perfection cannot be known by humankind, except through a glass darkly. But for the speaker in "Golfo," the real and the ideal are being perceived as different from what was heretofore imagined, foreseen, forethought; they are clouded but nonetheless desirable.

Hence, in "Golfo" the speaker begins to realize that he must now confront the indeterminacy of "nube"-"sol," "roca"-"mar," and "nada"-"todo." He must free himself from his precursors' predetermined (Platonic) vision of reality and discover his own. He dimly intuits in this text, as well as in "¿Soy yo . . . ?", his ability to illumine, to express, to embody an idealism that is similar but different from theirs.

"Lo que viene y lo que va"

The text then moves across its final gulf into the enigmatic "centro" of lines 15 through 18. The "centro" encountered is one of *estar*; it is one of continual movement. The "coming" and "going" of line 16 recalls the "Y voy y vengo" of "¿Soy yo . . . ?" A *specialist* reader also recognizes it as prefiguring the jubilance of *Animal de fondo*, but here the speaker is wrestling with his condition "estoy" (ll. 9, 15), not categorizing the selfhood achieved.[24]

This is a condition in which the speaker begins painfully and painstakingly to adapt to a modification of his prior ideals.

"Desilusiones" has the same rhythm as "acariciando" ($\cup\cup\prime\cup\cup$). These are the only two words with that rhythm in the text, which hints that such adjustment is similar to that inexorable process of the sea's lapping the rocks. The speaker accepts that he moves from one state to another, one extreme to another, and that this process results in his adjusting to something that beforehand he would have considered less than ideal.[25] He begins to "des-ilusionar" the ideal of arrival, of attaining goals which the sun traditionally represents. In "*u*nen desil*u*siones," the /u/'s suggest the harshness of this insight, and they recall "cúmulo." The *cúmulo* is thereby associated with "el centro" (l. 15), in which the speaker feels himself to be.[26] The speaker's center is cumulus, a gulf that accumulates and contains "nube"-"sol," "roca"-"mar," "nada"-"todo."

The center of things is no sudden revelation of all ideals; it is no epiphany; nor is it a still, small point of quietude. The revelation here is more like a dismissing or stripping ("desnudarse") of illusions; there is no immediate fulfillment. What is revealed is analogous to what is experienced when one travels by train or boat. The departure and the arrival involve mixed emotions: upsets contingent on parting and forgetting always interfere with pleasure from greeting and finding.

"Llegada y partida" is another reappraisal of Platonism, for the latter posits that by keeping on striving toward the next ideal, man jubilantly approximates the Ideal Form. Jiménez's "llegada y partida" is comparable to the ironic twist Yeats (299–300) gives Platonism in "What then!": "'What then?' Sang Plato's ghost. 'What then?'"

The speaker realizes that he has to gather together ("unir" or "recoger") his disillusions into his "golfo." The conjoining, "viene y . . . va," is not immutably fixed, it is one that needs to be dynamically reformulated. In addition, the "clouded" perspective is not negative; it symbolizes the transformations, the movements from one extreme to another noted in this text, for a cloud can ac*cumul*ate, incorporate, integrate, mediate between sun and sea. It is an extensive space that can develop dialectically an intense center, a process that entails disillusionment and euphoria.

Vitally, this syntagma is a return to the "roca" in order to envision the desired "roja"—a connection suggested by antanaclasis. The speaker would build from rock, not from sand, nor from the sky, the ideal life and love.

This is the existential resolution in the sonnetic form. The speaker begrudgingly intuits the new condition into which he enters. He is not elated, but he recognizes that it is *his* vision. He must accept what he suppressed after "¿Soy yo . . . ?," namely, that "coming" and "going" (*différance*; indeterminacy) are constitutive of reality, that "beggarly" dynamics—the "pilluelo" meaning of "golfo"—must be embraced.

The /o/ then is a circle of paradox, but not a totality. The symbolic gulf has not attained an intense depth, as it will in *Animal de fondo*, nor has the symbolic sun yet risen. The /o/ is also a sign for the self, which will need to be continually remade. The self is a being that strains and stresses to integrate, incorporate, the extremes; one that struggles to encounter that enigmatic and elusive center the energy of this text dimly intuits.[27]

Conclusion

"Golfo" may have begun as a lover's reflections on his imminent happiness and then moved to another pole, a poet's reflections on his changing aesthetic. However, by its closure it has synthesized these concerns into a spiritual code: the indeterminacy of the ontological and metaphysical condition of modern man.

Another feature of "Golfo" is that in it the speaker is caught in a "gulf" between nineteenth-century idealism (i.e. Platonism) and twentieth-century existential anguish; he achieves not resplendent vision but precarious insights, because he is still forging for himself his vision of modernity. "Golfo" reflects this indeterminate state. For this reason it may not be wholly satisfying as a Modern poem; but it is eminently enjoyable as a post-modern text.

In "¿Soy yo . . . ?," I argued, the 'dark' actant, "Mr. Hyde," dimly sensed that self, truth, reality would be constituted by a play of differences. "Golfo," written thirteen years after that text arrives at comparable enigmatic conclusions.

I believe that Jiménez's tentative insights in such basic texts on selfhood should be contrasted with the magisterial assurance of his "Dr. Jekyll" persona, which literary history continues to attribute to his entire vision.

Of course, Jiménez is correctly known for supreme success and confidence, because he is the one who wrote:

> ¡No le toques ya más,
> que así es la rosa! (*Piedra y cielo, LP* 695)

He is also the poet who is renowned for apparent serenity, because he wrote:

> Juan Fiel
>
> Contra el fluido ébano
> el arbusto de nácar.
>
> Juan Fiel, a medianoche,
> toca las granas rosas
> con sus llamas blancas.
>
> En un fondo más alto
> que el mirador de ópalo,
> la parada mar plana. (*La estación total, LP* 1258)

However, it is surprising that this artist, "Dr. Jekyll," in major deliberations on the self and its goals, should achieve insights that are tentative, indeterminate, deferred. This irresolution, of Jiménez's "Mr. Hyde," should be given careful consideration in future accounts of his *Obra*.

In "Golfo," therefore, "Dr. Jekyll" understands that *his* ideals must be similar but different from previous idealism; he intuits his Modern task as a blending and fusing of the contraries of "light" and "dark," heaven and earth, feeling and thought. "Dr. Jekyll" senses that art, love, self shall be constituted by that which is secure and the same ("roca") and that which is nebulous, indeterminate, unknown. "Golfo" also shows the tentative nature of "Dr. Jekyll's" insights; it reveals the shadow of "Mr. Hyde" lurking in the wings, waiting to undermine, even overwhelm, the resplendent solar vision of the Modern *Obra*.

5

A Resplendent Self:
"Yo y Yo"

Jiménez's most arresting exploration of selfhood after "Golfo" is "Yo y Yo," which first appeared in 1919 in *Piedra y cielo*, a significant volume in the second phase of the *Obra*.[1] But unlike "Golfo," "Yo y Yo" is "Dr. Jekyll's" vibrant affirmation of selfhood, that is, until its closure, when "Mr. Hyde" suddenly deconstructs the text's idealism.

The text displays many formal and ideological features which mark it as prototypical of Jiménez's version of Modern poetry ("poesía desnuda"). For *modern* readers, "Yo y Yo" is a remarkable instance of "organic unity," and it is appropriate in studying this phase of the *Obra* that *modern* reading describe in detail numerous linguistic features that contribute to that coherence.

However, as "Yo y Yo" finally deconstructs itself, a *modern* must be accompanied by a *post-modern* reading of the text, in order to trace the signs of dispersal, which although present throughout, are recognized only in the closure.

Here is the version of the poem that appeared in 1919:

Yo y Yo

I   1   Me buscas, te me opones,
       2   como la imajen
       3   del chorro, al chorro, en el espejo de agua.

II   4   ¿Cómo hallaré el camino eterno
       5   que da el espejo al alma de mis ojos,
       6   si vienes tú del fin de ese camino,
       7   con igual fuerza que este afán sin cuna,
       8   que, como tú de ti, no sé de dónde, de mí salta?

III 9   Todo, en torno, es de luz.
   10 ¡Mas yo no puedo ir a ese sinfín que anhela el alma,
   11 por este punto—¡el suyo!—a que me sales
   12 tú al encuentro!

IV 13   ¡Ay, fuerza de mi imajen—¡vida!—
   14 más poderosa que yo, ay! (*LP 699*)

I and I

I 1   [You] search for me, [you] oppose yourself to me,
  2 like the image
  3 of the jet, to the jet, in the mirror of water.

II 4   How will [I] find the eternal road
  5 which the mirror gives to my eyes' soul,
  6 if you're coming from the end of that road,
  7 with strength equal to this incunabular zeal,
  8 which, as you [spring] from yourself, leaps from I know not
       where in me?

III 9   All, round about, is in light.
  10 But I cannot go to that endlessness the soul craves,
  11 through this point—theirs!—at which you come out
  12 to meet me!

IV 13   Oh, strength of my image—life!—
  14 more powerful than I, oh!

Like "Golfo," "Yo y Yo" is more of a "text" than a poem. It is also a Modern text, and therefore contains—to a remarkable degree—a noteworthy concentration of defamiliarized linguistic features and poetic figures. To interpret these, I have divided the text into five sequences: the title and line 1; lines 2 & 3; stanza 2; stanza 3; stanza 4. The interpretation, which is diachronic (i.e. line by line), will specify modernity and post-modernity of style and thought in four of the text's rhetorical classes: syntax, figures, patterns, and semantics.

Syntax

The title and first line of the poem are fertile text for the *modern* reader who believes that in the selection and rejection of parts of speech *langue* is poeticized.

First, a *modern* (formalist) reader, especially one who has become intrigued by the importance of the conjunction "y" in Jiménez's prior texts on selfhood, asks what significance obtains from the fact that the conjunction that appears in the title ("y") never reappears in the text, but is present as a comma in line 1?

A coordinating conjunction normally coordinates separate and distinct entities: Jack *and* Jill. The "y" in "Yo y Yo," however, conjoins the *same* entities. This alerts the reader to the larger poetic context of *desdoblamiento*, doubling of the personality, or alterity, multiple selves. That, certainly, is a concern of the second phase of the Jiménez *Obra*. With Rimbaud's "Je est un autre" (*Oeuvres* 270) it became one of the traditions of Modern poetry. But a reader knows that in most of the Moderns exploration of multiple selves led to loss of self, to alienation or heteronymity. The title thereby alludes to that tradition while positing its own difference: the selves are separate, but not perceived as separated.[2]

The fact that no coordinating conjunction "y" is found in the text itself obliges the *modern* reader to consider that the same subject consists of distinct selves which will be conjoined in some manner yet to be specified. But in what manner? The *modern* reader looks to the text itself, in its entirety, to signify that coordination, in the belief that ideal Modern coordination is far too complex for any pre-formed part of speech to convey, or for any pre-existent signified to transmit.

Line 1, "Me buscas, te me opones," replaces the conjunction with a comma: "Me buscas [y] te me opones." This asyndetic comma assigns each verbal activity its discrete space. It juxtaposes around itself the paradoxical activities denoted by the verbs "searching for" yet "opposing." For the *modern* reader, the comma signifies a novel site around which distinct energies interact; it is analogous to a magnetic field of tension generated when two forces come close; it signifies the absence of complete coordination, while foregrounding the temporary nature of whatever conjoining these verbal energies achieve.

Second, a *modern* reader notes that the subject pronouns that appear in the title remain unexpressed in the first line. However, although line 1 elides subject pronouns, it clearly implies the interaction of a second and a first person singular subject ("[tú]"/"me"). A first person is referred to but only pronominally ("me"); a second person ("[tú]") is implicit but is *not* designated explicitly. Nevertheless, it is clear that two subjects are involved in the "searching" and "opposing" of the verbal activities.

Elision of the subject pronoun is of course basic to Spanish grammar (in which respect it differs, say, from French). But this Modern text is using that idiosyncratic grammatical feature to signify ways in which subjectivity is avoided. The text presents subjects that are denuded—"naked"—of any particular characteristics, so no reader, old or new to the *Obra*, may assign to either "[tú]" or "me" any specific and individualizing characteristics. Initially, these anonymous subjects are, in effect, little more than indeterminate bundles of potential energy, so, rather than "subject," the semiotic term "actant" again more adequately describes their function (see chap. 1). "[Tú]" and "me" exist *in potentia*: "naked" signifiers for first and second person actants that will be constituted as the text unfolds. They allow the Modern artificer to signify his intention to create a uniquely personal sign, one in which signifier and signified will be totally integrated, not arbitrarily connected through social and cultural bonds.[3]

Third, the *modern* (structuralist) reader asks, what added significance obtains from the fact that the Modern poet selected pronouns and verbs to initiate this utterance? The verbal energies of the first line are separated but share one significant element, "me": "*Me* buscas, te *me* opones." "Me," which here is both direct and indirect first person object pronoun, is a marked feature of the line from its frequency of occurrence, twice in just seven words. The same morpheme creates the appearance that the object of the antagonistic verbal activities is identical. Without the direct and indirect presence of "me," actants would achieve no coordination at all, subjects ("[tú]") would be totally separated, selves the title purports to explore would split apart, suffer fragmentation, alienation, and loss.

By selecting pronouns to initiate this text the Modern artificer appeals to the enigma of selfhood and alludes to the notion of an ideal *Self*, one capable of containing and coordinating all. Whether self will be fully constituted as subject becomes an enigma that pertains—for the *modern* reader—to this text's hermeneutic code.[4] On the other hand, a canny, *post-modern* reader—one inspired by Benveniste—will note that by selecting an object ("me"), not a subject pronoun ("yo"), as the initial reference to self, the speaker foregrounds the self's pronominal status.[5] A *post-modern* reader will assume that self will remain pronominal, that self—to adapt *Webster*'s (1816 col. 3) definition of the pronoun—will have "no fixed meaning," except "one of relation and limitation" which it will acquire as the text unfolds.

In addition to the selection of pronouns, the fact that verbs—rather than, say, nouns—were also selected to initiate the text is equally significant.

Verbs were foregrounded; they were placed, by the Modern artificer, in an utterly unmodified—"naked"—state at the outset. When anonymous verbal activity is placed in an original state of dynamic opposition and paradoxical tension ("search" and "oppose"), the reader's normal habits and knowing patterns of response are short-circuited. Verbs so used impersonalize the actants. The reader has nothing familiar—a noun, for instance—with which to identify, on which to hang some commonly shared significance. The reader is thereby prevented from prospectively imagining the subjects to which these verbs refer. This again accords with the Modern artificer's avoidance of conventional signs and pre-existent signifieds, and with the ideal that the poem in its entirety, not in its particularity, fuse signifier and signified in luminous signification.

The foregrounding of verbs also gives full play to a paradox that emerges from transitive and intransitive verbal constructions found in the line. In the construction "me buscas" there is an actant whose marked characteristic is transitive movement, that is, movement away from itself; there is also a second actant, the object "me," whose distinguishing feature is to receive the "searching" action of the first actant. In the construction "te me opones," there are also two actants: one actant is characterized by intransitive movement, that is, movement back on to itself and away from its object ("me"), which is the second actant of the construction and the indirect recipient of the "opposing." [6]

A *modern*, linguistic analysis thereby uncovers four actants—a transitive "[tú]" and an intransitive "[tú]," a direct "me" and an indirect "me." This discovery contradicts the title and problematizes the text's hermeneutic code.

In addition, the transitive-intransitive opposition contains connotative depth. The transitive action "me buscas" connotes movement through space, from one site to another; it symbolizes an active and outer impulse. On the other hand, the intransitive action "te me opones" connotes movement within a more confined space. It symbol-izes passive and inner impulses. The *deep* structure of these verbs therefore suggests a basic dichotomy between exterior and interior, body and mind, spirit and flesh, soul and world. At the same time, the title and the use of "me" indicate a major ideal of this poem: the will to imag(e)inatively transcend such subject-object dualism, by constitut-ing a *Self* that would contain all.

To summarize the first sequence: it appears that the speaker of the title and line 1 considers the poem to be an ontological search, which will end harmoniously with the emergence of a *Self* that contains all, a *Self* from which all will emanate.[7] The *modern* reader will accept this claim and will see the title as a synthesis of the artifact's coherent but paradoxical grasp on reality; it is a manifestation of the poet's inte-grated "Dr. Jekyll" persona. The *post-modern* reader, on the other hand, will be suspicious and will see the title as an attempt to force coherence, to give unity *a posteriori* to a text's thought and vision; it manifests the "scriptor," "Mr. Hyde." Readers are therefore on the lookout for holistic desires and frustrations latent in this text.

The verbal play and linguistic legerdemain in the first sequence also have their effect. The *modern* reader, having noted just two actants in the title, interprets them as indicative of post-romantic dualism. This reader appreciates the fact that the Modern poet skillfully worked the *surface* text in line 1 so that it appeared to involve only two actants ("[tú]"/"me"). Two actants seem easily translatable into the dyad "Yo y Yo" of the title. The fact that in his *deep* text the Modern poet con-cealed four actants is a testimony to his ingenuity for condensing and displacing.

However, *post-modern* readers believe, after Lacan, that such du-alism is endemic to the post-Oedipal stage of life (see chap. 1); they seize on this grammatical prestidigitation, this graphemic illusionism, as an indication of cracks the implied poet must paper over. These readers see the artist at his fabulating best and suspect that self is of a more complex fabrication, that it can be no simple conjoining of four actants. They suspect that later the speaker will manifest ideological preferences which will deconstruct whatever ingenious fictions the im-plied Modern poet labored so hard to spin.

Figures of Speech

The text's second sequence belongs more to the *post-modern* reader who has learned, from de Man and Hillis Miller, that figure on figure figured is writing's game (see chap. 1).

Lines 2 and 3 contain the imagery that generates the rest of the poem:

> 2 como la imajen
> 3 del chorro, al chorro, en el espejo de agua.

> 2 like the image
> 3 of the jet, to the jet, in the mirror of water.

The image is spatial: the rising and falling of a vertical jet of water is reflected in a horizontal pool. A virtual (or reflected) jet, "la imajen / del chorro," is opposed to one that is real (or three-dimensional), "al chorro." Similitude ("como") links this to the combination of transitive and reflexive movement found in the second person actants of line 1. The virtual jet correlates with inner and passive phenomena; the real jet with active and outer realities.

The image of a jet of water and its reflection in a pool confirms the speaker in his first ideal for selfhood. Just as the real jet appears to contain the virtual jets, and just as "me" (l. 1) appears to contain the conflicting dynamics the text explores, so *Self*, as "Dr. Jekyll," may contain contrary and antagonistic selves.

The second line, "como la imajen," is in fact a simile in embryo. As experience has taught that a simile elucidates the object to which it refers, the *modern* reader expects the simile to reduce to a more conventional world view the rather enigmatic tensions found in the first line. Such expectations are frustrated, however, by the apparent arbitrariness of the poetic syntax here. In the first place, the simile is left in an unusual state of incompletion at the end of the second line, and, in the second place, it is quickly transformed into a metaphor when it is taken up in the third line.

The embryonic simile, "como la imajen," is in fact located in the most incomplete line of the poem, which is to say that it is automatically foregrounded.[8] Such foregrounding directs the reader's attention on to an abstract noun ("imajen"). An abstract noun, in run-on position, in an uncompleted utterance is sufficient deviation from the implied poet's norm to warrant inspection.[9]

Rhyme has not determined the position of "imajen," so attention shifts to its semantic—inter- and intratextual—connotations. Of the various allusions in the lexeme "imajen," those sememes associated with love and beauty, and with religious and inner spiritual development seem most relevant.

Intertextually, "imajen" suggests a love code. *Specialist* readers know that within the *Obra* "imajen" alludes to "la amada" (as does "el chorro").[10] The embryonic simile therefore hints that this message is addressed to the beloved "[tú]"—Zenobia, the poet's wife. On one level, therefore, the implicit "[tú]" of line 1 is the speaker's amatorial ideal.

Intratextually, "imajen" is foregrounded in so far as it is repeated in the closure (ll. 13–14), by which time aesthetics have become the text's prime concern. This indicates that poetic image rather than self has developed into the text's dominant concern. Indeed, such a move is initiated in lines 2 and 3, in the syntagma "como la imajen / del chorro, al chorro," where "imajen" is the first element to be presented, and by virtue of its position, intensely foregrounded. This directs the reader's attention, in the first place, to the virtual jet ("la *imajen* / del chorro"), and, then, only in the second place, to the real jet. On another level, therefore, the implicit "[tú]" of line 1 is the speaker's ideal poetic image.

Two additional intertextual allusions in "imajen" are relevant: religious belief and inner spiritual idealism.

"Imajen" hints at a religious code, in so far as it is a distant echo of the biblical "graven image." The religious code is actualized in the text in such nouns as "camino eterno" (l. 4) and "luz" (l. 9)—Saul blinded by light on the road to Damascus—(and even in "cuna" [l. 7], which can mean manger or cradle). This suggests a religious parallel for the speaker's quest: God as the "Light"; Christ as "the way, the truth and the light." On another level, therefore, this utterance is addressed to the speaker's religious alter-ego.[11]

The simile "imajen" is set in opposition to the metaphor "water mirror," which triggers associations with Narcissus. The speaker is therefore addressing the perils of self-reflection, that inveterate quest to conjoin self to other, the lower to the higher self. On another level, therefore, this utterance is a dialogue between the speaker and his spiritual double.

"Imajen" is therefore another polysemic lexeme, but its connotations are limited to four, that is, to the speaker's latent concerns: for art and for love, for religious and for inner spiritual impulses.

The simile ("como la imajen / del chorro, al chorro,") begun in line 2 is, in line 3, transformed into a metaphor. "El chorro" is not reflected in "el agua," a locution which could complete the simile, but in "el espejo de agua." A "water mirror" is a metaphor which moves the simile's point of reference from the empirical world ("jet," "mirror") into a realm created and defined by language alone ("water mirror"). The text thereby foregrounds the fictive, the imag(e)inary, that which appears to be; it becomes preoccupied with image first, and second with empirical reality: refle[x/ct]ive, then transitive; mind, then body; inner, then outer.

The *modern* reader will note, here, that the speaker prioritizes imagination when he addresses his ideals for love and art, for religious and inner spiritual idealism. This reader sympathizes with the Modern poet who wished to make all cohere in "imajen," to "balance all, bring all to mind." [12] The *post-modern* reader, however, will note that the Modern poet is being thwarted in his valiant attempt to discover his self, because the "text" arranges reality so that the illusory supplants the concrete or three-dimensional. This reader can interpret these utterances only as a dialogue between the speaker's "imaginary" and "symbolic" selves.

Analysis of figures of speech ends by noting that the speaker's first insights into self are metaphorical. The fact that the origins of self are a fiction, an "imajen," is what returns to haunt the speaker in the poem's closure.

Structural Patterns

The *modern* reader discovers a pattern in the text's nouns, which is also encountered in its verbs, adjectives, sounds, and stanzaic form.

Line 3 is striking for the repetition of "chorro" which, it turns out, initiates a pattern of noun repetition in the poem. The poem contains twenty-two nouns, of which six are repetitions. Three of the six, "alma," "espejo," "imajen," foreground the interior, self- reflective nature of the exploration (the intransitivity of l. 1); two others, "fuerza," "chorro," stress its vitality; and the sixth, "camino," expresses, in its unmodified state, the speaker's desire for transitivity—that his quest link him with exterior reality. Noun repetition therefore fictionalizes a Modern ideal: that a struggle between exterior and interior ideals ("road" versus "soul") will result in the discovery of inner regeneration ("strength," "jet").

The noun pool in general supports this interpretation. Nouns range from the relatively concrete—"espejo," "camino," "ojos,"—to the totally abstract—"fuerza," "afán," "encuentro." All other nouns fall somewhere between these extremes of concretion and abstraction.[13] In addition, patterns of de-concretion and de-abstraction make the concrete nouns less concrete, and the abstract less abstract. The text's most concrete nouns are modified by abstract phrases: "camino *eterno*," "espejo *de agua*," and "*el alma* de mis ojos." Its most abstract nouns are concretized: "fuerza" (l. 7) and "encuentro" (l. 12) are personified, although weakly; "afán" (l. 7) is modified by "cuna" ("cradle," "source"). Therefore a movement away from the utterly abstract and the totally concrete is a feature of this text's "naked" energy.

Line 4 is significant, with regard to verbs, in that it contains the poem's only future tense. Apart from "hallaré," all verbs are present indicative. This indicates that the speaker is concerned with the present moment, and with the paradoxical and antagonistic activities of "searching" and "opposing" objects in present time and space.

In addition, verbal aspect is significant. The text's eleven verbs are in the active not passive voice.[14] Also, in relative terms, there is a gradation in the activity denoted, which ranges from the dynamic action of "salta[r]" (l. 8) to the static states of "no sé," "es," "anhela" (ll. 8, 9, 10). The remaining seven verbs denote a type of activity that falls somewhere between those dynamic/static extremes.

Moreover, in the text's phonemic structure there is a pattern of mediation. By far the majority of vowels and consonants are articulated in the mid position.[15]

A comparable structural pattern occurs in the deployment of adjectives. In keeping with a "naked" style, there are only three: "eterno" (l. 4), "igual" (l. 7), and "poderosa" (l. 14). The last refers to the power of the "imajen"; the first, "eterno," to eternal ideals (religious, spiritual, amatorial, aesthetic). The adjective in mid position, located more or less in the middle of the poem, functions anagrammatically to signify the equalizing ("igual") of contrary forces and urges which the

Modern poet encounters through wrestling with the energies this text generates.

Furthermore, there seems to be a pattern to what is otherwise an unremarkable stanzaic form. There are fourteen lines in this text: the requisite number for a sonnet. The text is brought to a close with a two line stanza: as were sonnets that ended with a couplet. In addition, the text is divided into four sections, as was the English—Shakesperian, Spensarian—sonnet. A *modern* reader can appreciate the poem's structure as a reflection of the implied poet's struggle with form, with tradition. For the *specialist* reader of Jiménez's *Obra*, it hints at the poet's talent for subjecting the already constituted to a process of transformation; his desire to modify, not reject, the classical, the formal impulse; his need to be original, but within his tradition.

A pattern thereby emerges, for the *modern* reader, in which poetic energy and imagination move away from polarities bounded by concrete/abstract, dynamic/static, outer/inner, image/world, self/other, tradition/innovation. Actions move toward that site in which actants might coalesce. The *specialist* reader recognizes this as the quest of the implied poet who, around 1949, toward the end of his creative life, wrote that he saw his work as a quest to discover an elusive point of intuitive grace (*LP* 1343–44).

Modern readers delight in believing they have uncovered such patterns because they were educated—by Jakobson in particular—to see them as constitutive of Modern poetry.[16] The *post-modern* reader, however, knows that such patterns are the formulations of an historically selected discourse, and that all they can explore is fictive being. The pleasures from such insights exist for both readers—although the pleasure is that of Jekyll and Hyde between Scylla and Charybdis.[17]

Semantics

The remainder of the poem pits rhetorical question against emotive response. Lines 4–8 are an interrogative in which the speaker questions the goals he set out to achieve ("¿Cómo hallaré . . . de mí salta?"). The question is never answered, but after posing it the speaker is surrounded by light: "Todo, en torno, es de luz" (l. 9). This illumination provokes two exclamations, one of which (ll. 10–12) is spoken by an explicit "yo" ("¡Mas yo no puedo . . . tú al encuentro!"). However, the other exclamation (ll. 13–14) introduces a completely different tone of voice into the text ("¡Ay, . . . ay!").

Lines 4 and 5 contain a first person actant, implicit in "hallaré" (l. 4). This actant—the implicit "[yo]"—is endowed with inner, spiritual vision ("el alma de mis ojos" [l. 5]), and glimpses eternal ideals ("el camino eterno" [l. 4]). It gazes with the soul's eyes (as opposed to the proverbial mind's eye). The implicit "[yo]" therefore fuses two ideals: the traditional faith of culture in the unquestioned superiority of religious *and* spiritual insights.

For the speaker, this is a passive experience ("que *da*"); it is also an "espejo" or mirror-image. In addition, that mirror-image is, once contrasted with the "fuerza" and "afán" with which "imajen" is actualized in line 7, a negative experience. Furthermore, in the context of this poem's lexicon, the syntagma "el camino eterno" is a cliché. It has the ring of biblical language, and associates with the "surrounding light" of line 9 (Saul's journey to Damascus). A *post-modern* reader again follows Riffaterre (*Semiotics* 39–42, 208) in interpreting clichés as displacements, as manifestations of latent content, which the text is developing in condensed fashion. "El camino eterno" is an allusion to pre-existent ideologies that impressed the implicit "[yo]" in the past, but are called into question at the moment of writing.

Lines 6, 7, and 8 confront the implicit "[yo]" with three more paradoxical and antagonistic actants, all of which challenge its religious faith in traditional spiritual values. In lines 6 and 8 the implicit "[tú]" of line 1 is referred to explicitly as "tú." The "tú" is dyadic: it is actualized as a subject pronoun ("tú") and a prepositional pronoun ("ti"). The former springs from the latter: "como tú [saltas] de ti."

Deictics link these two second person actants to the implicit "[yo]." They come from "*ese* camino," implying that the three of them are distant in both time and space.[18] As line 6 established "el camino" as "eterno," the goal ("el fin") and/or source ("cuna") of these actants must be that which has always been considered by culture to be "eternal." As the implicit "[yo]" is a mirror-image of religious and inner spiritual ideals, its eternal goal will be Eden or Heaven. As the "tú"/"ti" actants are mirror-images of ideal love and beauty—which, in Petrarchan fashion, are glimpsed on a road that leads to eternity—their goal and origin will be the realm of the Platonic Absolutes.

The passivity, the reflexivity, of these actants is vigorously challenged in line 8 by a "mí" actant. It experiences "*este* afán," which implies that it is closer to present time and space. In contrast to "tú"/"ti," its origin is mysterious and unknown ("sin cuna"); it springs from some undefinable ("no sé de dónde") space within the implicit "[yo]" who senses the dynamism of a "leaping image" ("imajen . . . que . . . salta").[19]

"Salta[r]" (l. 8), the verb that represents the strength of the "mí" actant, is the most dynamic in the text. In addition, the poetic syntax, by postponing "salta" until the very end of line 8, makes sure that it receives maximum emphasis. Such defamiliarization helps to foreground the "mí" actant; to mark it positively as a uniquely felt immanent force, whose original impulses the speaker must pursue.

The "mí" actant signifies the speaker's impulse to go beyond what is already constituted and predicted; it represents a self that demands more of itself in the here and now. In this respect it differs from the implicit "[yo]" which contents itself with established truths. In aesthetic terms, the "mí" is the Modern poet's need for challenge, his desire to be an original artist, articulate his own "andar/voz/ritmo," explore the unknown, discover the unique, resolve antinomies, dissolve post-romantic (or post-Oedipal) dichotomies. For the *specialist* reader, the "mí" correlates with the "yo eterno" or higher self, and with the implied poet's desire to discover in aesthetic practice an ethical praxis.[20]

However, the speaker experiences a dilemma, as the tone and syntax of lines 6–8 indicate. The elided syntax of these lines implies that all actants are felt by the speaker to have "igual fuerza." The speaker cannot pursue the "mí" to the exclusion of the implicit "[yo]," nor can he forsake these and pursue the "tú"/"ti" actants. A balance must be found.

Line 8 does juxtapose the actants—"como tú de ti / de mí salta"— but it separates them by the unknown:

> 8   . . . tú . . . ti . . . , no sé de dónde, . . . mí . . .

As in prior texts, commas indicate that the actants—"tú"-"ti"-"[yo]"-"mí"—are close, but that they do not coalesce; there is no complete fusion or harmonious integration. Commas signify that actants remain separated while reacting in an area of unknown, mysterious, and enigmatic tension. In addition, line 8 is the longest in the poem, and, rhythmically, the most tense. For a *modern* reader, its jerky sounds create a kinesthetic image of the extreme agitation the speaker experiences when exploring such contradictory impulses.[21] It is at this point in the text that disintegration of self, fragmentation into arbitrariness, become most possible.

By the end of stanza 2, the *modern* reader infers that the speaker's self would be a coalescence of all four actants. The *post-modern* reader, on the other hand, is enthralled by the commas, which are signifying a mere provisional coordination.

With stanza 3 the enigmatic tensions and contradictory drives generate light, not darkness:

> 9   Todo, en torno, es de luz.
> 10 ¡Mas yo no puedo ir a ese sinfín que anhela el alma,
> 11 por este punto—¡el suyo!—a que me sales
> 12 tú al encuentro!

> 9   All, round about, is in light.
> 10 But I cannot go to that endlessness the soul craves,
> 11 through this point—theirs!—at which you come out
> 12 to meet me!

"*Ese* sinfín" (l. 10) relates to "*ese* camino" (l. 6), an infinitude that promises escape from the limitations of time and space. Such unbounding is, in traditional fashion, what the soul craves: "que anhela el alma" (l. 10). This is the traditional faith of the implicit "[yo]" in purely spiritual fulfillment and religious vision, against which, in line 10, an explicit "yo" speaks: "Mas yo no puedo ir a ese sinfín que anhela el alma."

With line 10, self ceases to be designated either by an object ("me") or by a prepositional ("mí") pronoun. Self becomes a subject pronoun ("yo"); but self remains pronominal.

This explicit "yo," the regenerated "Dr. Jekyll," declares its unwillingness to undertake a journey to the infinite, to surrender the integrated actant (*Self*) to any of the subsidiary actants the text has explored. Its reasons (in ll. 11 and 12) are that the "tú" actants (love and poetry) have made manifest a form of spirituality the implicit "[yo]" has always desired.

Actantial opposition has resulted in the emergence of an explicit "yo," which uncovers in present time *and* present space ideals hitherto considered unattainable by a consciousness bounded by time and space. This explicit "yo" claims, in perplexed surprise and consternation, that its struggle has surrounded it with a light, the resplendent sun it so desired, within which it envisions what it calls "este punto" (l. 11). That this vision was a complete surprise is indicated in the unfamiliar expression "[¡]tú al encuentro!," which, in all probability, is a transform of the familiar and colloquial greeting "tú por aquí." Such deviation permits the text to foreground the unexpectedness of the discovery of this "point."

"Este punto" associates, for the *modern* reader, with "este afán" (l. 7)—the only other noun in the text modified by the demonstrative "este"—to indicate that the explicit "yo" was impelled toward this vision by the zeal of the dynamic "mí." However, the "tú" actants are also located at this point: "a que me sales / tú al encuentro" (ll. 11–12). The explicit "yo" perceives "este punto" as a space in which the activities of the second person actants (love and poetry) are integrated with those of the first person (religious and inner spiritual vision). It is *their* space: "¡el suyo!" It is the center of energy to which all patterns in the text so far converge, where all urges flourish in a state of mysterious tension, enigma, process; an area in which actants of the protean fiction "Yo y Yo" thrive in coherent but continual strife and transformation.[22]

A *modern* reader will note that, in stanza 3, all actants coalesce and that they give voice to the explicit "yo," the "Dr. Jekyll" persona, who speaks of a novel and unexpected fulfillment in its ideals. Such readers believe that the Modern poet in art discovers a strong, vibrant, dynamic "imajen" which leads him beyond narcissistic self-engrossment. These readers focus on the positive marking for "imajen" and see it as the Modern quester's momentary experience of *true* reality.

A *specialist* reader will interpret the "light" generated by this "point" as signifying the attainment of the solar vitality after which the Modern poet has quested. "Light" and "point" signify the desired integration of *Self*.

Despite all this, *post-modern* (Lacanian) readers, who sardonically interpret the stanza as the speaker's "imaginary" fulfillment, one never obtainable in the "symbolic" realm of post-Oedipal reality, have those suspicions confirmed by the rest of the text. Between lines 12 and 13 the ideal Modern poet, the explicit "yo," comes upon a ditch over which imag(e)ination could not leap; the text, that is, reaches an aporia.[23]

Stanza 4 clearly breaks the euphoric tone and mood, the glorious vision, of the preceeding lines. In it, the closure, a reader finds not a representative nor an interrogative utterance, but an expressive one in which pain ("¡Ay!") is conmingled with lamentation. The speaker now confronts the imag(e)inative insights of the text. It is "imajen" that is active and dynamic, that has strength ("fuerza"), and that possesses a life ("vida") and a power ("poderosa") of its own: "imajen," not the explicit "yo."

By surrounding "vida" with exclamation marks, the text refers the *modern* reader back to the only other occurrence of exclamation marks in the text—"¡el suyo!" (l. 11)—to signify that "punto" not explicit "yo" has "¡vida!"

The speaker of the concluding lines, which are framed by "¡Ay!" to foreground disillusionment, laments that the explicit "yo" is an "imajen," whose insights are achieved only in fiction, in *poesis*, in imag(e)ination. The speaker is also pained to realize that the "punto"—although an image that leaps for life—is generated by actantial opposition with and within a text, and that any unique form of coalescence must be a linguistic point of no rest but of perpetual configuring.

The implied Modern poet attained such insights in the exploratory voices of the first twelve lines, but the implied post-modern poet, in the closure, realized that fictions created in order to understand self are self-generating, that they reflect only upon language's ingenuity, and not upon the unplumbed depths of the human mind or soul.

The comma, which figures prominently in this sequence of lines, has figured that coordination from line 1, where it displaced the conjunction "y." The comma, unlike the period or the semicolon, marks out a temporary and undefinitive space in which such configurings occur. It corresponds to the pronominal status self attained in the text, the only status self ever achieves for a post-modernist, one constituted by its relationships, not by any inherently fixed worth.

The coordination in the conjunction "y," searched for in prior texts on selfhood, proves to be provisional. Moreover, it is ironic that at the very point of specular luminosity, when "Dr. Jekyll's" ideals for art, love, and life appear to have been reached, the "Mr. Hyde" persona, self-as-image, rears its self-reflexive, post-modern head.

Conclusion

In "Yo y Yo" the speaker experienced the selfhood for which the Modern poet quested. It is therefore appropriate to place that quest in a broader perspective, that is, within a tradition of selfhood established by Modern poets.

One such conception is the fragmented or heteronymous self. Rimbaud, as noted, was claiming—in 1871—that "Je est un autre"; this fractured self became a common concern of many twentieth-century poets (Pessoa, for instance). In fact, most of Jiménez's contemporaries encountered some form of split or alienated self. In the 1920s, for example, Antonio Machado encountered, in the persona of Abel Martín, "la esencial heterogeneidad del ser" (228, 233). Eliot concluded "The Hollow Men" (1925) with "the Shadow": "Between the idea / And the reality / Between the motion / And the act / Falls the Shadow," (*Poems* 91–92). Yeats in *A Vision* (1925) described what amounts to a perpetual struggle of antithetical selves, and in the conclusion to "Byzantium" (1930) his speaker cried out in despair of "Those images that yet / Fresh images beget" (244).

"Yo y Yo," written between 1917 and 1918, signals from the outset its determination to differentiate itself from such a conception of selfhood. In fact, it begins by exploring what might be termed an overself, a *Self* that can contain all; it then undermines this self and explores the self as a point of integration of disparate and contrary urges. But it concludes in as dispirited a fashion as the work of many contemporary poets by encountering self as image; the latter is a deconstruction of the ideal faith and optimism implicit in the previous selves.

The overself, although the opposite of what Rimbaud was asserting, is curiously analogous to what American poets (Emerson, Whitman) were affirming at approximately the same time as the French *poète maudit*. The overself was in effect explained by Hillis Miller (*Stevens' Rock* 22–24), when he observed that for Emerson "the strong affirming self is the bedrock fiction beneath which one cannot and should not go," and that for both Emerson and Whitman "each self affirm[s] itself . . . as the axis of all, the incorporator of all: 'I am large, I contain multitudes.'" The title and first stanza of "Yo y Yo," in particular the conjunction and foregrounding of "me," allude to an Emersonian bedrock self, a *Self* on which all could rely, from which all might emanate. The *specialist* reader of Jiménez recognizes that such an aggrandized ego is an important thread to the *Obra*.

For instance, in the sonnet "Nada," at the beginning of the *Obra*'s second phase, the speaker declares: "A tu abandono opongo / la elevada torre de mi divino pensamiento; / . . . / buscaré en mis entrañas mi sustento . . ." (*LP* 19).

By *Piedra y cielo*, in "Ruta," the speaker certainly perceives himself as having already assumed such a mantle: "Todos duermen, abajo. / Arriba, alertas, / el timonel y yo. / . . . Yo, los ojos / en lo infinito, guiando / los tesoros abiertos de las almas" (*LP* 763). A clear articulation of this conception of self occurs in *La estación total*, in the well-known poem "El otoñado": "Rico fruto recóndito, contengo / lo grande elemental en mí (la tierra, / el fuego, el agua, el aire) el infinito" (*LP* 1140).

The pursuit of such an aggrandized ego may have satisfied the Modern poet's desire to fulfill the role of a Romantic hero, an ideal Romantic poets bequeathed their heirs, the late romantics (or *simbolista-modernistas*). That such desires are ill suited to the Modern age is implied by Nemes (*Inicios* 173), when she labels "El otoñado" perhaps the most narcissistic poem in the language.

But, "Yo y Yo" does not persist in developing the overself, it modifies it, transforms and deconstructs it into the concept of selfhood as point of integration of all other selves or impulses. "Este punto" is experienced as an imaginative transcendence of all dichotomies, one that leaps for life in paradoxical recognition that *all* is subject to transformation—structures, traditions, ideals. This is a vision that recognizes that only in the dialectical interplay of such opposing tensions is the "point," "life," self, achieved.

This endeavor is tacitly presented as a spiritual ideal worthy of imitation. It is, I believe, a more modest conception of selfhood than that implicit in the overself, for whereas the latter contains all (space and time), the integrated self is experienced within surrounding space and time, as a single site, a point of fulfillment in the infinite and eternal. In pursuing this quest Modern poets may be fulfilling the role of seer, which befell them during the Symbolist epoch, when faith in God declined.

Such an ideal must also be criticized for being narcissistic. However, the mirror-image the anchorite Narcissus encountered entrapped him in sensual and spiritual darkness.[24] The explicit "yo," the regenerated "Dr. Jekyll," is not trapped; it attained its insights neither by sequestering itself from the tensions inherent in reality, nor by embracing an already constituted system of belief. The explicit "yo" asserts that the mirror-image it encountered led not to stagnation and sterility, but through strenuous activity toward light.

The *specialist* reader, following Olson in particular, notes that this quest to fuse contrary impulses persists throughout the Jiménez *Obra* and culminates in its final book of poems, *Animal de fondo*. In "Soy animal de fondo," for example, the point is one of depth: "Este pozo que era, solo y nada más ni menos, / que el centro de la tierra y de su vida" (*LP* 1340). Its most forthright expression occurs in the "Notas" which accompany that book, where Jiménez explains his life's work thus: "Mis tres normas vocativas de toda mi vida: la mujer, la obra, la muerte se me resolvían en conciencia, en comprensión del 'hasta qué' punto divino podía llegar lo humano de la gracia del hombre" (*LP* 1343–44).

As in "Golfo," it is arrival ("llegar") that is foregrounded in these "Notes." The arrival or "punto" here, for the implied poet, is one at which the human experienced the divine. In the context of "Yo y Yo" this is equivalent to the belief that religious and inner spiritual impulses wrestle, in actantial opposition, with the cultivated ideals for art and love, and that this struggle results in the articulation and vision of a higher self.

The *specialist modern* reader must also note, again following Olson's insights, that Jiménez's originality stems from a precarious balance in his vision. His "imajen" is dependent on the past, as well as on the future; its originality is that it moves away from both and encounters "their point" ("¡el suyo!"[l. 11]), a point at which past ideologies are transformed by present realities into future ideals.[25]

In its second stage, therefore, "Yo y Yo" presents selfhood as a glorious and euphoric sensation, one experienced as a momentary thriving in creative tension with surrounding realities—self as an elusive point of intuitive grace. The mystical component to this vision is understandable, for Jiménez was impelled toward it by the deep admiration he had for the work of San Juan de la Cruz, and by the inspiration he derived from Eastern literatures (Tagore in particular). In this conception of self, Jiménez certainly differs from most major contemporary poets (although Stevens's "supreme fiction" [31] is surely comparable: an imag(e)ination that sustains a human kind).

From this perspective, the speaker in "Yo y Yo" attains the unique self, the coalescence of antagonistic impulses, the resplendent, solar light, on which he meditated in "¿Soy yo . . . ?" and "Golfo." This speaker, one could argue, experiences a self that is the same ("lo mismo"), yet different; a self that fuses and blends the contraries: one that is integrated, but only at dynamically elusive points in space and time.

However, as the *post-modern* reading argued, the end of this text presents a third conception of self: self as image. This is the shadow of "Mr. Hyde," which lurks behind the luminosity of "Dr. Jekyll." Only a *post-modern* reader will uncover the presence of such a 'dark' and destructive actant.

When *specialists* allude to this idea, they do so from a positive perspective. They note with approval that in Jiménez self is totally identified with the *Obra*, and that this reading is authorized by the implied poet who boasts that the fate of his corporeal self is utterly immaterial to him, because: "Al lado de mi cuerpo muerto, / mi obra viva" (*LP* 963). Coke-Enguídanos (101), for instance, most recently distinguished between the poet's "empirical self" which dies, and the "lyrical 'yo'" which lives.

This interpretation is aided and abetted by the abounding faith in the *Obra*, as Villar (62) recently observed, which Jiménez proclaimed between 1916 and 1936, the *Obra*'s second phase. In addition, it was during these years, Blasco recently pointed out, that Jiménez was influenced by Ortega's denial that: "la realidad auténtica esté en el sujeto o en el objeto; está, por el contrario, en la mutua relación, relación que es *creación* del arte" (144). Ortega thereby sustains Juan Ramón's optimism during the second phase of the *Obra*, encouraging him in the belief that to live in art, for art's sake, was the supreme attainment of any Modern quester after truth.

But, an uncanny, *post-modern* reading of this contorted sonnet must come back to the negative marking acquired by "imajen" and "espejo" as the text develops. A post-modern, deconstructive perspective must focus on the speaker's horror that self is merely a linguistic construct. It must emphasize the amount of anguish expressed in the closure, where it was realized that "point" is as much a reflection as any "eternal road." This reading is overlooked in idealizing interpretations of the *Obra*; only *post-modern* reading strategies detect it.

Nevertheless, it is quite apparent that in the closure to "Yo y Yo," the speaker realizes, to borrow Hillis Miller's words (*Stevens' Rock* 345) that "any stability or coherence in the self is an effect of language. The self is a linguistic construction rather than being the given, the rock, a solid *point de départ*." Self is a figure of a figure, with no referent in empirical reality and no embodiment as truth.

Such a conception of selfhood is not pursued in the second phase of the *Obra*, but is found in the late (post-1936) phase of Jiménez's "Work." It resurfaces in *Espacio*, to which I now turn, where the *post-modern* reader is intrigued by the "héroe" who discovers not a *Self* that contains all, nor a self that continues to integrate all disparities, but a self that is totally hollow, "un hueco" (*TA* 878).

This reader also notes that Jiménez suppressed "Yo y Yo" from *Leyenda*, that final and extensive anthology of his work which he attempted to complete during the last years of his life. A *post-modern* reader interprets this as suppression from the *Obra* of those rare moments in which the poet glimpsed with horror the independence of language and text, as well as the presence of the uncanny, different other. It is this 'dark' other that Modern artificers can never succeed totally in suppressing, despite the consummate mastery with which they spin their Modern imag(e)inative insights.

Post-Modern:
An Aesthetic for Twilight

6

An Integrated Self
Disintegrating:
Espacio

Espacio is the next major text in the *Obra* in which the speaker addresses the problematics of selfhood. Indeed, those concepts of self that preoccupied the speaker in previous texts resurface in the pages of this long prose-poem (*TA* 851–80). However, as the final sequence of *Espacio* was published in 1954, twenty-five years after "Yo y Yo" (1919), it is not surprising, with the lapse of a quarter of a century, that the speaker's ideals for self are assessed from a less idealistic standpoint.

Between 1919 and 1954 Jiménez published major works, which the next chapter will reassess from the vantage point of *Espacio*'s vision. In *Espacio* the speaker does re-confront the negativity the Modern *Obra* avoided; he struggles to synthesize it with the positive idealism literary history attributes to the "Work," but in certain instances, he fails.

The Text

Espacio is a long prose-poem of almost eight hundred lines (approximately 7,500 words), written "Por La Florida, 1941-1942-1954" (*TA* 880). It is divided into three "Fragmentos." The "Fragmento Primero" and the "Fragmento Tercero" are extensive (3,300 and 3,600 words respectively); they are separated by a shorter, rhapsodic, almost jubilant "Fragmento Segundo" (600 words).

The noun "fragmento" immediately intrigues a *post-modern* reader, who will note that the "Work" is now presenting "fragments," as opposed to the coherent wholes which were the artificer's concern in the

131

Obra's second—Modern—phase. In the *Obra*'s third phase, a *post-modern* reader will conclude, the speaker will settle for fragmented perceptions; he will offer no totalizing vision of reality.

Indeed, a *modern* reader who, for example, checks the use of the conjunction "y" in these "fragments," will encounter no pattern. "Y" registers both coherence and dispersal throughout; it appears that no artificer controls its use (or rhythm, for that matter), or invests it with any special signified. Hence, a *modern* reading of this text would probably prove unfruitful. Indeed, once *Espacio* is contrasted with the Modern *Obra*'s pride (in coherence of form and terseness of style), its focus is found to lie elsewhere. Albornoz (in "Estudio de la obra") has offered the most succinct interpretation of *Espacio*. She writes that it is the "punto culminante de la obra juanramoniana . . . síntesis y re-capitulación." [1] That is, *Espacio* is concerned with ideas, it is an intellectual *summa*tion of the *Obra*. Hence, a *post-modern* reading strategy, with its focus on rhetorical contradictions, more befits its style.

From the point of view of selfhood, *Espacio* is more of a "synthesis" than a "culmination" of the "Work." In other words, it re-poses the following basic rhetorical questions: "¿Soy yo o . . . soy el mendigo?" Am I a self or an other? Am I a 'bright' or a 'dark' actant, light or shadow, day or night? Have I illumined my spatio-temporal locus ("punto") with my love, my work, my life, or have I attained no enlightenment at all?

The speaker in *Espacio* poses those questions in a more aphoristic and philosophical manner. "'Y para recordar porqué he vivido', vengo a ti, río Hudson de mi mar" (*TA* 864), is one example of his phrasing. The speaker now is concerned with the extent to which his life and work have answered humankind's basic metaphysical concerns: why am I living? what am I doing? and where am I heading?

The text itself alludes to such concerns by its foregrounding of the lexeme "suma," a word charged with religious significance, since St. Thomas Aquinas's *Summa Theologica*.[2] A *post-modern* reader will begin to pay particular attention to this lexeme's occurrence, because the speaker in *Espacio* questions its worth, whereas as a Modern poet he had once asserted that "la rosa" was his "suma": "A ti me lego, rosa. Sé tú, desnuda, mi descanso; sé tú la suma, para mí, rosa, mujer ya casi y obra ya, de mujer, muerte y obra" (*Leyenda* 532, "Hacia otra desnudez" no. 1011).

The worth of "suma" is challenged by a rhetorical question in *Espacio*'s "Fragmento Primero." The speaker asks: "¿Qué es, entonces, la suma que no resta; dónde está, matemático celeste, la suma que es el todo y que no acaba?" (*TA* 853).

Nevertheless, a few pages later the speaker implicitly provides an answer to that question:

Grande es lo breve, y si queremos ser y parecer más grandes, unamos sólo con amor, no cantidad. El mar no es más que gotas unidas, ni el amor que murmullos unidos, ni tú, cosmos, que cosmillos unidos. Lo más bello es el átomo último, el solo indivisible, y que por serlo no es ya más pequeño. Unidad de unidades es lo uno; ¡y qué viento más plácido levantan esas nubes menudas al cenit; qué dulce luz es esa suma roja única! Suma es la vida suma, y dulce. (*TA* 856)

In these thoughts the speaker is claiming that the ultimate ideal is a life lived with love (which lovers provide each other with in small doses, "murmullos," over time).

In addition to this, the first fragment provides a second implicit answer to the question it asked of the "celestial mathematician," when it subsequently affirms that the poetic image, in conjunction with love, is perfection: "suma gracia y gloria de la imajen" (*TA* 862).

Although "suma" is not used in the "Fragmento Segundo," the word "ideal" is selected to refer to the entire fragment's sense of wonder and ecstasy, which the speaker, as an integrated self, has experienced in the world.

The "Fragmento Tercero," however, does provide a third implicit answer to the metaphysical question, because it selects "suma" to refer to the speaker's "conciencia": "Difícilmente un cuerpo habría amado así a su alma, como mi cuerpo a ti, conciencia de mi alma; porque tú fuiste para él suma ideal y él se hizo por ti, contigo, lo que es" (*TA* 879). The speaker therefore believes that the cultivation of a heightened consciousness, a heightened mental, spiritual and sensual awareness is a "suma ideal."

By attending to the diachronic occurrence of the lexeme "suma," a *post-modern* reader has engaged the thoughts of a speaker whose basic concerns are those of the *Obra*: love, aesthetics, death, and spiritual (including existential) enlightenment. Following Eco (*Role* 26), I shall refer to these as the *Obra*'s "narrative topics," that is, "topics [that] rule the comprehension of the text at [its] higher levels." This means that by analysis of a lexeme ("suma") within a micro-text of the *Obra* (i.e. within *Espacio*), the *post-modern* reader has been able to engage the fundamental concerns of The Macro-Text (i.e. the *Obra*).

In addition, this analysis has revealed that, between 1941 and 1954, as Jiménez reflected on the extent to which he had approximated his ideals, the more anxious, more dubitative, did his tone become. By *Espacio*, "Dr. Jekyll" has relinquished absolute control of the "Work"; the 'dark' voices of "Mr. Hyde" are more frequently heard. The extent of the anguish that is latent in Jiménez's poetry during these years is rarely mentioned. Sánchez-Barbudo (*La obra* 123–24) is one of the few critics to comment on it. Coke-Enguídanos (141) is more cautious; she notes the "provisional and unfinished character" of the final fragment.

The Fragments

The task is quixotic, given that *Espacio* is an utterly alogical discourse,[3] but before any serious discussion of this text can be undertaken an attempt must be made to summarize ways in which its speaker confronts the fundamental "narrative topics" of the *Obra*. For this purpose, each "Fragmento" can be divided into a series of "discursive topics." The latter, to adapt Eco (*Role* 26), are "short sequences" of discourse, which "rule the understanding of microstructural elements." That is, a "discursive topic" is to a local structure what a "narrative topic" is to the structure in its entirety. In this case, discursive topics offer different perspectives on the *Obra*'s fundamental concerns (love, work, death, spiritual enlightenment). In most instances, the optimistic opinions of "Dr. Jekyll" are rebutted by the anguish of "Mr. Hyde."

The "Fragmento Primero" offers numerous reflections on love and aesthetics, from both positive and negative perspectives. The speaker reproaches Pierre Abelard for not embracing Héloise's sensual overtures: "hay que encontrar el ideal que existe" (*TA* 858), he exclaims. Love, woman, the real woman (*TA* 854) are lauded throughout. But, though he repeatedly asserts that love is the basis of all, the speaker continually emphasizes love's negative aspects: sexual contact is deprecated (*TA* 853; also 875) and only doomed lovers, like Héloise and Abelard, Othello and Desdemona, figure in his discourse.

Poetry is also presented from a positive and a negative light. The bird ("el pájaro") is used to symbolize art, song, poetry. In a euphoric hymn to song, the speaker proclaims: "Tú y yo, pájaro, somos uno" (*TA* 861). The "pájaro" (like the speaker) is a god ("nunca he visto tu dios como hoy lo veo" [*TA* 861]), which has given to all things whatever "sustancia" and greatness they possess (*TA* 861). Against this idealism must be set the despair the speaker voices, early in the "Fragmento Primero," over language's ambiguity, over the fact that a flower can be interpreted as a sexual symbol ("Y el idioma, ¡qué confusión!" [*TA* 853]).

As for death and spiritual enlightenment, reflections on this topic are scattered throughout the "Fragmento Primero." For example, the speaker dismisses both the notion that there is a grand design or pattern ("'Lo que sea'" [*TA* 860]), and the belief that there are natural endings or neat closures to life and work ("y hay que darle una lección al que lo quiere terminar, al que pretende que lo terminemos" [*TA* 856]). He stresses that life is a natural cycle; that it flowers and it fruits (*TA* 858). It is a tree that blossoms (*TA* 855), as well as a dead stump ("un tocón" [*TA* 858]); "¿Hay otra cosa más que este vivir de cambio y de gloria?" (*TA* 854), he exclaims.

Nevertheless, the "Fragmento Primero" ends by rapturously intoning a hymn to art, to love, and to light (i.e. life). Art creates an "universo májico" (*TA* 862), the speaker claims. He then addresses his art ("imajen"—recalling "Yo y Yo") and exclaims: "¡Vosotras, yo, podemos crear la eternidad una y mil veces, cuando queramos!" (*TA* 863).

Despite this euphoria, it is apparent that in the "Fragmento Primero" the speaker's attitude is neither exclusively that of "Dr. Jekyll" nor exclusively that of "Mr. Hyde"; it is a mêlée of both.

However, the "Fragmento Segundo" becomes "Dr. Jekyll's" chant for joy. This fragment treats the narrative topics from an idealistic perspective. In rhapsodic answer to the question "porqué he vivido" (*TA* 864), the speaker presents (by means of continuous spatio-temporal superpositions)[4] moments of intense fulfillment experienced in New York City (Washington Bridge, Broadway, the cathedral garden of St. John the Divine, Amsterdam Ave., Morningside Heights) and in Spain (Moguer, Madrid, Seville).

One impression left on a reader from this flow of euphoria is that the speaker believes that his life has been utterly fulfilled; it has been one of intense love (*TA* 865) which enabled him to create his "trabajo hermoso" (*TA* 866). The "second fragment" is therefore utterly positive. (However, we shall soon note that negativity creeps into its final lines.)

The "Fragmento Tercero," compared with the first and second fragments, is much more negative. There is a certain degree of recollected euphoria, but it is woven into a dense network of *angst*.

From the point of view of the self's reflections on its attainments, I would divide the fragment into five sequences (or micro-texts), each of which contains (to a greater or lesser degree) reflections on the *Obra*'s basic narrative topics.

In the first micro-text (*TA* 867–68), the speaker returns to the sea, because it alone is eternal and naked ("Desnudez es la vida y desnudez la sola eternidad . . ." [*TA* 867]), and again meditates on the metaphysical queries he has of life.

In the second micro-text (*TA* 869–70), the speaker reflects on what he refers to as "Destino." The following lines imply that in his philosophy, the concept "Destino" had displaced that of the Divine Logos, or Word (John 1 : 1), and that he thinks of it as inevitable:

> Mi Destino soy yo y nada y nadie más que yo; por eso creo en Él y no me opongo a nada suyo a nada mío, que Él es más que los dioses de siempre, el dios de otro, rejidos, como yo por el Destino, repartidor de la sustancia con la esencia. En el principio fué el Destino, padre de la Acción y abuelo o bisabuelo o algo más allá del Verbo. Levo mi ancla, por tanto, izo mi vela para que sople Él más fácil con su viento por los mares serenos o terribles, atlánticos, mediterráneos, pacíficos o los que sean, verdes, blancos, azules, morados, amarillos, de un color o de todos los colores.[5]

"Destino" is inevitable, though not predestined; it is a ship that follows certain winds ("levo mi ancla, por tanto, izo mi vela . . ."). It definitely has a negative aspect (the shipwreck), which is sudden and unexpected death (*TA* 870). But the speaker also insists on a positive (Berkeleyian) facet: "Pero si yo no estoy aquí con mis cinco sentidos, ni el mar ni el viento son viento ni mar; no están gozando viento y mar si no los veo, si no los digo y escribo que lo están. Nada es la realidad sin el Destino de una conciencia que realiza" (*TA* 872). "Destino" is therefore represented from the viewpoint of both personae, "Dr. Jekyll" (who imposes "realidad" with his "conciencia") and "Mr. Hyde" (who knows of terrible seas and shipwrecks).

The third micro-text is a long sequence (*TA* 870–75). It is a reflection on the speaker's varied but chronic existential anguish ("inquietud"), and it contains reflections on all of the *Obra*'s narrative topics.

First, the speaker notes that this "inquietud" is inherent: he calls it his "ritmo vejetativo" and "mi tercer ritmo" (*TA* 870), which he says is close to poetry's rhythm. The text definitely foregrounds "three": the speaker had earlier called this journey "mi mar tercero" (*TA* 868),[6] and at the end of the fragment he speaks of himself as "yo, el tercero, el caído" (*TA* 878). Although "tercero" is negatively marked, it is related to poetry and nature ("vejetativo") and therefore has positive elements within it.

Second, the speaker reflects on *desdoblamiento*. The speaker is disturbed that "dentro de mí hay uno que está hablando, hablando, hablando ahora." He calls this his "segundo yo, que hablas como yo y que no hablas como yo" (*TA* 871). His distress over the lack of an integrated self reaches such a nadir that he later exclaims: "Todos somos actores aquí, y sólo actores" (*TA* 874). Here, the speaker's anguish is acute.[7]

Third, the speaker reflects on love, which has become another cause of his anguish. The speaker is fixated (throughout *Espacio*) on the relationship of Othello and Desdemona. The love of this couple was far from ideal, yet the speaker exclaims: "Y Otelo con Desdémona será lo eterno" (*TA* 874).

Fourth, the speaker reflects on the benefits that accrue from a mature life. This sequence (*TA* 875–76) is positive. In contrast to the youthful beauty and innocence of Michelangelo's statue of David, the speaker champions autumnal ripeness as an ideal condition. He imagines man and woman developed in their maturity to their uttermost perfection. "¡Mujer de otoño; árbol, hombre! ¡cómo clamáis el gozo de vivir, al azul que se alza con el primer frío! ¡Quieren alzarse más, hasta lo último de ese azul que es más limpio, de incomparable desnudez azul!" (*TA* 875).

Fifth, the speaker reflects on death, in *Espacio*'s final sequence (*TA* 876–81). As artist, lover, and man, he jousts with a crab, which he defeats; his prize for winning is hollowness and total silence (outer and inner). The speaker is enveloped by a 'dark' actant: "alguien mayor que yo y el nuevo yo" (*TA* 878). This seems to be the darkness of death that drowns his light ("sol"). Then, in a final monologue, he harangues his "conciencia." Like Othello, he proclaims his desire to give his "conciencia" a final kiss ("para que el beso quedara . . . como un abrazo, por ejemplo, de un cuerpo y su conciencia en el hondón más hondo de lo hondo eterno" [*TA* 879]).

The speaker's final lament is that his "conciencia" will be recycled: "¿Y te has de ir de mí tú, tú a integrarte en un dios, en otro dios que este que somos mientras tú estás en mí, como de dios?" (TA 880).

In the "Fragmento Tercero," therefore, the views of "Dr. Jekyll" are outweighed by those of "Mr. Hyde." "Dr. Jekyll" sees positive elements in "Destino," in the creativity that issues from anguish, and in maturity. "Mr. Hyde" sees negativity in "angustia," in "desdoblamiento," in love, in work, in death, and in spiritual enlightenment.

Espacio, as an example of the third phase of the "Work," contrasts with such texts as "Golfo" and "Yo y Yo" from the *Obra*'s second phase. In these poems, the urge was toward mediation, toward a controlling stasis and the resolution of tensions. In the third phase, the speaker's attitude to life is fluid and dynamic (as is the style); the negative and the positive are accepted as warring actants in the reality of life and art.

Espacio and Negative Lexemes

With *Espacio* negativity resurfaces in the *Obra*, having been repressed in its second phase. However, whereas negativity dominates the *Obra*'s first (pre-Modern) phase, in its third (post-Modern) phase it blends the negativity of "Mr. Hyde" with the positive attitudes and feelings of "Dr. Jekyll." This can be demonstrated by analyzing the manner in which *Espacio* treats the negative lexemes of the *Obra*'s first phase.

First, let me demonstrate the presence of those negative lexemes in *Espacio*;[8] then let me discuss their incorporation into less negative semantic contexts.

The negative cosmology is present. Sun and moon are referred to in the "Fragmento Primero" as "mi nostaljia, como la de la luna, es haber sido sol de un sol un día y reflejarlo sólo ahora" (*TA* 852, and see 878). In addition, at the end of the "Fragmento Tercero" when the speaker kills the crab, he exclaims: "yo llegaba al sol con mi oquedad inmensa . . . y el sol me derretía lo hueco, y mi infinita sombra me entraba en el mar y en él me naufragaba en una lucha inmensa, porque el mar tenía que llenar todo mi hueco" (*TA* 878).

The negative bestiary reappears: "aquel cuervo muerto, suspendido por una pluma de una astilla, y los cuervos aún vivos posados ante él sin atreverse a picotearlo, serios" (*TA* 855). In the "Fragmento Tercero," in addition to the crab, which will be analyzed later, we find: "Un zorro muerto por un coche; una tortuga atravesando lenta el arenal; una serpiente resbalando undosa de marisma a marisma" (*TA* 876).

In addition, there are negative tree trunks (which occur in the same context as negative animals): "¡Un árbol paternal, . . . junto a una casa, solo en un desierto (seco y lleno de cuervos; aquel tronco huero, gris, lacio" [*TA* 855]). "Vi un tocón, a la orilla del mar neutro; arrancado del suelo, era como un muerto animal" (*TA* 858).

The "hombre enlutado" is not referred to. However, one of its metonymic counterparts ("sombra") is often in evidence. The "Fragmento Primero" refers to "la sombra que viene" (*TA* 859), as well as to "la noche inmensa" (*TA* 861). The "Fragmento Tercero" refers to "alguien mayor que yo" and to "mi infinita sombra" (*TA* 878).

However, though negative lexemes are present throughout *Espacio*, they are treated differently from the way they were in the first phase of the *Obra*. In the *Obra*'s pre-Modern phase, negativity dominates. In the *Obra*'s post-Modern phase, negative lexemes are frequently juxtaposed with positive attitudes.

For example, the "Fragmento Segundo" ends with an expression of intense fulfillment (of work, love, life):

Y entré cantando ausente en la arboleda de la noche, y el río que se iba bajo Washington Bridge, con sol aún, hacia mi España por mi oriente, a mi oriente de mayo de Madrid; un sol ya muerto, pero vivo; un sol presente, pero ausente; un sol rescoldo de vital carmín; un sol carmín vital en el verdor; un sol vital en el verdor ya negro; un sol en el negror ya luna; un sol en la gran luna de carmín; un sol de gloria nueva, nueva en otro este; un sol de amor y de trabajo hermoso; un sol como el amor... "Dulce como este sol era el amor." (*TA* 865–66)

Negativity in this passage is alluded to in the phrase "en el negror ya luna," to imply that life is coming to a close. But this negativity is one element in a most jubilant exclamation of the intensely profound fulfillment encountered in life (figured in the sun and the moon); the negativity, the fact that life dies, is incorporated toward the end.

As for the bestiary, negative animals ("cuervo," "zorro") are balanced by the "perro," which appears very frequently in the speaker's thoughts in *Espacio* and is almost exclusively positive. "No, este perro no levanta los pájaros, los mira, los comprende, los oye, se echa al suelo, y calla y sueña ante ellos" (*TA* 862). In the following exclamation from the "Fragmento Primero," "perro" is juxtaposed with a symbolic sun which is about to set on the speaker's life; it is therefore part of a positive-negative context:

> ¡Qué vivo ladra siempre el perro al sol que huye! Y la sombra que viene llena el punto redondo que ahora pone el sol sobre la tierra, como un agua su fuente, el contorno en penumbra alrededor; después, todos los círculos que llegan hasta el límite redondo de la esfera del mundo, y siguen, siguen. Yo te oí, perro, siempre, desde mi infancia, igual que ahora; tú no cambias en ningún sitio, eres igual a ti mismo, como yo. Noche igual, todo sería igual si lo quisiéramos, si serlo lo dejáramos. Y si dormimos, ¡qué abandonada queda la otra realidad! (*TA* 859)

The impact of "dog" here is both positive and negative: it does prod the speaker's memory, and he is led to reflect on the positive (Berkeleyian) impact mind can have on present reality. But the dog barks because all is ominously coming to an end.

Animals also figure in the final sequence of the "Fragmento Tercero": there is a positive flock of herons and a negative "army" of crabs. The positive "garzas" are in touch with nature: "Las garzas blancas habladoras en noches de escursiones altas" (*TA* 876). Although their impact on the speaker is also positive, because they recall those in Moguer, they are immediately followed by the speaker's utterly negative confrontation with a "crab":

> Plegadas alas en alerta unido de un ejército cárdeno y cascáreo, a un lado y otro del camino llano que daba sus pardores al fiel mar, los cánceres osaban craqueando erguidos (como en un agrio rezo de eslabones) al sol de la radiante soledad de un dios ausente. (*TA* 877)

This entire episode of the crab is of plurivalent negative significance (and it will be discussed as a whole below).

140

With regard to negative trees, they occur with positive ones. In the "Fragmento Primero" there are negative trunks, but the speaker sees them as enhanced by death: "Tronco de invierno soy, que en la muerte va a dar de sí la copa doble llena que ven sólo como es los deseados. Vi un tocón, a la orilla del mar neutro; arrancado del suelo, era como un muerto animal; la muerte daba a su quietud seguridad de haber estado vivo" (*TA* 858).

In addition, a negative treetrunk, to which "cuervos" are fixed, "aquel tronco huero, gris, lacio" (*TA* 855), is framed by a sequence dominated by life affirming trees. The sequence begins with: "Entramos por los robles melenudos;" and continues after describing the crows with: "Y un árbol sobre un río. ¡Qué honda vida la de estos árboles . . . qué llenura de corazón total queriendo darse . . . ¡Qué amigo un árbol, aquel pino, verde, grande, pino redondo, verde, junto a la casa de mi Fuentepiña!" (*TA* 855). Clearly, the speaker is balancing the good with the bad. The tree can be a stump, but it can also be that which stretches symbolically toward the sky, as the "Fragmento Tercero" implies with "¡Mujer de otoño; árbol, hombre!" (*TA* 875).

It is highly significant, from a Freudian perspective, that Jiménez, in his mature (post-modern) poetic imagination, returned to the negative lexemes that preoccupied him in the first phase of the "Work," and that he perceived them from both negative and positive perspectives. No longer is his vision solely that of a "Dr. Jekyll" or a "Mr. Hyde"; it is a mixture and melding of both. In this respect much of *Espacio* is, as Albornoz notes, an attempt to synthesize the poet's ideals.

In addition, this fusing of positive with negative helps a *specialist* reader understand the type of "culmination" *Espacio* attains. It is, as Albornoz says, a synthesis of the *Obra*. The lunar aestheticism in the first phase of the "Work" is a thesis; the solar aestheticism of the second phase is an antithesis. The third phase ("un sol en la gran luna de carmín" [*TA* 866]) is striving to synthesize both.

Espacio as Synthesis of Previous Texts on Selfhood

Espacio is also intriguing because of the way it treats those notions of selfhood which previous chapters have analyzed. In the first place, the actantial struggle between the 'bright' "Dr. Jekyll" and the 'dark' "Mr. Hyde" is more fully pursued. In the second place, there are sufficient semantic and imagistic intertexts in *Espacio* which allude to the texts previously analyzed in this study.

There is no doubt that the two actants, first diagnosed in "¿Soy yo quien anda esta noche?," are present. There is the 'bright' actant (of the "Work's" second phase) who affirms the intense fulfillment derived from life, love, work: "Alas, cantos, luz, palmas, olas, frutas me rodean, me envuelven en su ritmo, en su gracia, en su fuerza delicada; y yo me olvido de mí entre ello, y bailo y canto, río y lloro por los otros, embriagado" (*TA* 854). There is a 'dark' actant who looks at finitude with fortitude: "¡mírame bien a mí, pájaro mío, consuelo universal de mujer y hombre! Vendrá la noche inmensa, abierta toda, en que me cantarás del paraíso, en que me harás el paraíso aquí, yo, tú, aquí, ante el echado insomnio de mi ser" (*TA* 861).

However, in the "Fragmento Tercero" (1954), the 'dark' actant becomes less stoic, becomes 'darker'. Whereas the first two fragments accept the ups and downs, the "constante ir y venir" (Albornoz, "Estudio de la obra" 75) with relish (e.g. "¿Hay otra cosa más que este vivir de cambio y de gloria?" [*TA* 854]), the third fragment foregrounds 'darker' imagery, it compares life to "una pesadilla náufraga o un sueño dulce, claro, embriagador" (*TA* 870).

Besides the actantial struggle noted in earlier texts on selfhood, *Espacio* contains, for the *specialist* reader, allusions to those prior texts. Whereas the speaker in "¿Soy yo . . . ?" did not understand the nature of the "dark" and uncanny other inside him, *Espacio* recognizes it as a reality. The speaker refers to it as: "segundo yo, que hablas como yo y que no hablas como yo" (*TA* 871), an echo of "Y todo / es lo mismo y no es lo mismo." Although *Espacio*'s speaker is not at all easy with this intrusive, loquacious, and uninvited inner guest ("¡Calla, segundo yo, que hablas como yo y que no hablas como yo; calla maldito!" [*TA* 871]), he does accept and understand the intruder as part of his "Destino," which the speaker in "¿Soy yo . . . ?" failed to do.

Moreover, a *post-modern* reader will note that the fluid state of indeterminacy, of sameness and difference, first intuited in "¿Soy yo . . . ?," is brought to creative fruition in the style and vision of *Espacio*. In "¿Soy yo . . . ?" the play of differences resulted in amorphous form, constant motion, poly-perspectival textuality, lack of an individual essence, all of which are figured in the coming and going of the thoughts of the speaker in this prose poem.

Imagery found in "Golfo" also occurs in *Espacio*. For example, in

"Golfo" the *modern* reader found "la nube—blanco cúmulo—," and in *Espacio* he encounters: "¡y qué viento más plácido levantan esas nubes menudas al cenit; qué dulce luz es esa suma roja única!" (*TA* 856). These lines attest to one of the speaker's peak experiences; they express the supreme fulfillment the speaker experienced in life. But unlike "Golfo," where the clouds signified the speaker's indeterminate state, in *Espacio*, "esas nubes menudas" signify an intense delight in smaller—less idealistic—achievements.

In addition, some of the lexematic contrasts found in "Golfo" occur in *Espacio*. In particular, the contrast between "nada" and "todo" is to be noted. For example, the sea is "más muerte que la tierra, el mar lleno de muertos de la tierra, sin casa." Then immediately following this, the sea is a site of fulfillment: "'El mar que fué mi cuna, mi gloria y mi sustento; el mar eterno y solo que me llevó al amor'" (*TA* 857). These lines are from the "Fragmento Primero," and in the "Fragmento Tercero" the sea is again important. As he did in "Golfo," the speaker returns to it to think. He imagines a more perfect society (one, in particular, in which blacks are recognized, and in which they develop their full potential), and he reflects: "Allí la vida está más cerca de la muerte, la vida que es la muerte en movimiento, porque es la eternidad de lo creado, el nada más, el todo, el nada más y el todo confundidos" (*TA* 873). It is in the waters of such a state that the speaker envisions the blending together of all colors.

Also, the "nada"—"todo" opposition in this sequence impels the speaker to articulate an ethical vision. He implies that if society in general could accept what he has had to accept, namely, that death is very near life, that "nada" is interchangeable with "todo," then the worth of the blacks would be recognized, and they would cease to be exploited. This is an instance of the "ética estética" Jiménez always sought to express. As a Modern poet Jiménez rarely managed to incorporate such ethical concerns into the *Obra* (the *Diario* being the exception), but as a post-Modern, in his final "fragment," he succeeded.

As for "Yo y Yo," one of the distinctive features of that poem was the desire to achieve coordination. A *modern* reader would argue, as does Coke-Enguídanos (122–42), that the "Fragmento Segundo" and parts of the "Fragmento Primero" manifest a self that is integrated with itself and its desires. However for each instance of coordination a *modern* reader finds, a *post-modern* reader will find another that subverts it. For example, at the beginning of the first fragment the speaker exclaims in consternation: "Enmedio hay, tiene que haber un punto, una salida; el sitio del seguir más verdadero, con nombre no inventado que llamamos, en nuestro desconsuelo, Edén, Oasis, Paraíso, Cielo, pero que no lo es, y que sabemos que no lo es" (*TA* 853).

That, of course, is another way of referring to the "punto" achieved in "Yo y Yo." By the end of the fragment it seems that the speaker has re-discovered that "punto" in the immensity between the sky and the sea: "¡Espacio y tiempo y luz en todo yo, en todos y yo y todos! ¡Yo con la inmensidad! Esto es distinto; nunca lo sospeché y ahora lo tengo." But then he goes on to explain this as: "Los caminos son solos entradas o salidas de luz, de sombra, sombra y luz; y todo vive en ellos para que sea más inmenso yo, y tú sea. ¡Qué regalo de mundo, qué universo májico, y todo para todos, para mí, yo! (*TA* 862). This is an acknowledgment of the fact that there is no one true "camino eterno . . . de luz" which once encountered provides the self with a site in which it will always be eternally fulfilled. As he had begun to suspect in "Yo y Yo," the speaker implies that "caminos" are merely entrances and exits; they lead nowhere in themselves; they merely provide a structure along which light and shade, positive and negative may emerge, coalesce, defuse. Or, as he implies in "Golfo," they provide a structure which abuts in the joy of arriving, which is a pleasure that is forever mitigated by the sadness of departing.

An amatorial code also links "Yo y Yo" and *Espacio*. For example, the speaker in *Espacio* affirms his faith in the symbolic sun of love. The "Fragmento Segundo" ends with: "un sol de gloria nueva, nueva en otro este; un sol de amor y de trabajo hermoso; un sol como el amor . . . 'Dulce como este sol era el amor'" (*TA* 866). However, this is undermined by criticisms of Abelard's rejection of Héloise's love (TA 857–58), by aspersions the speaker casts on sexual love ("'amor e[n] el lugar del escremento'" [TA 853]), and by the speaker's insistence that "Otelo y Desdémona será lo eterno" (*TA* 874).

An aesthetic code also links *Espacio* and "Yo y Yo." The "Fragmento Primero" ends on the most idealistic note with regard to the power of the poetic image, as optimistic as the mid section of "Yo y Yo." The speaker has created what he refers to as an "universo májico" and continues:

¡Yo, universo inmenso, dentro, fuera de ti, segura inmensidad! Imájenes de amor en la presencia concreta; suma gracia y gloria de la imájen, ¡vamos a hacer eternidad, vamos a hacer la eternidad, vamos a ser eternidad, vamos a ser la eternidad? ¡Vosotras, yo, podemos crear la eternidad una y mil veces, cuando queramos! ¡Todo es nuestro y no se nos acaba nunca! ¡Amor, contigo y con la luz todo se hace, y lo que haces, amor, no acaba nunca! (*TA* 862–63)

The fragment ends with this resplendent affirmation of belief that perfect love and poetry combine to create what will be eternal. But a *postmodern* reader will note that in order to express this idealism the artificer resorted to a trick of language called *calambur*: "vamos a hacer" slips into "vamos a ser," and that he included these language games inside rhetorical question marks. In addition, the "Fragmento Primero" did not begin on this idealistic and affirmative note. It began by lamenting that the lexeme "flor" can be interpreted as conveying a sexual message, and then went on to protest the ambiguities inherent in language: "Y el idioma, ¡qué confusión!, qué cosas nos decimos sin saber lo que nos decimos. Amor, amor, amor (lo cantó Yeats), 'amor e[n] el lugar del escremento'. ¿Asco de nuestro ser, nuestro principio y nuestro fin; asco de aquello que más nos vive y más nos muere? ¿Qué es, entonces, la suma que no resta . . ." (*TA* 853).[9]

Hence, though *Espacio* alludes to ideals on selfhood found in prior texts, it modifies them by incorporating them into a negative-positive semantic context, which the melding of sun and moon, or, to be more precise, of sun *into* moon, signifies throughout. In fact, at the outset of the "Fragmento Primero" the speaker proclaims: "Como yo he nacido en el sol, y del sol he venido aquí a la sombra, ¿soy de sol, como el sol alumbro?, y mi nostaljia, como la de la luna, es haber sido sol de un sol un día y reflejarlo sólo ahora" (*TA* 852). And in a little known poem, "Calles de solisombra" (from *Romances de Coral Gables*), his mind figures a comparable blending: "Y hay un hombre que prefiere / la calle de sol y sombra / y pierde por ella todo / lo que no encuentra en la otra" (*TA* 898). The compound lexeme "solisombra," a neologism, provides a suitable figure for the fusion, but uneasy balance, that typifies much of Jiménez's post-modern vision.

Espacio and Three Conceptions of Self

Three conceptions of selfhood were implicit in "Yo y Yo." These three are again present in *Espacio*, and it is instructive to see how they are treated. "Dr. Jekyll" is manifest as a 'bright' actant, who alludes to an overself, and as a 'brighter' actant, who experiences self as a point of integration. "Mr. Hyde" is manifest as a 'dark' actant, who struggles to fuse and meld the negative and the positive, and as a 'darker' actant who sees all as disintegrating.

Overself

First, there is the notion of an overself, a self that might contain all. In the "Fragmento Primero" the speaker muses:

Hora celeste y verde toda; y solos. Hora en que las paredes y las puertas se desvanecen como agua, aire, y el alma sale y entra en todo, de y por todo, con una comunicación de luz y sombra. Todo se ve a la luz de dentro, todo es dentro, y las estrellas no son más que chispas de nosotros, que nos amamos, perlas bellas de nuestro roce fácil y tranquilo. ¡Qué luz tan buena para nuestra vida y para nuestra eternidad! (*TA* 857).

The above lines clearly figure a self that contains all ("las estrellas . . . chispas de nosotros"), and they also indicate a marked pantheistic element, which forms part of Jiménez's conception of the overself. This pantheism is found elsewhere in *Espacio*, where sparrows and herons are attuned to nature and to the speaker. In the "Fragmento Segundo" the sparrow and the speaker communicate: "el gorrión universal cantaba, el gorrión y yo cantábamos, hablábamos" (*TA* 865). And in the "Fragmento Tercero" the speaker hears "las garzas blancas habladoras" (TA 876) talking with the stars.[10] The implication is that the overself is in touch with all elements and communes with them. This is not pure pantheism. In Jiménez, the self has not dissipated into the natural setting, as it would in a strictly pantheistic experience. The self has retained awareness of itself and of all of nature that it contains.

Point of Integration

A second conception of selfhood found in "Yo y Yo" is self as point of integration of diverse impulses, a "punto" in space and time, which can be a space with multiple time frames condensed within it, or a point in time which contains multiple spatial planes or perspectives.[11] In *Espacio* there is a similar outlook. In the closure to the "Fragmento Primero" the speaker asserts: "¡Yo, universo inmenso, dentro, fuera de ti, segura inmensidad!" (*TA* 862). The implication is that there is a spatio-temporal immensity ("inmensidad, y todo y sólo inmensidad" [*TA* 862]) within which the speaker feels himself to be a "universo má-jico . . . inmenso." Earlier in the fragment he had alluded to this notion, claiming that the cosmos is nothing more that mini-cosmoses joined together:

> Grande es lo breve, y si queremos ser y parecer más grandes, un-amos sólo con amor, no cantidad. El mar no es más que gotas uni-das, ni el amor que murmullos unidos, ni tú, cosmos, que cos-millos unidos. Lo más bello es el átomo último, el solo indivisible, y que por serlo no es ya más pequeño. Unidad de unidades es lo uno. (*TA* 856)

Self is like a planet in the cosmos; a point within a vast network of space; or, as the speaker later says (TA 879), a star in a galaxy.[12]

The "Fragmento Segundo" is in effect a successive, poly-perspectival meditation on self as point of integration of all experience. It presents numerous spatial and temporal superpositions to imply that they flourish in the mind of the speaker. The impact of this ecstatic idealism is to annul spatio-temporal limits and to condense all that ever impacted on the speaker's senses into a successive temporal profundity. Coke-Enguídanos (133–40) has convincingly argued that this self is in touch with what Bergson called the "dureé réelle," and that *Espacio* exemplifies "Bergson's palimpsestic concept of consciousness" (135). In concrete terms, a temporal point (1942) and a spatial locus (New York City) are expanded by imagination to contain and condense every moment and every space the speaker had found charged with significance.

Despite this euphoric optimism, the speaker's vision in the "Fragmento Tercero" is more negative. He perceives the self as a point of integration that flourishes within a larger negative network of disintegration. In a sequence referred to as "esa tarde de loca creación," in which the speaker's euphoric experience is interrupted by his talkative double ("segundo yo"), there occurs the following representation of integration within a vaster network of chaos:

> Es como el viento ese con la ola; el viento que se hunde con la ola inmensa; ola que sube inmensa con el viento; ¡y qué dolor de olor y de sonido, qué dolor de color, y qué dolor de toque, de sabor de ámbito de abismo! ¡De ámbito de abismo! Espumas vuelan, cho-

que de ola y viento, en mil primaverales verdes blancos, que son festones de mi propio ámbito interior. Vuelan las olas y los vientos pasan, y los colores de ola y viento juntos cantan, y los olores fuljen reunidos, y los sonidos todos son fusión, fusión y fundición de gloria vista. (*TA* 871)

The self as point of integration within a larger immensity (wave within sea) is what is figured here. It is represented as a fusion of the five human senses with the four traditional terrestrial elements, all of which fuse together ("ámbito," "fusión") but then defuse ("abismo").[13]

This vision reaches a culmination toward the end of the fragment when the speaker rhetorically asks if he and his "conciencia" are not a star within the universe. He protests that his consciousness and his body have fully loved each other with a deep love, "con un convencimiento doble que nos hizo vivir un convivir tan fiel como el de un doble astro cuando nace de dos para ser uno?" He then asks: "¿y no podremos ser por siempre lo que es un astro hecho de dos?" (*TA* 879). The imagery presents first separation, then fusion. However, the implied answer to that rhetorical question is quite clearly "no," for the two parts must separate.

Integrating Self Disintegrating

Hence the "Fragmento Tercero" undermines both of the speaker's idealistic conceptions of selfhood (overself and integrated self) by placing their positivity within a negative framework. In addition to this, a *post-modern* reader cannot fail to note that a third conception of self, one which struggles to integrate experience, and which despairs, is foregrounded by the end of *Espacio*.

In *Espacio*'s final "fragment," the speaker refers to two personae. One he calls the "segundo yo"; it is talkative. The other he calls "yo, el tercero, el caído." Both of these are recognized only in the "Fragmento Tercero," and the text identifies both as part of this "tercer" experience. Both compete against each other to undermine all sense of harmony and euphoria.

At the beginning of the third fragment the speaker explains that "se me apareció mi mar tercero" (*TA* 868). He then proceeds to indentify "mi tercer ritmo" (*TA* 870) within him (one that is "vejetativo [y] . . . más cercano . . . al de la poesía" [*TA* 870]). This "ritmo" is presented in a positive light (it fuses human senses with terrestrial elements); it is this that the "segundo yo" interrupts:

> Deja este ritmo timbres de aires y de espumas en los oídos, y sabo-res de ala y de nube en el quemante paladar, y olores a piedra con rocío, y tocar cuerdas de olas. Dentro de mí hay uno que está hablando, hablando, hablando ahora. No lo puedo callar, no se puede callar. Yo quiero estar tranquilo con la tarde, esta tarde de loca creación (no se deja callar, no lo dejo callar). Quiero el silen-cio en mi silencio, y no sé callar a éste, ni se sabe callar. ¡Calla, segundo yo, que hablas como yo y que no hablas como yo; calla maldito! . . . Y ése [segundo yo] era el que hablaba, qué mareo, ése era el que hablaba, y era el perro que ladraba en Moguer, en la primera estrofa." (*TA* 871)

At this point in the text the "segundo yo" undermines a euphoric and profound experience. The personae, "segundo" and "tercero," are in competition; one subverts the other; neither one gains mastery of the self. These personae foreground the 'dark' actant's struggle to blend the irreconcilable contraries. The 'dark' actant recognizes that reality is an amorphous struggle, a play between sameness and differences.

Although this vision is negative, the one represented in the text's last sequence is much more so, because there the personae are obliterated. That last sequence (of one hundred lines) begins after an aposiopesis (...).[14] In it the speaker quixotically attacks a swarm of crabs ("un ejército cárdeno") which is threatening the (symbolic) sun. The speaker is challenged by the most aggressive crab, and he attacks it "con el lápiz de mi poesía y de mi crítica, sacado del bolsillo." The crab ("un cáncer . . . un cangrejo . . . el david") grabs hold of the pencil and the speaker ("el literato filisteo") begins to swing the crab around and around above his head: "yo lo levanté con él cojido y lo jiré a los hori-zontes con impulso mayor, mayor, mayor, una órbita mayor, y él aguantaba" (*TA* 877).

The result is that the speaker fails to send the crab into orbit and ends up crushing it underfoot:

> Lo aplasté con el injusto pie calzado, sólo por ver qué era. Era cáscara vana, un nombre nada más, cangrejo; y ni un adarme, ni un adarme de entraña; un hueco igual que cualquier hueco; un hueco en otro hueco. Un hueco era el héroe sobre el suelo y bajo el

cielo; un hueco, un hueco aplastado por mí, que el aire no llenaba, por mí, por mí; sólo un hueco, un vacío, un heroico secreto de un frío cáncer hueco, un cangrejo hueco, un pobre david hueco. (*TA* 877–78)

The speaker then experiences silence and emptiness. He had revealed such hollow silence to all the world and feels utterly hollow himself ("qué monstruoso de oquedad erguida"). He thinks that circumambient space is deserted, but he then feels that "alguien mayor que yo y el nuevo yo venía." This greater spirit is not positive in nature, for what is next represented seems to be the contrary of baptism (i.e. it is a kind of black baptism as opposed to black mass). The sun melts his hollowness and converts him into "sombra," which is thrown into the sea. In the negative space of sun, sea, and shadow, there is a revolution, a chaos, a total and utter hollowness: "Revolución de un todo, un infinito, un caos instantáneo de carne y cáscaras, de arena y ola y nube y frío y sol. . . ." The result of this chaos is: "Y en el espacio de aquel hueco inmenso y mudo, dios y yo éramos dos. Conciencia..." (*TA* 878).

Hence, the hero overself is found to be hollow, while the self that struggled to integrate all contraries disintegrates into chaos.

After "Conciencia...," the text's third and final aposiopesis, the speaker harangues his "conciencia" for quitting his body; he emphasizes how much he has loved it; he protests that it will forget him and will abandon him for another "god": "te esparzas en lo otro (¿qué es lo otro?)" (*TA* 878); and he begs that he be allowed to give it one final kiss before it leaves him for ever.

A *modern* reader finds in the phrase "dios y yo éramos dos" one of the most depressing notes in *Espacio*. The speaker realizes that self and god are distinct, two entities not one: a clear contraversion of the assertion that "the gods had no other substance than mine," as well as an implicit rejection of the notion that a "Dr. Jekyll" persona can make conflicitng realities cohere at a central point of elusive grace.

Hence, *Espacio*'s final space is not one of integration, but of separation; it is one in which self does *not* incorporate or integrate the uncanny, the negative other into its self. It is a space in which the uncanny other, "the Other" of Lacanian discourse, has superseded Self, leaving it as a sad and abandoned "pelele negro" (*LP* 1003). The final experience of the third, the *post-modern* self—"yo, el tercero, el caído"— must be assessed as utterly negative.[15] Soul slips away from body (as, in Lacan, the signified always slips under the sign); lover is not eternally bound to the beloved; poet is no longer contained within the magnificent artifice of eternal beauty, for which he labored so intensely, in such optimistic faith, to create.

Further tragic, post-modern implications are to be found in this final vision by analyzing the lexemes "cangrejo" and "beso" (both of which occur in the final fragment of the "Fragmento Tercero").

The noun "cangrejo" (whose semantic range is extended by the use of "cáncer" [i.e. death])[16] had never before appeared in Jiménez's poetry. A *post-modern* reader asks why it should suddenly appear at the very end?

The crab is called "el pobre david." Although it dies, the crab does metaphorically slay its Goliath: Jiménez, the Modern artist. The crab thereby signifies the failure of the hero to impose his solar vision on reality.

In addition, as a general symbol the crab "depends on the moon and grows with it" (Vries 115); it thereby signifies a return to the lunar pessimism with which the *Obra* began. Crab also symbolizes disunity, disintegration. T. S. Eliot's famous lines toward the end of Prufrock come to mind: "I should have been a pair of ragged claws / Scuttling across the floors of silent seas" (*Poems* 15). The crab as such is a negative opposite for the "pájaro," which has symbolized the supreme achievement of art and love in *Espacio*, and indeed throughout the *Obra*'s second phase (see Font 112).

The "cangrejo"—"cáncer" lexeme must be read as a sign of the re-emergence of all negative forces the *Obra* succeeded in repressing during its second phase. The crab signifies those negative realities the "Work" had avoided facing: amatorial, aesthetic, thanatotic, spiritual.

Aesthetic failure is apparent, because imagery links the crab to the *Obra*. The speaker battles it "con el lápiz de mi *poesía* y de mi *crítica*" (*TA* 877; my italics). When the crab grabbed that pencil, the artist tried to send the crab into orbit (into "una órbita mayor"). This implies that the artificer tried to immortalize the crab in his art, transform its total negativity into positivity, its darkness into light (its hollowness into fullness). But he fails, and therefore in the final battle, the total signified (the *Obra*) is found not to contain all signifiers; the supreme artificer is found not to be forever a part of the artifact he created. It is "yo, el tercero, el caído" who realizes these failures in his aesthetic ideals.

The "beso" in the final sequence is equally pessimistic. It refers not just to the spiritual-metaphysical quest ("conciencia"—"cuerpo"), but also to the speaker's amatorial ideals.[17] His desire to give his "conciencia" one final kiss is an allusion to his insistence throughout *Espacio* that: "Y Otelo con Desdémona será lo eterno" (*TA* 874). In Shakespeare's play, Othello's last words are: "I kiss'd thee ere I killed thee: no way but this; / killing myself to die upon a kiss." In addition, Verdi's opera on Othello ends with the haunting phrase: "un baccio, un altro baccio."

The context for "beso" is therefore one of suspicion, betrayal, hate, and distrust. "Beso" foregrounds spiritual and amatorial failure, and, in the last analysis, views both of them from a negative perspective. As such, "beso" here undermines the spiritual, amatorial, and aesthetic idealism which "beso" symbolized throughout the Modern *Obra*, the second phase of the "Work" (see Santos-Escudero, "Dios, beso completo" 384–88).

W. B. Yeats linked human and spiritual love when he lamented that the tragedy of sexual intercourse is the perpetual virginity of the soul. This perhaps can provide some insight into the last tragic sequence of *Espacio*. The meaning in Jiménez's context would be that the speaker has failed to accomplish the fundamental goals of his life's work; he has not discovered the essence, the soul, of either art, or love, or self. Spirit has remained untouched, in the speaker's love for woman, in the speaker's quest to attain the higher, integrated self, and in the speaker's quest to make his word eternal.

Espacio began with a speaker declaring that he was equal to the gods: "'Los dioses no tuvieron más sustancia que la que tengo yo.' Yo tengo, como ellos, la sustancia de todo lo vivido y de todo lo por vivir" (*TA* 851).

If the extremism of this claim is not apparent at the beginning of the first fragment, by the end of the third fragment, when it is almost repeated (*TA* 880), it stands revealed as a hollow boast. For not only is the speaker's tone utterly changed at the end of the third fragment, his claim is truncated: he does not affirm that "Yo tengo como ellos la sustancia de todo lo vivido y de todo lo por vivir." The speaker has not come full circle, there is no idealized "eterno retorno" as some readers insist, for by the end of *Espacio* the speaker has lost his conviction.[18] The categorical assertion of the godliness of the self is revealed to be conceited and petulant—perhaps even more narcissistic than "El otoñado."

Hence, *post-modern* readers will treat with suspicion the speaker's assertion that he is equal to the gods. They will see it as a compensatory ploy: Jiménez's way of requiting the extremely powerful attraction formal religious discourses had exercised on him in his formative years.

In conclusion, in its final sequence *Espacio* undermines that ideal faith and optimism that the *Obra* in its second phase sustained. It finds no harmony between artificer and artifact, lover and beloved, body and soul. It concludes that self and god, lover and beloved, poet and *Obra* "somos dos" not "uno." It recognizes that a final shadow covers all; that the overwhelming power of the negative is inevitable.

Despite this *post-modern* reading, it must be stressed that the speaker articulates this negative vision only in *Espacio*'s final sequence of one hundred lines, the "Leyenda de un héroe hueco." *Espacio*'s last phase is 'dark,' the darkest of any Jiménez text. But it would be incorrect to read *Espacio* in its entirety as a totally negative poem. A *modern* reading clearly detects that the "Fragmento Tercero" contains many 'bright' moments of recollected euphoria which it balances with 'dark' moments of pessimism. In this respect, *Espacio* is typical of the post-Modern phase of the *Obra*, in which the speaker expresses both manic highs of ecstasy and extreme lows of utter despair. This blending of the negative with the positive is, in my opinion, characteristic of Jiménez's post-modern vision.

As such a fluctuation does not characterize the Modern phase of the *Obra*, I would like now to describe, in much sharper detail, differences between Jiménez's Modern and post-Modern poetry.

7

Modern and Post-Modern Visions: *Obra* and *Leyenda*

"Yo, el tercero, el caído"—from *Espacio*'s final sequence, sometimes referred to as "Leyenda de un héroe hueco" (Albornoz, "Estudio de la obra" 105)—presents an image of the poet that is utterly distinct from the confident and ecstatic self of "Yo y Yo," and from the undecided self of "¿Soy yo . . . ?"

These texts represent three phases and impulses within the *Obra*. "Yo y Yo" together with the second (or middle) phase of the "Work" represent a supreme achievement: a climax in the speaker's faith and optimism in life, love, and work. This, I have argued, is the Modern *Obra*: a consummate and self-sufficient artifice.

The Modern phase of the "Work" distinguishes itself from the other two in its treatment of negativity. If the Modern impulse encounters negativity (as it does in the closure to "Yo y Yo"), it suppresses rather than confronts it. In the first (or early) phase, negativity (nostalgic melancholia, mournful crepuscularity) predominates; optimism is subdued and overwhelmed. This is the pre-Modern phase of the *Obra*. In the third (or late) phase, negativity is confronted, mixed and balanced with positive impulses, thoughts, and feelings. The poet's optimism reaches euphoric heights in this phase, at the same time as his despair reaches its nadir. This is the *Obra*'s post-Modern phase.

To reconcile such contradictory impulses, images, voices, or personae, let me discuss the transformations wrought throughout the *Obra*'s three phases on its basic "narrative topics": love, work, death ("la mujer, la obra, la muerte" [*LP* 1343–44]).[1] What follows is a fictionalized reconciliation of the *Obra*, my "legend" of the Juan Ramón *Leyenda*.

The Pre-Modern *Obra*

During the *Obra*'s first phase, the positive elements in love—adolescent entrancement, youthful, sensual delectation—are backgrounded by a sense of failure and disgust. The predominant reaction to love throughout the first phase of the "Work" is therefore negative, an attitude exemplified in this very early stanza from *Rimas*: "Ni perfumes, ni brisas, ni flores, / calmarán mi fatal padecer: / mis amores son vagos amores / que no encuentran aquí su placer" (*PLP* 168).

As for the *Obra*: the positive element is the belief that poetry brings the Ideal near to earth—"Algo del más allá, que llega hasta la vida / por una senda de nostalgia" (*PLP* 1273). However, that feeling of "nostalgia" totally overwhelms the poet's attitude to aesthetic ideals throughout the first phase of the "Work." It is the suffering the poet undergoes which becomes the predominant aesthetic topic. The moon comes to signify such negative sentiments; it frequently represents—as in the following stanzas from *Jardines lejanos*—the ideal beauty and love the poet always fails to achieve:

> ...El piano está soñando.
> En los cristales violetas,
> un poeta va llorando
> desencantos de poetas...
>
> El melancólico brillo
> de no sé qué dulces oros
> cuenta un romance amarillo
> de rosas y de tesoros...
>
> Hay claridades de luna
> en un naciente lejano...
> Sobre mi corazón, una
> mano llora en un piano...
> Llanto... Silencio...
> La luna. (*PLP* 490)

Disillusionment, melancholia, suffering: these are the constants of the first phase of the "Work."

As for "la muerte," it is, of course, absolute negativity. However, during the first phase of the "Work," the poet makes numerous valiant attempts to view it stoically, and he frequently describes death as more fulfilling than life. The following alexandrines from *Elegías* can exemplify these attitudes: "La golondrina canta—El poeta está muerto ...—, / ¡Oh, qué dulzura tiene el viento vespertino! / Parece que una inmensa flor azul ha entreabierto / su cáliz que perfuma lo eterno y lo divino" (*PLP* 889).

However, this optimistic stance is never convincing, and the predominant feeling toward death throughout the *Obra*'s first phase is negative. As another metaphor of *Elegías* puts it: "Lenta obsesión de muerte . . . se obstina / en arañar el alma" (*PLP* 886) of Jiménez throughout these early years.

Hence, in the pre-Modern *Obra*, any positivity found in the basic "narrative topics" of the "Work" is eventually incorporated into a general negative reaction to the world.

The Modern *Obra*

Estío can be advanced as the indisputable start of the Modern phase of the "Work."[2] Its "Canción de despacho" (cited in full in chap. 3) bids farewell to the past. *Estío* was published in 1916. In that year, in New York, Jiménez also referred to his past (thought and style) pejoratively: "una manera antigua y recargada; / amontonada / barrocamente . . . [una] nubarronada de poesía" (*LP* 309). *Eternidades*, with the Modern gems "Intelijencia, dame" and "Vino, primero, pura," appeared in 1918. *Piedra y cielo*, with "Yo y Yo," was published in the following year.

After this, the Modern *Obra* is concentrated in *Poesía* (*en verso*) and *Belleza* (*en verso*), both published in 1923; it next reasserts its dominion in *Canciónes*, 1936, which contains one third of the poems ("Canciones de la nueva luz" [*LP* 1186–1208]) which will appear in 1946 as *La estación total*.

In the work published during these years, 1916 to 1936, Jiménez reveals utter faith in his ideals, and he represents a self that is fully integrated. His supreme idealism can again be seen in the manner in which his Modern *Obra* treats the fundamental narrative topics.

"La mujer" and love encounter their symbol of perfection in *Poesía* (1923), in the well-known "¡Amor!":

> Todas las rosas son la misma rosa,
> ¡amor!, la única rosa;
> y todo queda contenido en ella,
> breve imajen del mundo,
> ¡amor!, la única rosa (*LP* 909)

Later, in the "Canciones de la nueva luz," the naked female body becomes a symbol of perfection achieved: "La rosa: / tu desnudez hecha gracia" (*LP* 1197).[3]

"La Obra" became the poet's overriding concern with *Poesía* and *Belleza* (1923). As the poem "Obra y Sol" implies, the "Work" became for him a world unto itself: "¡Abierto libro mío; / cielo estrellado de la noche!" ([*LP* 1079], cited in full in chap. 4).

As part of this faith and idealism, the magisterial optimist also proclaimed that his personal death was of no importance at all: "Al lado de mi cuerpo muerto, / mi obra viva" (*LP* 963). He refers to the body as "este pelele negro" and proclaims that the real self is eternal:

> ¡Y yo, esconderme
> sonriendo, inmortal, en las orillas puras
> del río eterno, árbol
> —en un poniente inmarcesible—
> de la divina y májica imajinación! (*LP* 1003)

"La muerte" in this phase of the *Obra* is therefore idealized. The fact that death can have a negative impact on the speaker is repressed. Two well-known indications of this occur in the poems "Morir es solo / mirar adentro" (*LP* 899) and "La muerte es una madre nuestra antigua" (*LP* 1028).

Hence, each of the *Obra*'s basic "narrative topics" is treated with total idealism in the middle phase of the "Work."

Modern idealism, however, does not end in 1936 with *Canción*; it persists beyond, into *La estación total* and *Animal de fondo*. For example, *La estación total* (1946) proceeds with the idealization of love and woman. The poem "Flor que vuelve" (*LP* 1167–69) lauds them as: "Amor y flor en perfección de forma," (*LP* 1168). Also, the poet expresses his utter conviction in the eternal truth and beauty of his poetic word. In "Poeta y Palabra" (*LP* 1171–72), he proclaimed he had discovered: "la vibrante palabra muda, / la inmanente, / única flor que no se dobla, / única luz que no se estingue, / única ola sin fracaso."

As for death, even in 1946 (in *La estación total*) the speaker denies that death threatens the self. In a poem entitled "Espacio" (*LP* 1164), which is *not* the prose-poem, the dead woman's "conciencia" is represented as forming part of the immense totality that surrounds the speaker.

La estación total and *Animal de fondo* also contain ecstatic and euphoric poems of spiritual perfection in which no trace of negativity is found. "Desde Dentro," the first poem in *La estación total*, begins "Rompió mi alma con oro" and ends: "Ella, Poesía, Amor, el centro / indudable" (*LP* 1135); such ecstasy is also developed in "Su Sitio Fiel" (*LP* 1170).

Leyenda has recently provided additional Modern gems. The following makes clear that the Modern impulse had faith in idealism and was self-sufficient: "Yo me quisiera detener / en cada cosa bella, / hasta morir con ella; / ...y con ella, en lo eterno, renacer" (*Leyenda* 316, no. 483). In addition, the Modern seer was conscious of realizing his ideals:

Con mi cuerpo y con mi alma

La mesa, el banco, el catre se los hago con mi cuerpo.

El sol que dora su mantel, el aire de la sombra de su árbol, la noche
que los cubre con estrellas, se los hago con mi alma.

(*Leyenda* 443, no. 756)

In the Modern phase, the speaker, "Dr. Jekyll," a Berkeleyian idealist, believes he can achieve all. Another poem, "Ilímite," asks: "¿Qué es vida sino este ilimitarse, este sentirse totalizado en fundición de único?" (*Leyenda* 510, no. 957).

Hence, the Modern impulse persists in the *Obra* to the very end. In addition it is seen in the poet's style: virtually all Jiménez's texts cohere; they resolve their paradoxes into organic wholes.

However, the optimism and abounding energy together with the dynamic idealism of this phase begin to lose momentum. For instance, "Juan Fiel" ([*LP* 1256], cited in full in chap. 4) metonymically represents that Modern persona, "Dr. Jekyll." "Juan Fiel" is the Modern aesthete whose exclusive concern was to re-touch his "scarlet roses" until he brought them to a paralysis of perfect form ("la parada mar plana"). This is the artificer, the "Dr. Jekyll" who put his faith in "los nombres," in "intelijencia," as well as in the unquestioned powers of "la poesía desnuda" to create perfection of life, love, "Work."

However, in such phrases as "el arbusto de nácar" and "la parada mar plana," "Juan Fiel" implies that there is within him a "Mr. Hyde" who is conscious of stasis, rigidity, paralysis. This text hints, that is, at the "detainment" ("la ola detenida" [*LP* 1326]) the Modern impulse suffered. The Modern speaker became conscious of restraint and hardening.

In fact, even while he was forging the resplendent "naked" beauty of his Modern canon, Jiménez recognized a negative, antivital impulse, by alluding in *Belleza* (1923) to his *Obra* as: "pétrea mujer desnuda, / hermosa piedra mía" (*LP* 1068).

It is as though Jiménez's Modern beauty began to turn against itself, to become uncanny: "'*Unheimlich* and motionless like a stone-image,'"—one of the many expressions Freud encountered in his studies of the uncanny ("Uncanny" 375).

Jiménez's struggle with the hardening, the petrification of beauty is represented in "La conquista," a significant poem from *La estación total*. The text, which I have analyzed elsewhere, struggles with negativity and succeeds in fusing negative ("lo falso") with positive ("lo bello") dynamics. I argue that in "La conquista" there is a recognition that art is a momentary "conquista" of negativity, as opposed to its being an eternally resplendent force for beauty, which is what it was conceived to be in the Modern phase of the *Obra*. "La conquista" is post-modern: it struggles to reintegrate the sensual and human, which the Modern style and mind had repressed, and to balance them with earlier aesthetic ideals.[4]

As I said in chapter 1, Jiménez's truly Modern impulse is expressed during the years of High Modernism in Western life and letters. This impulse begins to diminish after 1936, when Jiménez ceased to reside in Spain, which means that it controls the "Work" for approximately twenty years: 1916–36. As Juan Ramón published poetry from 1896 to 1956, sixty years, his High-Modern impulse, therefore, is dominant for a little more than one-third of his creative life. In the context of the entire *Obra*, therefore, I see the Modern Jiménez, "Dr. Jekyll," the supreme stylist, the seer, the 'bright' actant, that magisterial optimist monumentalized in the *antolojías*, as one aspect of a more total mask.

The 'darker' shadows (pre- and post-Modern) constitute that mask's additional facets.

The Post-Modern *Obra*

It is hardly necessary to demonstrate that the years following 1936–39 were years of transition and turmoil. The Spanish Civil War and World War II say it all. In addition, one might note that *Finnegans Wake* appeared in 1939, *La familia de Pascual Duarte* in 1941, and Borges's *Ficciones* in 1944. There is a completely different vision in these books, which I have been referring to as post-modern. Yeats captured it, elliptically, in his *Last Poems* (1939). In "High Talk" (331), he implied that during these years artists climbed down off their "high stilts." In "The Circus Animals' Desertion" (336), he implies that poets re-learned to "lie down where all the ladders start, / In the foul rag-and-bone shop of the heart."

And in effect, a different impulse is to be detected in Juan Ramón after 1936. The faith and optimism of the preceding years are attenuated and mixed with doses of doubt and despair. A preference for the abstract and the mental is modified by a concern for the human and the sensual. The texts in which this impulse is detected are the first and third parts of *La estación total* (1946), *Animal de fondo* (1949), *Espacio* (1954), and *Leyenda* (1956).

Jiménez's post-modern impulse can be defined as an impulse to fuse contraries. It can be characterized by its awareness of the process of anti-idealization, prevalent in the West, to which Yeats alludes in his *Last Poems*. The post-modern is more aware of limits, but strives, in Jiménez's words, to move the human toward the divine, or, in Hassan's terms (123–38), to raise earth toward heaven (as opposed to dismissing earth as irrelevant).

Jiménez's post-modern impulse is manifest in the post-1936 poetry, but it is also evident on occasion in the Modern phase of the *Obra*. The impulse, to balance and blend positive and negative, is present, for instance, in the *Diario* (1917), in the following playful poem, titled "Sky":

> Como tu nombre es otro,
> cielo, y su sentimiento
> no es mío aún, aún no eres cielo.

> Sin cielo, ¡oh cielo!, estoy,
> pues estoy aprendiendo
> tu nombre, todavía...
>
> ¡Sin cielo, amor!
> —¿Sin cielo? (*LP* 289)

As the poet spoke little English at the time he wrote this poem, the text plays the positivity of the noun "cielo" against the negativity of the noun "sky." Also, it uses "cielo" to mean "heaven" ("¡oh cielo!" i.e. good heavens!) to indicate that the speaker at the moment of articulation lacks such a firm spiritual and existential foundation. It also plays with love ("amor"), for in the vernacular "cielo" can mean "my loved one." In this poem the speaker is therefore aware of negativity (aesthetic, spiritual, amatorial), but balances them playfully with positive turns of phrase.[5]

In *Poesía* there is an uncanny poem, "Desvelo," strange, that is, in the context of the "Work's" second phase:

> Se va la noche, negro toro,
> —plena carne de luto, de espanto y de misterio—,
> que ha bramado terrible, inmensamente,
> al temor sudoroso de todos los caídos;
> y el día viene, nino fresco,
> pidiendo confianza, amor y risa,
> —niño que, allá muy lejos,
> en los arcanos donde
> se encuentran los comienzos con los fines,
> ha jugado un momento,
> por no sé qué pradera
> de luz y sombra,
> con el toro que huía—. (*LP* 838)

Negativity is in the ascendant here, and this may well be the most uncanny poem in the published *Obra*'s second phase. It clearly represents a Manichean struggle in which the speaker wills a precarious balance between the opposing powers.

These poems from the *Diario* and *Poesía* indicate that a post-modern attitude is present within the High-Modern phase. However it in no way threatens the solar optimism of the "Work."

The post-modern vision emerges more frequently in parts of *La esta-ción total*. Indeed, the poem "Flor que vuelve," a line of which was cited earlier, is particularly pertinent; it is post-modern in its blending of the sensual and the abstract. Though it idealizes love and woman, it places them within a concern for the human body, sensuality, and sexuality: "Amor y flor en perfección de forma, / en mutuo sí frenético de olvido, / en compensación loca; / olor, sabor y olor, / color, olor y tacto, olor, amor, olor" (*LP* 1168).

The poem "Luz tú" is interesting in this respect. "Luz tú" is part of "Las canciones de la nueva luz" (of *La estación total*), but it did *not* appear in *Canción* in 1936. It is therefore a text from "el otro costado."[6] It emblematizes the struggle between positive and negative in concrete as well as symbolic terms:

> Luz vertical,
> luz tú;
> alta luz tú,
> luz oro;
> luz vibrante,
> luz tú.

Y yo la negra, ciega, sorda, muda sombra horizontal. (*LP* 1241)

The "tú"/"yo" opposition here is sufficiently indeterminate to imply that this text represents a struggle to balance the *Obra*'s major narrative topics (love, work, death, spirit). The balance between the positive and the negative is tenuous, although it appears to be achieved.

In addition, the poem "Su sitio fiel," from the first part of *La estación total*, though apparently a Modern poem has a trace of negativity. Moreover, it figures the concept of self as point of integration, and contains numerous images relevant to the present study. However, unlike Jiménez's Modern verse, this poem hints at negativity. For all of these reasons I cite it in full:

> Las nubes y los árboles se funden
> y el sol les trasparenta su honda paz.
> Tan grande es la armonía del abrazo,
> que la quiere gozar también el mar,
> el mar que está tan lejos, que se acerca,
> que se oye latir, que huele ya.

> El cerco universal se va apretando,
> y ya en toda la hora azul no hay más
> que la nube, que el árbol, que la ola,
> síntesis de la gloria cenital.
> El fin está en el centro. Y se ha sentado
> aquí, su sitio fiel, la eternidad.
>
> Para esto hemos venido. (Cae todo
> lo otro, que era luz provisional.)
> Y todos los destinos aquí salen,
> aquí entran, aquí suben, aquí están.
> Tiene el alma un descanso de caminos
> que han llegado a su único final. (*LP* 1170)[7]

No one would deny that the tone here is utterly assured, even ecstatic. However, in the phrases "el cerco universal se va apretando," and "Cae todo / lo otro," there is a hint of the negative power against which the speaker struggled.

Finally, although *Animal de fondo* is euphoric, its vision is frequently post-modern, precisely because its thrust is struggle and achievement. Sánchez-Barbudo persistently commented on how struggle and failure were mixed with euphoria in these final, mystical poems. Indeed, in *Animal de fondo* an integrated self sings of its visionary experience of oneness, of total integration with circumambient space. The self in these poems has attained that higher point where the human meets the divine.

Its first text, "La trasparencia, dios, la trasparencia," is at pains to distinguish the negativity of the speaker's prior traditional religious instincts from the positivity of his present discovery:

> No eres mi redentor, ni eres mi ejemplo,
> ni mi padre, ni mi hijo, ni mi hermano;
> eres igual y uno, eres distinto y todo;
> eres dios de lo hermoso conseguido,
> conciencia mía de lo hermoso.
>
> Yo nada tengo que purgar.
> Toda mi impedimenta
> no es sino fundación para este hoy
> en que, al fin, te deseo; (*LP* 1289)

The impediment of the past (the negative) became the pediment for the present: the speaker's unique religious experience.

The poem "Soy animal de fondo" is a consummate expression of the euphoria, ecstasy, and *aletheia* present in the book. Self is a bird-like animal in flight, cut through by light and by the sun's rays; its stature is extended as it flies through the air and over the sea. Its contours are stretched by this experience to such an extent that it becomes as profound as a well ("pozo"); it thereby touches the earth. This depth of space contains numerous levels of time (from childhood to the present). In the conclusion to the poem, self experiences other as part of itself:

> Y tú eras en el pozo májico el destino
> de todos los destinos de la sensualidad hermosa
> que sabe que el gozar en plenitud
> de conciencia amadora,
> es la virtud mayor que nos trasciende.
>
> Lo eras para hacerme pensar que tú eras tú,
> para hacerme sentir que yo era tú,
> para hacerme gozar que tú eras yo,
> para hacerme gritar que yo era yo
> en el fondo de aire en donde estoy,
> donde soy animal de fondo de aire
> con alas que no vuelan en el aire,
> que vuelan en la luz de la conciencia
> mayor que todo el sueño
> de eternidades e infinitos
> que están después, sin más que ahora yo, del aire. (*LP* 1340)

In the final lines above, the speaker refers to a "dream of an eternal and infinite" self, which is a self that remains intact after ("después") the struggle that brought it into existence has been concluded. The implication is that the selfhood experienced by the speaker is different from this; it is not of such duration ("sin más que ahora"). That is, negativity is alluded to; the texts betray the speaker's awareness of all he had to overcome in order to arrive at the point of integration.

The final lines of "Soy animal de fondo" provide an insight into the speaker's intuition of self as point of integration within a vaster network. In addition, the figure selected, "animal de fondo de aire," foregrounds the tenuous nature of such integration. That figure is accompanied in some of the final poems by additional compound lexemes, such as "alaluz" and "cuerpialma"—both of which connote coalescence, while at the same time implying the fragility of that achievement.

The poem "Río-Mar-Desierto" is another important post-Modern text, for it implies that the positive (river-sea of life and "Work"), represented by the compound "ríomar," entails the negative (desert of death) represented by "desiertoríomar" (*LP* 1325).[8]

Animal de fondo may be one of the most ecstatic books of Modern poetry; nevertheless, it foregrounds its spiritual (religious, ontological) and aesthetic struggles. In that respect, it is post-modern.

The post-modern awareness is frequently expressed in *Leyenda*, which was compiled during years in which Jiménez was reflecting on the entire span of his life, and while he was attempting to bring the *Obra* to a close. The most intriguing texts in *Leyenda* assess from a level perspective, even from a detached and ironical point of view, just how far the speaker succeeded in lifting earth toward heaven.[9]

In words that echo (for this *post-modern* reader at least) Yeats's "rag-and-bone shop of the heart" Jiménez wrote in *Leyenda*:

Hasta tú, la muerte linda

¡Qué sol este más roñoso, gusanera de calleja!
¡Y qué podre esta, salida de la matriz de la tierra!
¡Vaya arsenal arrumbado de eternidad de trastienda!
Parece que dios está enfermo de lepra eterna.
¡Hasta tú, la muerte linda, tú, mi palomita limpia, pareces,
    mugrienta y fea!

(*Leyenda* 692, no. 1286).

One of the thrills (*jouissances*) of reading *Leyenda* is the discovery of texts such as these which so clearly deconstruct the *Obra*'s Modern self-sufficiency and optimism. Even death ("¡Hasta tú, la muerte linda[!]") is visualized without rose-tinted blinkers.

Leyenda de-idealizes the *Obra*'s major concerns. The first poem is at pains to note that when the mature mind returns to the place of its childhood "las casas no eran palacios ni catedrales los templos" (7).

Later, it refers to the sun as a visitor, which is ominous, given the sememic limits this study has described (chap. 3) for the lexeme "sol": "El visitante ilúmine / del salón inmortal es el sol que se hunde" (45, no. 68). Jiménez's post-modern consciousness, in *Leyenda*, is aware that it does not remain in all; it recognizes that perfection is limited to *a* time and *a* place: "Eterno fui yo en un valle. ¡Qué grande felicidad!" (642, no. 1204; see also chap. 3). The mature poetic mind also knows that "Work," "love," and spirit are never to perfection brought:

> Rosa, lo he realizado todo en mí:
> amor, poesía, en forma y alma:
> ¿qué me falta?
>
> (*Leyenda* 603, no. 1159) [10]

As for spiritual perfection, the speaker in *Leyenda* refers to "la sombra" that covers all. In one of the first poems the speaker asks:

> ¿Soy esa imajen en dos que está dentro de tus ojos?
> ¿Dos nadas dentro de ellos, la sombra infinita, sólo?
>
> (*Leyenda* 10, no. 6)

Shortly afterwards, the speaker concludes "¿Sombras, lumbres?" with this assertion: "Y aprendí a vivir, seguro de llama negra, en la sombra" (15, no. 15).

The poetic word and the *Obra* in *Leyenda* suffer a comparable anti-idealization. For example, *Las tres presencias desnudas*, which consists of texts from collections formerly titled *Poesía* and *Belleza*, contains many negative doubts about the future of the *Obra*: "di ¿te hundirás también como yo? Di, di ¿te hundirán también; y el sol, un día, será sobre tus esparcidos restos tristes (tu hueso seco en descubierta fosa) primavera y olvido, putrefacción no deseada ver, inmunda flora?" (495, no. 914). And in the last book of the anthology, entitled *De ríos que se van*, there occurs this rough gem:

> Solo guardo un tizo negro
>
> ¡No le cojí el oro a dios!
> ¡Qué lástima! El viento seco
> zumbó por mi corazón
> buscándome el pensamiento.

¡Un oro que se perdió,
pudiendo ser gloria! Pero
de toda la bendición
sólo guardo un tizo negro.

Con él le escribo a mi dios
este sufrido dicterio;
"¡Si me cantas la canción,
no me cuentes más el cuento!"

(*Leyenda* 692, no. 1285)

Finally, in one of the last poems, written possibly after Zenobia's death, or while she was hospitalized, the speaker asks his wife if their home is really as empty as he feels it to be: "¿Este huevo vacío, esta blancura huera de nuestro nido mío sólo y ya no nuestro? (701, no. 1300).

Hence, Juan Ramón's post-Modern vision, that is, the vision the *Obra* articulates after the paralyzing and petrifying of its Modern idealism begins to set in, is at times as empty as that "huevo vacío," as empty as the shell of that "cangrejo/cáncer" of *Espacio*'s "Fragmento Tercero," as "hueco" as "yo, el tercero, el caído" of the same fragment. But at other times Jiménez's post-Modern vision is not as negative as this; it is even euphoric: it balances the human with the divine, by discovering the "hasta qué punto" to which the human might ascend.

Probably in reaction to the excessive mentalism and purity of the *Obra*'s Modern style and mind, the post-Modern *Obra* strives to synthesize and blend the senses with the spirit, the intellect with the imagination, the ideal with the real.[11] In this fervent desire to blend the negative with the positive—to move metaphorical earth toward metaphorical heaven—the "Work" manifests both manic highs as well as excessive lows.

This fact—that Jiménez's post-Modern vision contains contradictory impulses (terrestrial and celestial)—needs to be emphasized, because it is one a *post-modern* reader could overlook. As we have seen, the perspectives of *post-modern* readers lead them to focus on disintegration and desolation, and to demonstrate that truth and selfhood are illusions of language. Such impulses are certainly present in Jiménez's post-Modern *Obra*, but only in the 'darkest' ruminations of its 'dark' actant. In addition to that aspect of Jiménez's post-Modern

Obra, there are the dynamics of a 'dark' actant, one which sees difference emerging from sameness, which struggles with all logical contradictions, and which attempts to embrace all their tragic implications.

This 'dark' actant, who struggles to discover light in darkness, should represent Jiménez's post-modern "leyenda."

Postscript

This study has implied that Jiménez's is an *Obra* which matures as it evolves, but one which obeys no recognizable archetypal patterns of growth.

Despite the fiction Jiménez attempted to represent in his *antolojías*, his *Obra* does not begin in innocence and light, move on to idealism, and later embrace the wisdom—or foolishness—of more advanced years. Taken in its entirety, Jiménez's *Obra* does not banish darkness and impose resplendent light. Jiménez's vision is conflictual and, as a legacy to posterity, extends no satisfying resolution, no "parada mar plana."

"Successive," a word the poet himself preferred, perhaps best indicates the *Obra*'s many movements. At first it is a "nightingale" ("ruiseñor"); then it is a "lark" ("alondra") and other birds of light, as well as a "butterfly" ("mariposa de luz"). It subsequently becomes an "animal de fondo de aire" and an "alaluz." Finally it is a "crab" ("cangrejo"). The logic of such successive maturation is one that belongs to the *Obra* itself; it is not one that pre-existed the evolution of this unique "Work."

In addition to this, and again despite the *antolojías*, the poetic persona of Juan Ramón Jiménez is more complex than history and criticism have allowed. He is a poet of different masks. I have argued that he contains the darkness of a "Mr. Hyde" and the light of a "Dr. Jekyll." As the former, he is a "modernista" and a post-modern, a pessimist, a sensualist, riddled with anguish and self-doubt. As the latter, he is a jubilant and optimistic aesthete, a purifier of the senses, who asserted and practiced devotion and faith with respect to the Spanish poetic word; it was with and through that word that he realized for his culture the ideals of the European High Moderns, and in so doing he also extended the vision of his own mystic tradition.

Jiménez is also at times an admixture of these polarities, a poet of "solisombra," of darkness and light, one who did struggle to face the "mendigo," make it a part of the "poeta con sol." As such, Jiménez wished to meld the black with the white, to embrace what had terrified him in 1904: the "traje negro" with the "barba blanca." It is this melding of contraries which produces, in my opinion, some of Jiménez's most intriguing texts.

Such a successive *Obra* and such complex personae required, I have argued, multivalent reading strategies, and—by way of conclusion—I should like to ask: How might a *specialist* reader of the Jiménez *Obra* assess the *modern* and *post-modern* readers' insights into language and selfhood?

From the point of view of language: the *specialist* should approve of the complex linguistic patterning the *modern* reader described for Jiménez's "poems." The existence of such organic precision in the Jiménez artifact had previously been posited but never specified in such detail. *Specialists* should be pleased that there is a *modern* reading strategy capable of accounting for some of the structural and linguistic ingenuity their poet was always reputed to display.

However, the *specialist* will be disturbed by the *post-modern* reader's insistence on the negative and the uncanny. The *specialist* will not be convinced by what de Man describes as "the rhetorical, symbolic quality of all language" (*Allegories* 111). Hence, the *specialist* will reject the *post-modern* reading of the *Obra*: that "empirical reality is illusory," and that "truth . . . [and] human specificity may be rooted in linguistic deceit" (*Allegories* 156). The specialist will resist these notions because they run counter to his humanistic formation.

From the point of view of selfhood: the *specialist* will approve of the *modern* reader's apt selection of texts that present the evolution of Jiménez's desire to understand the self, to articulate "the transparency of the self to its own experience of selfhood, the unmediated presence of the self to itself" (de Man, *Allegories* 165). The *specialist* will derive pleasure from the notion that in a very early text ("¿Soy yo . . . ?"), there is latent (for example, in the conjunction "y" and in the compounding of spatial and temporal modalities) a desire to conjoin all experience at a center, a desire that is almost realized in "Yo y Yo," and which is finally manifest in "'soy animal de fondo de aire' (sobre tierra)" (*LP* 1339).

The *specialist* sees in this endeavor a High-Modern poet "able to imagine himself as a coherent and self governing entity," one who achieves "identity, integrity, harmony, tranquillity, maturity, selfhood." [1] It is with this self of Lacan's "Imaginary" order that the *specialist* sympathizes.

However, the *specialist* will treat with distrust Lacan's belief that selfhood may be figured only in "Symbolic" order: which means that "one's destiny as a subject will always be one of indefinite displacement," that selfhood is an invented unity, a "product of successive inventions," of "attempts to find ways round certain inescapable factors of lack (*manque*), absence and incompleteness in human living." [2] *Specialists* will want to refute this *post-modern* reading of the *Obra*; they will want to reject de Man's assertion (*Allegories* 111) that: "the idea of individuation, of the human subject as a privileged viewpoint, is a mere metaphor by means of which man protects himself from his insignificance by forcing his own interpretation of the world upon the entire universe, substituting a human-centered set of meanings that is reassuring to his vanity for a set of meanings that reduces him to being a mere transitory accident in the cosmic order." However, before *specialists* reject this reading out of hand, they might ponder the fact that Jiménez had also glimpsed that life may after all be nothing more than "mere metaphor":

> ¡Ay, fuerza de mi imajen—¡vida!—
> más poderosa que yo, ay! (*LP* 699)

In addition, in the post-modern account of selfhood, the *specialist* might detect echoes of Jiménez's concept of "Destino," as well as his discussion (in notes and lectures late in life) of successiveness and simultaneity as conditions of human living.[3] Indeed, the Lacanian notion that self "can be grasped only as a set of tensions, or mutations, or dialectical upheavals within a continuous, intentional, future directed process" (Bowie 131) may increasingly appear to the *specialist* as a fair representation of Jiménez's view of selfhood in such texts as "¿Soy yo . . . ?," "Golfo," "Yo y Yo," and *Espacio*. The *specialist* on Jiménez might even agree with de Man, who, with respect to Rilke (*Allegories* 51), noted: "The full complexity of his poetry can only appear in the juxtaposition of two readings in which the first forgets and the second acknowledges the linguistic structure that makes it come into being."

Hence, *specialist* readers might well be caught in a bind at the end of their assessments, because they will see both positive and negative aspects in the *post-modern* readings of the *Obra*.

The *specialist* in prudence could hold the *Obra*'s contradictory impulses in mind, and see that both readings are latent in Jiménez, and that the *Obra* is enriched, deepened, even prescient, by containing both.[4]

Jiménez could therefore remain a "Dr. Jekyll," a "Mr. Hyde," and a curious mixture of them both. "Dr. Jekyll" is the Modern idealist, the artificer immortalized in the anthologies and the histories of literature. "Mr. Hyde" is a pre- and post-Modern poet: a pessimist and a doubter, enthralled by the uncanny, a persona revealed in "el mendigo," "el hombre enlutado," "el fantasma," "el cangrejo," "el tercero, el caído," "el huevo vacío." Despite these polar contradictions, there is in Jiménez the "engulfer" of "Golfo" and *Espacio*, who mixed "Dr. Jekyll" with "Mr. Hyde," who saw beyond the confines of his own amatorial, aesthetic, thanatotic, and spiritual traditions, and who struggled to incorporate vital aspects of those traditions into his own.

Leyenda puts it more simply. It says: "yo renové, yo cambié el mundo que yo vi en espresión de vida y en espresión de muerte" (646, no. 1211).

Those 'bright' and 'dark' personae, who ceaselessly changed and renovated what they encountered, constitute some of the *difference* Juan Ramón Jiménez bequeathed to Modern Hispanic poetry.

Notes

Preface

1. For example, Angel del Río writes of "La pureza lírica de Juan Ramón Jiménez" (289). See also Brown (79–82).

2. Although the organization of each analysis emerged from a detailed study of the text, Traugott and Pratt (14) imply the desirability of this type of organization; and it is one that has similarities with that implied by Culler ("Literature").

3. Nineteen fifty-six is the final date for compositions included in *Leyenda*, which contains poetry from 1896 to 1956, exactly sixty years. In 1954 *Espacio* appeared in its entirety (see Albornoz, *Jiménez* Escritor, 348). Sánchez-Barbudo's division is found in *La segunda época*. Further discussion of this issue is found in chapters 1 and 7 and in my "Etapa histórica."

4. I avoid the English term "modernist" throughout this study because the Spanish term "modernista" connotes only a *fin de siècle* style of writing.

5. As these texts are analyzed line by line, I have provided for each a literal translation into English.

6 Hamburger (42–80, 110–47), in "Lost Identities," "Masks," and "Multiple Personalities," discusses alterity in Western poetry from 1860 to 1960. Carreño (1–46) has a far-ranging discussion on "desdoblamiento." For Juan Ramón, Villar studies it from a biographical and pyschological perspective (i.e. Juan Ramón's neuroses); so do Coke-Enguídanos (97–100) and Young (*Line*, 77–8, 129–30, 160–61, 278–79 n. 89).

Chapter 1

1. Debicki (*Poetry*) both argues and demonstrates this type of approach.

2. For a recent novel account (and bibliography) of these methods of analysis, see Eagleton (43–53, 95–116, 223–25, 226–27).

3. For discussion and analysis of this issue, see my "The Rhetoric of Existential Anguish in a Poem (LXXVII) by Antonio Machado," in *Hispanic Review* 53.2 (1985): 163–80.

4. On this, see Culler, *Deconstruction* (210ff).

5. Eliot, *Selected Essays*: "Tradition and The Individual Talent" (13–22)

and "The Metaphysical Poets" (281–91). The term "objective correlative" appears in "Hamlet" (*Selected* 145); for a discussion of it, consult Preminger, *Princeton* (581–82).

6. Debicki (22–29, 230) successfully applied "defamiliarization" in his recent reading of contemporary Spanish poetry.

7. Gullón on "space" (in Machado's poetry), and Cano Ballesta on "time" (in Lorca's poetry), are also pertinent studies. See Gullón, *Una poética* (132–51). See also Juan Cano Ballesta, "Una veta reveladora en la poesía de García Lorca (Los tiempos del verbo y sus tiempos expresivos)," rptd. in *Federico García Lorca*, ed. Ildefonso-Manuel Gil (Madrid: Taurus, 1973), 45–71. I applied the notion of spatial figures in: "Algunas configuraciones" (3–8), and in "The Love Poem."

8. For rhetorical figures in Culler, see "Resistance and Recuperation," (in *Structuralist* 178ff). His discussion of metonymy and synecdoche is too complicated for general use; it is derived from a book now translated as *A General Rhetoric* by Group μ, trans. Paul B. Burrell and Edgar M. Slotkin (Baltimore: Johns Hopkins University Press, 1981). In the present study, synecdoche means "part for whole" (arm for human body); metonymy is "whole for whole" (arm for weapon).

9. From Benveniste, three chapters from section 5 of *Problèmes* are particularly relevant: "Structure des relations de personne dans le verbe" (225–36), "La nature des pronoms" (251–57), "De la subjectivité dans le langage" (258–66). The following studies are also valuable in inculcating linguistically oriented reading strategies: Raymond Chapman, *Linguistics and Literature* (London: Edward Arnold, 1973); E. L. Epstein, *Language and Style* (London: Methuen, 1978); Roger Fowler, ed. *Essays on Style and Language* (London: Routledge, 1966); Geofrey N. Leech, *A Linguistic Guide to English Poetry* (London: Longman, 1969).

10. In Traugott and Pratt: classes of nouns and verbs (99–101), speech-acts (229), deictics (275); for surface and deep structure (17–18, 167).

11. The use of the word "artificer" throughout this study is inspired by Forrest-Thomson's rigorous study of Modern poetry (*Poetic Artifice*).

12. For further discussion and application of *différance*, see chapter 2.

13. As early as his (unpublished) dissertation, in the section on Yeats, de Man wrote of "the irrevocable inferiority and defeat of the natural image" (69). Then, in *Blindness* (135) he observed: "Since [love] expresses all its feelings by means of images it speaks only in figures." See also Culler (*Deconstruction* 243–80) for a critical discussion; Norris (90–125) provides a good overview of American deconstruction. The anthology by Harari, and the review article by Lewis, as well as the essays by Rorty (chapters 6 and 8) are indispensable.

14. Freud's *General Introduction* deals with parapraxes as "errors" (Part 1); Part 2 discusses dreams (see esp. chaps. 7, 9, 10). For "The 'Uncanny'," see *Collected Papers* vol. 4, pp. 368–407, and *Complete Psychological*, vol. 16, pp. 398–401.

15. It is not my intention to apply Barthes's codes in this study. However, I do find the "hermeneutic" code helpful in explaining certain devices. My application of the codes is very free: e.g. to denote the various discourses that constitute a text ("love code").

16. Benveniste's essays (see n. 9) also undermine the notion of subjectivity; they therefore move toward a post-modern world view.

17. My construal of intertext is quite broad. In Spanish poetic criticism Pérez-Firmat has argued that intertexts must be literary and must be cited the text in hand. Against this narrow view, Andrew P. Debicki (*Poetry* 81–101, 233 n. 5, 225 n. 23, & Index p. 231) has argued that non-literary codes (social, political, economic) must also be considered as intertexts, to which the text in hand may merely allude. I follow Debicki in my construal of the intertext.

18. The term *poetee* stems from Prince's *narratee*: "some*one* whom the narrator addresses" (my emphasis; see Tompkins [*Reader* 7]).

19. I have at all times tried to avoid sexist language by using the plural forms. I limit "he/his/him" to a *male* writer and/or his work.

20. In England the term "modernism" dates from 1910, when an exhibition entitled "Manet and the Post-Impressionists" was mounted. Robert Wohl, *The Generation of 1914* (Cambridge: Harvard University Press, 1979), describes a pre-1912 generation in France as pessimistic and a post-1912 generation as energetic. Perkins (10–30) gives a comparable (nostalgic withdrawal) account of pre-1910 poetry. For Modernism's "high" style, see Beebe. For good accounts of Modernism: Howe (11–40); Gullón (Jiménez, *El modernismo* 13–43), and Siebenmann (208–24).

21. The distinction between Dr. Jekyll and Mr. Hyde, which is Luis Cernuda's (*Prosa* 1016–20), I shall apply systematically to the Jiménez *Obra*. Unlike Cernuda's, my use is not moralistic.

Chapter 2

1. See Jiménez, *Nueva antolojía* (97–8). Although Albornoz's task was to re-present Jiménez to a new Spanish audience, she deliberately passed over some two hundred early poems, published between 1900 and 1903, and selected "¿Soy yo . . . ?," the twelfth poem of the middle section, "Jardines místicos," of *Jardines lejanos.* This surprised her readers; see, for example, José Hierro's review in *Cuadernos Hispanoamericanos* 284(1974):387–99. I assume that Albornoz wished to signal her conviction that it was with this poem that a reappraisal of the *Obra* could begin, and in effect, I am taking up that suggestion.

2. *PLP* 429–30. In *SA* 50 and *TA* 734, line 9 has "verde" instead of "blanco". The version in *Leyenda* (113–14 no. 168) has fourteen sixteen-syllable lines, in addition to the following changes: line 5 has "veo" instead of "hallo," and lines 25–28 read: "...Voy y vengo... ¿Y yo ¡yo! no me había ya dormido? / Mi barba está blanca... Y todo no es lo mismo y es lo mismo." The

Leyenda version is significantly titled "Mi posible." There is no sustained commentary on this poem that I know of. Aguirre ("Window" 114–15) does mention it.

3. Exceptions to this pattern are in lines 2, 3, and 21, where the basic rhythmic nucleus is used twice. (More detailed analysis of Jiménez's use of rhythm is pursued in chapter 4.)

4. Here is a chart of the vowels, with percentages:

		no.		*norm.*
/i/	52 =	9.63%	8.6%
/o/	64 =	11.85%	9.88%
/e/	65 =	12.04%	12 %
/a/	68 =	12.59%	13.7%
/u/	11 =	2.04%	2 %

There are more /i/ and /o/ vowels than is the norm (see last column) given by Alarcos Llorach (*Fonología* 192), but that is due to the rhyme scheme in i-o. The next to last column gives each vowel as a (rounded) percent of the text's *total* sounds.

5. First person pronouns: "yo" (6×); "me" (2×); "mío, mi" (1×). Nouns: "mendigo, caer, tarde, nubes, viento, voz" (2×); "noche, cuarto, ventana, luna, cielo, andar, ritmo" (1×).

6. See, for example, Sánchez-Barbudo (vol. 1, 33ff). The death figure prowls around the outskirts of a garden (i.e. the body [ll. 3–4]), it lurks in the evening shadows and in the moonlight (i.e. the end of time [ll. 4, 9–10]), and it leaves on the beholder a white beard and mourning clothes (i.e. shroud [ll. 15–16]).

7. In *Leyenda*, this became: "...Voy y vengo... ¿Y yo ¡yo! no me había ya dormido?" The initial "y" is transposed to the second sentence. For paratactic versus hypotactic, see Smith (*Closure* 98–109).

8. Ulibarri (73) implies in comments on another poem that "y" joins contradictory urges.

9. The text has this order: "el mendigo que rondaba mi jardín al caer la tarde." Space precedes time. One might thereby argue that the transposition of space into the syntagmatic slot in which the reader is expecting a time clause is an adumbration of the spatio-temporal disturbance ("voy y vengo") that is to follow.

10. See, for example, Culler (*Pursuit* 169–217); B. H. Smith ("Narrative" 214–15ff). Culler (169–70) defines "story" as a "sequence of actions or events," and "plot" as the "discourse that orders those actions or events" (i.e. the order in which the events manifest themselves in the discourse). In Russian Formalism, this difference corresponded to "fabula" and "sjuzhet," respectively.

Eco (*Role* 27) writes: "The *fabula* is the basic story stuff, the logic of actions or the syntax of characters, the time-oriented course of events. It need not necessarily be a sequence of human actions (physical or not), but can also concern a temporal transformation of ideas or a series of events concerning inanimate objects.

The plot is the story as actually told, along with all its deviations, digressions, flashbacks, and the whole of the verbal devices."

11. In the above tabular representation of the text, (10) through (5) represent linear (story) sequence; plot sequence is: (5), (10), (8), (7), (9), (6). The plot presented to the reader switches, therefore, between present and past time modes: present (ll. 1–6), past (ll. 6–11), present (ll. 11–14), past (ll. 14–15). Present is superimposed on past, past on present.

12. The gradual loss of delineation is to be observed by contrasting stanza 1 with stanza 6. In stanza 1 the speaker clearly located himself in a particular space—"¿Soy yo quien anda esta noche, / *por mi cuarto* [?]"—which he differentiated from the beggar's. When stanza 1 is repeated, beginning with line 20, the speaker has ceased to locate himself in the specific space of his room: "¿Soy yo, o soy el mendigo [?]," he merely asks. The syntagma "quien anda esta noche / por mi cuarto" is elided.

13. If the intonation arrow drops on the last syllable of the question, the implication is that the speaker is in front of a closed window. If the arrow rises, the speaker is in front of an open window.

Aguirre ("Window" 115) writes: "Whether the window is open or closed, the tonality of the symbol changes little." Although I do find a change of outlook here, I think my analysis is documenting ideas Aguirre suggested. I believe that Juan Ramón in this poem is intuiting a way to overcome the polarities Aguirre (105) describes as: ". . . melancholy hopelessness (the self in the street looking at the window of the "other") to *taedium vitae* (the self in the room), and from these to either despair (the self concentrating his gaze upon the mirror) or melancholy hope (the self looking out of his window at the "other" in the street)."

14. A reader notes that the speaker wishes the experience were a dream. Line 8, "yo no me había dormido?" becomes in line 26, "no me había ya dormido?" There is a difference in intensity, which became even stronger in the *Leyenda* version: "¿Y yo ¡yo! no me había ya dormido?" The repetition underlines the fact that the "yo" wishes it were all a dream for then he would not have to dread his insights.

15. Classified by point of articulation, from back to front of mouth, Spanish consonants are:

BACK	velars	[k g x]
	palatals	[ĉ l y ñ]
MID	alveolars	[s l n r r̃]
	dentals	[t d f ø]
FRONT	bilabials	[p b m]

The velars are, phonosymbolically, 'dark' and ominous; the bilabials are 'bright' and soft. For remarks on phonosymbolism in English, see Fónagy, in Malmberg *Readings*, 282–305.

16. In W. B. Yeats's poetry, beggars are more carefree; in *Responsibilities*, see "The Three Beggars" (109–10) and "Beggar To Beggar Cried" (112); in *The Wild Swans At Coole*, "Tom O'Roughley" (139).

17. This explanation does help explain the selection of "mendigo" over the paradigmatically similar noun, "pordiosero." Laplanche and Pontalis (300–301) write: "Freud showed that parapraxes, like symptoms, are compromise-formations resulting from the antagonism between the subject's conscious intentions and what he has repressed." As instances of parapraxis, all of which begin in German with the prefix 'ver-', they give: "slip of the tongue, misreading, slip of the pen, bungled action."

18. The portrait is in the Sala Zenobia-Juan Ramón Jiménez at the University of Puerto Rico, Río Piedras. It is reproduced on the dust jacket of this book. See also *Leyenda* 246.

Juan Ramón lived in the "Sanatorio de Rosario" (in Madrid) from the end of 1901 until September 1903, when he went to live with Dr. Simarro (also in Madrid). See Albornoz (*Jiménez* Escritor 344).

19. Aguirre ("Window") takes "cuarto" as a negative force symbolizing melancholy, "l'éternel ennui" (114), and I agree entirely that by the end of the first phase of the *Obra* this is its connotation. For example, part of the prose preface to *Laberinto* reads: "Ambientes y emociones de un Watteau literario un poco más interior y menos optimista . . . Es el alma, ansiosa de una elegancia espiritual que lo invadiera todo, que todo lo cambiara. . . . Si el vivir cotidiano tuviera sus frondas de jardín con pajarillos líricos, sus horizontes de campo . . . sus estancias apacibles, con rosas, con ventanas abiertas y con mujeres ideales!" (*PLP* 1173).

Despite this, I believe, and shall argue again in the next chapter, that the *Obra* appeals to a garden and a room filled with sunlight, both of which existed prior to the melancholy and nostalgic "cuarto" found throughout most of the early "Work."

20. Hillis Miller ("Williams' *Spring*" 428) links *aletheia* to creation, and he comments: "in art alone is the hidden truth of nature uncovered . . . in art a new object is brought into existence." Then in "Stevens' Rock" (20), he explains "the traditional metaphysical structure of *aletheia*" as "the appearance of something visible out of the abyss of truth." Culler (*Deconstruction* 186) defines *aletheia* as "the unveiling or making present of what has been hidden[.]"

21. There is a well known poem on this topic in *Poesía*, i.e. in the second phase of the *Obra*; it begins, "Poder que me utilizas, / como médium sonámbulo" (*LP* 901). One can argue, therefore, that subsequently the poet adjusted to the strange, uncanny power that he experienced for the first time in "¿Soy yo . . . ?" This is the power that kept him in touch with "la realidad invisible," and which he harnessed for creative ends. (For sources of commentary on mystery in J. R., see chap. 5, n. 19, below.)

22. Some notion of the power of the imagination to totally possess a human being is indicated by the case of Antonio Gaudí. It is reported that Gaudí, absorbed in the construction of "la Sagrada Familia," became utterly oblivious to prosaic reality and was hit by a tramcar while crossing the street. The injuries he sustained were fatal, and he died penniless and unrecognized in a hospital, in a beggarly state.

23. I overstate the case slightly. However, Juan Ramón insisted that the only thing that distinguishes poetry from prose is "rima." "—No hay prosa y verso . . . lo que les diferencia es la rima" (Gullón, *Conversaciones* 114, and see 115−16). In addition, Young (*Line* 52) says Juan Ramón detected the "echo of eternal music" (Shelley's words) in both prose and poetry. For me, that is rhythm.

24. See Jiménez, "Poesía y Literatura: I" (*Trabajo* 37): ". . . la poesía . . . será fatalmente rítmica . . . eso dicen los bailarines auténticos, los poetas del ritmo absoluto . . . En realidad, el poeta . . . es un bailarín abstracto[.]" Yeats concludes "Among School Children" with: "O body swayed to music, O brightening glance, / How can we know the dancer from the dance?" (214).

25. Culler (*Deconstruction* 97) writes: "The term *différance*, which Derrida introduces here [*Positions*, pp. 39−40/28], alludes to this undecidable, non-synthetic alternation between the perspectives of structure and event. The verb *différer* means to differ and to defer. *Différance* sounds exactly the same as *différence*, but the ending *ance*, which is used to produce verbal nouns, makes it a new form meaning "difference-differing-deferring." *Différance* thus designates both a "passive" difference already in place as the condition of significa-tion and an act of differing which produces differences."

By describing the play of differences here and elsewhere in the *Obra*, I am attempting to domesticate Derrida's ideas for the purposes of what I. A. Richards termed "Practical Criticism."

26. A *modern* reader would claim that this condition is figured in the poem. For example, in the chart that analyzed the syntax above, it can be shown that segments of the *ambiente* are coordinated (in C, D, F); parts of the self are coordinated (in A, E, G). However, "yo" is not coordinated with "other," nor is "other" ever coordinated with inner or outer *ambiente* in the poem.

27. The term "destined" is deliberately used, because in *Espacio* Juan Ramón sees life as "Destino." For a reproduction of this painting, see *Leyenda*, "edi-ción de bibliófilo," facing p. 410. Also, compare "El retrato" in *Leyenda* 324, no. 498.

Chapter 3

1. Aguirre ("Symbolism" 71) writes of "Arias otoñales" that "Jiménez's landscape is a metamorphosis of [the myth of] Arcadia, the ideal region of pas-toral and rustic love, functioning as a world of art and love, a paradise of music and poetry." (See also p. 79 of same, for Symbolist poets who used similar landscape.)

The *post-modern* reader in this chapter questions the extent to which this Arcadia is present in the first phase of Jiménez's work. This reader will imply that such metaphors are in effect nostalgic cries for the loss of the "imaginary" pre-Oedipal state in which a child recognizes no distinction between itself and an object (see chap. 1).

2. One could argue that, as Jiménez was not well known in Spain from 1940 until quite recently, this private script belonged to a very small "minoría" of

readers. Added to this is the fact that darkness was successfully banished to the distant recesses of the pysche during Jiménez's years in Madrid. It resurfaced only when the poet was forced to live in exile from his native land.

3. Olson, in his study of the rose, the fountain, the circle—in *Circle of Paradox*—can be said to be studying true symbols. Images and symbols of decadence, indexed to an aestheticized, indolent beauty—"hojas secas," "parques viejos," "pinares," "rosas mustias," "verdeoro el jazmín"—are more typical of Jiménez's early work. Such symbols lack the uncanny and ominous negativity which is present in the words I shall study. Aguirre ("Window" 114) writes that "the evening, the park, the rain, the autumn leaves" are objects "much favoured by symbolist and *modernista* poets alike."

4. Compare Aguirre ("Symbolism" 64) who is studying "words/objects which suggest that between them and the poem's 'I' there exists a *fusion* rather than a mere *correspondance.*"

5. The symbol with multiple connotations in Juan Ramón is studied by Gullón (*Estudios* 161–68). I cite Greimas and Courtés on "lexeme" and "sememe" in chapter 1. My application of their description is: to trace the "historical development" of the lexeme through the *Obra*. This diachronic procedure determines the lexeme's sememes. For example, it will demonstrate "sol" is indexed to "muerte" in the first phase of the work, and that hence we can speak of a sememe "dead"-"sun."

6. Freud in "The Uncanny" (*Collected Papers*) writes: "The subject of the 'uncanny' . . . undoubtedly belongs to all that is terrible—to all that arouses dread and creeping horror" (368). He adds: ". . . aesthetics . . . concern themselves with what is beautiful, attractive and sublime, that is with feelings of a positive nature, with the circumstances and the objects that call them forth, rather than with the opposite feelings of unpleasantness and repulsion" (368–69). Also pertinent to the present reading, Freud writes: "The German word *unheimlich* is obviously the opposite of *heimlich*, *heimisch*, meaning 'familiar'; and we are tempted to conclude that what is 'uncanny' is frightening precisely because it is *not* known and familiar" (370). He adds: ". . . the uncanny would always be that in which one does not know where one is" (370). For "free energy and bound energy," see Freud (*Complete Psychological* vols. 1, 16, and 17); for succinct explanation, see Laplanche (171–73).

7. In "J. R. J. & T. S. Eliot" (164–65). The malevolent figure appears at the beginning of the third part of "Ash Wednesday": "At the first turning of the second stair / I turned and saw below / The same shape twisted on the bannister." *Collected Poems* (99).

8. See "Recuerdos" in *Ninfeas* (PLP 1473) and *Rimas* (PLP 196), where these lines occur: "el ígneo sol de mayo / sonriendo se moría, / una canción de luces suspirando." In addition, a poem in *Arias tristes* defines the moon by apposition thus: "Luna, mis lágrimas son / para ti, para ese encanto /—visión, sombra, novia, blanca—" (PLP 224). Aguirre ("Symbolism" 77) discusses this poem.

9. Compare these remarks by Aguirre ("Symbolism"): "The symbolism of the moon is complex and varied, and at times contradictory. Depending on

context, it can relate to barrenness and fertility, to reason and intuition, to death and love. I believe that in Juan Ramón's poetry the symbol retains part of its traditional association with death" (76). He later adds: "If we accept that the sun symbolises life and love, the moon is often seen to be endowed with other connotations." And: "The poet belongs to a world in which the sun becomes a negative symbol" (78).

10. Santos Escudero (70–82) discusses this positivity for the second phase of the *Obra*.

11. See "Creador segundo" (LP 1178): "¿Qué me importa, sol seco? / Yo hago la fuente azul en mis entrañas."

12. In Albornoz (*Jiménez* Escritor 27–32). See also below in present chapter.

13. The moon is also a madonna, not just a prostitute, in the early work: "mujer casta y armada" (*PLP* 1223; see also 157, 932, 1159).

14. Mario Praz, *The Romantic Agony* 1956; rpt. (Cleveland and New York: World Publishing Co., 1968), studied excesses of "algolagnia"—how suffering is inspired by death, sexual deviation, *femmes fatales*, unobtainable aesthetic ideals.

15. The dog is not exclusively negative in the early work. It is found in a peaceful setting: "ladran / los perros lejanos: el valle / parece un valle del alma" (*PLP* 307). See also: *PLP* 135 (*Rimas*), *PLP* 541, 627, 633 (*Pastorales*), *PLP* 719 (*Las hojas verdes*), *PLP* 1163 (*Poemas mágicos y dolientes*), and *LIP I*, 250; *LIP II*, 218, 286.

16. Sánchez-Barbudo (vol. 1, 29–30) notes that in the poem there is: ". . . vivísima inquietud . . . y conciencia de la inutilidad de todo ("para qué sirve . . ."), si siempre un abismo nos ha de separar del infinito."

17. For an erotic reaction to the beloved, see *LIP II*, 453. Her departure is perceived by the lover in these terms: "Mi anhelo apasionado / vino hasta mi alma desde el fin a donde ibas / y fue, cien veces, perro, ladrándole al ocaso."

18. This is unusual, for negative canine lexemes rarely occur in the second and third phases of the work.

19. Trees and trunks are associated with peace and hope in *PLP* 241, 959, 986, 987, 1005.

20. A Freudian reading would interpret a trunk as phallic. The pustulating sexuality occurs in relation to the "sapo." For example, in *Arias tristes* a melancholy or sad "sapo" in the light of the moon accompanies the speaker who fantasizes about a virgin's body (*PLP* 242–24, 338). In *Pastorales* (*PLP* 540, 571–72, 663) the "sapo" again forms a part of scenes of unrequited sexual passion: "un sapo / extático y mudo, que ama / tristemente, desde lejos" (*PLP* 540).

21. The figure intrigues him: "y sus ojos quietos tienen / un brillo extraño que atrae" (*PLP* 280). See Young's comments on this ("J. R. J. & T. S. Eliot" 164).

22. For "enlutado," see also: *PLP* 1512; *Leyenda* 28 no. 42; and *LP* 39. (After the *Sonetos* it does not appear.)

23. The narcissism in this poem could be interpreted as an attempt to discover within self the seeds for future growth. Not for many years will Jiménez

learn to transform a negative self-love (narcissism) into a positive self-love that permits regeneration.

24. Aguirre ("Window") discusses Jung's assertion that "man cannot invent symbols." Aguirre writes that symbols represent "units of human *feeling*, human experience, . . . they also stand for statements of the rational mind" (104). I note that in this interpretation "symbol" has a basis that is extrinsic to the *Obra*. The lexeme as I study it has an intrinsic foundation only. I am also intrigued by the following quotation, translated in Aguirre ("Symbolism" 64), from Gilbert Durand, *L'imagination symbolique* (Paris, 1968), pp.10–11: "the sum of all the symbols on a single theme clarifies the symbols by their relations one to another, it gives them a supplementary symbolic 'power'." This is how I argue the lexeme can function.

25. Debicki (*Poetry*) has made extensive use of intertextuality in reading contemporary Spanish poetry; see chap. 1, n. 17.

26. See also, *Leyenda* 122, no. 178.

27. The ephebe's sense of a lack of priority is the equivalent of death for the young poet (*Anxiety* 10). Jiménez's "mendigo" could thereby represent poetic death: that the strong precursor poet will kill his originality. Later, Bloom (*Anxiety* 147–48) concludes: "The strong poet peers into the mirror of his fallen precursor and beholds neither the precursor nor himself but a Gnostic double, the dark otherness or antithesis that both he and the precursor longed to be, yet feared to become." And ". . . the anxiety of influence [is that] each poet [fears] that no proper work remains for him to perform." Jiménez is in that anxious state during the first phase of his *Obra*.

Chapter 4

1. It is mentioned twice in *Sonetos espirituales*, *LP* 21, 39; and see *LP* 890; see also chap. 3, n. 22, above.

2. See also "Perro Divino" in *Piedra y cielo* (*LP* 749); "un dios azul perro manso" (*TA* 886); and numerous references to the friendly dog (*LP* 314; *Leyenda* 7 no. 1; 496 no. 917). See Santos Escudero (246–50) for "El símbolo del perro y lo divino."

3. See also "Muy tarde" (*LP* 948), which Sánchez-Barbudo explicates (*Cincuenta* 76–9); and "El pajarito verde" series (*LP* 939, 965). Santos Escudero (chap. 14) describes positive bird symbolism.

4. The words are Yeats's, from the last stanza of "Adam's Curse" (79). For this period of the life, consult Nemes (*Vida* 499–597; *Inicios* 124–50).

5. See Olson (83) for an interpretation of the entire poem.

6. The distinction is Barthes's, in "From Work to Text," Harari (73–81).

7. This interest has been studied by Young in *Line*, and in "Luisa and J. R.," *Revista de letras* 6 (1974): 469–86; "Anglo-American Poetry in the Correspondence of Luisa and J. R. J.," *Hispanic Review* 44 (1976): 1–26; "North American Poetry in the *Diario*: A Preliminary Assessment," in *Estudios sobre J. R. J.* (Puerto Rico: University de Mayaguez, 1981), 171–79. By the present author, see: "Enticing Yeats to Spain: Zenobia and J. R. J.," *Yeats Eliot Review*

5.2 (1978): 5–12; "William Butler Yeats: Un 'lírico del Norte' en la poesía de J. R. J.," *Insula* 416–17 (1981): 8; and two items cited below in the bibliography, "'Naked' versus 'Pure' Poetry" and "W. B. Yeats and J. R. J." On Emily Dickinson, see: Harriet S. Stevens, "Emily Dickinson y J. R. J.," *Cuadernos hispanoamericanos* 166 (oct. 1963): 29–49; A. M. Fagundo Guerra, "The Influence of Emily Dickinson on J. R. J.'s Poetry," Ph.D. diss., University of Washington (1967); Carl Cobb, "J. R. J. and Emily Dickinson," *Revista de estudios hispánicos* 4 (1970): 35–48. On T. S. Eliot, see Cándido Pérez Gallego, "J. R. J. y T. S. Eliot," *Cuadernos hispanoamericanos* 376–78 (oct.-dic. 1981): 911–25; also, Young, "J. R. J. & T. S. Eliot." On Robert Frost, see Howard T. Young, "Lo que dicen los árboles: La amistad literaria entre Robert Frost y J. R. J.," *La Torre* 29 (1981): 289–309. On Lindsay, Masters, and Sandburg, see my "J. R. J. and the Illinois Trio." On Walter Pater, see my "An Inquiry."

8. See Jiménez *Diario*, ed. Sánchez-Barbudo, p. 118.

9. Corominas, under "golfo" (162–64), gives maritime and vernacular meanings for the word: "ensenada grande, la anchura del mar, alta mar." He notes that the derivation "engolfarse" can mean "abismo" (162). For "golfo" as "pilluelo, vagabundo," he writes: "particularmente frecuente en voces jergales," and "vagamente denigratorio." A derivation from "golfo" is "golondra," which is associated with "alondra"—and which offers fascinating material for *post-modern* speculators.

10. For remarks on a Renaissance love code in Juan Ramón's poems of these years, see my "The Love Poem as *vita nuova*." For *Sonetos*, see Nancy B. Mandlove, "The Ordering of Experience: A Study of Juan Ramón Jiménez's *Sonetos espirituales*," *Hispania* 63 (1980): 666–73.

11. Navarro Tomás provides indispensable information on this aspect of the work. See "J. R. J. y la lírica tradicional," in Albornoz (*Jiménez* Escritor, 307–24).

12. For "ritmo"/"rima," see chap. 2, nn. 23 and 24. I also discuss rhythm in my "J. R. J. and the Illinois Trio" (190ff).

13. For further discussion of the amphibrach, see my "Algunas configuraciones" (4ff).

14. For vocalic norm, see chap. 2, n. 4.

15. Hillis Miller ("Stevens' Rock" 28). For *aletheia*, see chap. 2, n. 20. "Visto" (l. 7) could be classed as an adjective ("fin *visto*"). Although it is not chromatic, it is linked to colors in the sense that "blanco—rosa—roja" represents what was *seen*.

16. In Vries (*Dictionary of Symbols* 269) indigo is "1. night, evil[.]" Webster's (1150) says that "indigo blue . . . is synthesized as a blue crystalline powder with a coppery luster." It adds: "a variable color averaging a dark grayish blue that is redder and deeper than night blue." Corominas, under "indigo" (448), gives its derivatives, which include "individual, individualismo, individualizar." Under "añil," Corominas (288) offers: "color azul oscuro."

17. In the poem "Yo y Yo," to be analyzed in the next chapter, the poet employs this device at the symbolic center of the text.

18. Predmore (106), the only commentary I have found on the poem, writes: "El sentido de desencanto en este poema es tan fuerte como en cualquier otro pasaje de gran desilusión del *Diario*." He also adds (107): "aquí, en este momento desalentador, [el sueño] es como un puerto de la nada, una negación de la 'fe', la 'vida', y la 'voluntad' que le pueden conducir a una nueva primavera de amor y renacimiento." My reading is not as negative as this.

19. Corominas, under "coger," gives "recoger" and observes: "en la ac. religiosa es invención de los místicos españoles" (121).

20. Predmore (105) believes "el cambio de color . . . [es] originado, es de suponer, por el sol poniente." Ulibarri (74) writes of "el sol que desaparece."

21. Jiménez's positive response to the land can be seen, for example, in "¡Ya!" (*Diario, LP* 471).

22. For Pater and the maturation of beauty, see my "An Inquiry" (195). For purchase of Pater's works, see Young (*Line* 276, n. 68).

23. A *modern* reader notes that the tactility, visibility, and acccessibility of "el pie desnudo" contrasts with "el sol que no se ve," which remains forever covert, invisible, inaccessible. This, also, is foregrounded in the rhythm: the rhythmic unit *que no se ve* ($\cup\cup\cup\prime$) terminates with a stressed syllable, enforcing the notion of inaccessability and concealment. A cluster of three unstressed syllables is rare in this text; it occurs only four times. It does begin to appear in the next line, *a ca ri cián* ($\cup\cup\cup\prime$); however, it is expanded with an unstressed syllable ("do"). Hence, a *modern* reader notes that rhythm does not seal off the image here, it leaves it open to future possibilities. Again, rhythm is subtly furthering semantic differences.

24. In the famous "Soy animal de fondo," both "estar" and "ser" are selected:

> "En el fondo de aire" (dije) "estoy",
> (dije) "soy animal de fondo de aire" (sobre tierra),
> ahora sobre mar;
>
> .   .   .   .
>
> Pero tú, dios, también estás en este fondo
>
> .   .   .   .
>
> que es el pozo sagrado de mí mismo.
>
> .   .   .   .
>
> Este pozo que era, solo y nada más ni menos,
> que el centro de la tierra y de su vida. (*LP* 1339–40)

25. Reference to "desilusiones" may imply a fear—understandable in the twenties—that experimentation (with text, with sonnetic form) might follow the course of many of this century's *isms* and dissipate into triviality and mere play. This may indicate the onerous burden felt by the conscientious and original artificer, at the beginning of his Modern period. He is aware of his tradition and is brooding on the transformations to which—in the originality of his *Diario*—he is *subject*ing it, but he clearly senses that he has finally broken into the style that will distinguish him as a Modern poet.

26. For the clearest equation of "mar" with *Obra*, see *Leyenda* (531 no. 1009). Also, in *Leyenda* (584 no. 1129), "mar" is conjoined with "centro": "Tú, mar desnudo, vives, en el centro de la vida." The "cumulus center" leads on, in my opinion, to such exultant *cloud* poems as "Huir azul" and "Soy animal de fondo" where the "golfo" has really been converted into "un fondo," and where the speaker is conscious of the struggle (i.e. the negativity) involved in achieving that state (i.e. positivity).

27. Ulibarri (74) reaches a similar conclusion in his remarks on the conjunction "y": "Todo esto ilustra una oscilación constante de la realidad, nunca fija, nunca inerte. La conjunción sirve de instrumento que junta los extremos y proporciona la avenida para el tránsito de dos vías para los múltiples y confusos elementos de la realidad."

Chapter 5

1. Carreño (42) briefly mentions "Yo y Yo," noting that a subjective "yo" contemplates a transcendent "tú" in the water, and that the transcendent longing remains unfulfilled in so far as it is a mere image. Villar (56) comments on the poem. He sees the poet as lamenting his inability to unite with his inner, immortal self, to travel along the roads of his unconscious to meet the eternal self. He claims that the "image" is the immortal self, which is more powerful than the physical self.

The significance of *Piedra y cielo* is noted by Predmore (210), who writes that it "resuelve, por fin, el conflicto de las fuerzas de una personalidad dividida."

2. For *desdoblamiento*, see preface, n. 6. For distinction between convention and tradition, see chap. 1.

3. For the distinction between "motivated" and "arbitrary," see Alonso (31–32).

4. For hermeneutic code see Barthes (*S/Z* 19, 210, 262); Culler (*Poetics* 210). Eagleton (138) notes that this code is "concerned with the tale's unfolding enigmas."

5. In, for example, "Structure des relations de personne dans le verbe" (225–36) Benveniste discusses "je" and "tu" and suggests why Rimbaud's "Je est un autre" signifies alienation (230). See also chap. 1, n. 9.

6. Jiménez could have selected the non-reflexive "oponer" because paradigmatically it is very similar to the reflexive "oponerse," but then intransitive connotations (interiority, passivity, reflexivity) would have been lost.

7. A further response to this line concerns the total anonymity of the actants. Owing to the non-personalization of the actants, the reader assumes that "me" designates the speaker of the text and "[tú]" the *poetee* (see chap. 1, and chap. 1, n. 18). This act of communication is therefore construed as a private dialogue which excludes as *de trop* both reader and implied poet. This is in accord with the Modern poem's ideals of objectivity, with the implied Modern poet's conscious attempt to obliterate personality from the artifact, as well

as with Modern art's ignoring of the *addressee*—its dehumanization (Ortega). This situation aggravates the *modern* readers' inferiority complex: they know that Modern art is a private speech-act from which they are excluded; they know that they are voyeurs. Added to this is the fact that "New Criticism" instructed them that their knowledge of poet and work, of literature and life, is invalid for a just comprehension of the project.

8. In lines 2 and 3, the enjambment is strong and abrupt, hence "imajen" is foregrounded. With lines 11 and 12, the enjambment is weaker, with the result that the lines run quickly together; hence, neither "sales" (which, like "ima-jen," ends in accented /a/ + closed /e/) nor the short line 12 is foregrounded.

9. See also my remarks on intuition as "norm" and "deviation," in "Specialist Reader" in chapter 1.

10. See, for example: "Y el peso de tu alma y de tu carne / sobre mi carne, / no me deja correr tras de tu imajen" (*LP* 310). Also: "El chorro de agua . . . como una mujer nueva . . ." (*LP* 840).

11. Cole demonstrated that the "religious instinct" is an integral part of Jim-énez's work. For "graven image," see Exodus 20:4; for God the "Light," see John 1:7; for "Christ, the way . . . ," see John 14:6; for Saul and blinding light, see Acts 9:2. Young (*Line* 159) notes that "St. Paul's vision on the road to Damascus" preoccupied Juan Ramón in *Espacio*. In the "Tercer Fragmento," written in 1954, the phrase "yegua de San Pablo" occurs (*TA* 869).

12. This adapts Yeats ("An Irish Airman . . ." 133): "I balanced all, brought all to mind."

13. Additional concrete nouns are: "chorro, agua, cuna, luz." Additional abstract nouns are: "imajen, alma, fin, sinfín, punto, vida."

14. +Action (dynamic) verbs would include: "saltar, buscar, oponerse, salir, venir, dar, hallar." −Action (static) verbs would include: "poder, saber, ser, anhelar."

15. There are approximately 33 high /i u/ and 33 low /a/ vowels, but 87 mid / e o/ vowels. There are 25 back (velars and palatals) and 27 front (bilabial) consonants, whereas there are 107 mid consonants (labiodental, interdental, dental, alveolar). See chap. 2, n. 15.

16. Jakobson's influence on the linguistic analysis of poetry is paramount (see chap. 1). In the bibliography I cite works in which "patterns" form an important part of his analysis.

17. Compare, Culler (*Deconstruction* 87–88): The "double procedure of systematically employing the concepts or premises one is undermining puts the critic in a position not of skeptical detachment but of unwarrantable involvement, asserting the indispensability of causation while denying it any rigorous justification. This is an aspect of deconstruction which many find difficult to understand and accept."

18. However, they are not as distant as "aquel."

19. Bly first pointed out the "leaping image" in Spanish poetry. Albornoz ("Estudio preliminar" 60–61), Gullón (*Estudios* 195–203), Young (*Line* 157–59) emphasize the importance of mystery, magic, the occult in Jiménez.

20. For "yo eterno," see Young (78), who defines it as "that inner para-

digm against which all others must be matched." For a discussion of its place in Jiménez's theorizing, see Blasco (95, 209–10, 220).

In the first chapter of *La rebelión de las masas*, Ortega describes the higher man as he who demands more of himself.

21. In all other lines, except line 8, a stressed syllable is surrounded by two or three unstressed ones. In line 8, there is one unstressed only accompanying each stressed syllable, which creates a tense, jerky sensation. Smith (*Closure* 177–78) discusses kinesthetic imagery.

22. Basilio de Pablos first pointed out the dynamics of continual regeneration and transformation in Jiménez's later vision.

23. Norris (49) defines aporia as a point at which thought has encountered a self-engendered paradox beyond which it cannot pass.

24. See Frenzel (346–50) for spiritual darkness in Narcissus. Sánchez-Barbudo (vol. 1, 99–118) confronts the issue of Narcissism in Jiménez. It could be argued, following Lacan, that any conception of self is narcissistic. Only by looking into a mirror and seeing an image of its total body does the child begin to develop an ego, an integrated self-image. To accuse Jiménez of narcissism is therefore to note that he was more sensitive than most to the process of becoming human, or that he was preoccupied with Lacan's postulations *avant la lettre*.

25. The negative marking for "camino eterno" and "imajen" indicates the speaker's dispirited attitude toward the past. He comes to see the "eternal road" as *one* among several equally valid "images." In *Leyenda* (587 no. 1135), we find: "Camino sin mi vida no es para mí camino; es objeto, no es destino." In addition, the overwhelming verbal activity in "Yo y Yo" is the present, an energy that militates against pursuing into the future ideologies that already existed in the past.

Chapter 6

1. "Estudio de la obra" (89). Albornoz begins this "Estudio" (63–64) of *Espacio* with: "*Espacio*: Culminación, Recapitulación y Crítica de la 'Obra'." The opinion of *specialist* readers is that *Espacio* is a synthesis. Albornoz (63–64) provides a full bibliography, but indispensable works on *Espacio* are: Howard Young, "Génesis y forma de *Espacio*," *Revista hispánica moderna* 34 (1968): 462–70; and Font, *Espacio*.

I do not wish to claim that form is utterly disregarded in *Espacio*. I believe that form is not reified, as it was by the Modern artificer. Font has commented on rhythm, for example. I encounter a lax rhythm throughout (comparable to amphibrachs).

2. For a recent discussion of Juan Ramón and Aquinas, see Coke-Enguídanos (31–34).

3. Font (*Espacio* 12) cites a letter by Juan Ramón published by Enrique Díez Canedo in which the poet writes of *Espacio* as: "una escritura de tiempo, fusión memorial de ideología y anécdota sin orden cronológico, como una tira sin fin desliada hacia atrás en mi vida."

4. The technique is studied by Bousoño (*Teoría* 303–36). An additional example of spatio-temporal superpositioning occurs in the "third fragment" in references to "Sitjes, Villa Vizcaya, Santiago Rusiñol, Deering, Cau Ferrat." Deering was an American millionaire who bought the house next to Rusiñol's, Cau Ferrat, in Sitjes. He furnished it with Spanish antiques, and when he had filled it he bought the house opposite, built the overhead bridge that connects the two, and furnished the second house with more antiques. He grew tired of the place (around 1920), and moved all the antiques to the Villa Vizcaya, a mansion he built in 1914–16 in Miami, which is now the Dade County Art Museum.

5. For commentary, see Olson (181–82) and Albornoz ("Estudio de la obra" 76–77).

6. It seems that Juan Ramón's first sea was the Mediterranean; that his second was the North Atlantic ("que me llevó al amor"); and that his third was the South Atlantic: "No, no fué allí en Sitjes . . . en donde se me apareció mi mar tercero, fué aquí ya; era este mar, este mar mismo y verde, verdemismo; no fué el Mediterráneo azulazulazul, fué el verde, el gris, el negro Atlántico de aquella Atlántida." The South Atlantic is the sea of *Animal de fondo*, but when he wrote the above lines in *Espacio* in 1953–54 he would have been in Puerto Rico. Hence it would make more sense if his third sea were the Caribbean.

7. The line should be read as a rejection of *La vida es sueño*'s faith in an after-life (cf. Font *Espacio* 164–65).

8. I limit myself to those studied in chapter 3. However, I do mention the sea below. I study the sea in more detail in my "Otra lectura de *Espacio*: temas y símbolos," in *Actas del Congreso Internacional Conmemorativo del Centenario de Juan Ramón Jiménez*, Huelva: Excma. Diputación Provincial, Instituto de Estudios Onubenses (1983), 619–24.

9. For a discussion and development of this paradox, see my "'Naked' and 'Pure' Poetry" (513–14).

10. As mentioned in chap. 5, residues of Romantic thought may well be part of the concept of the overself. There is the belief that the artist, the human mind, humankind creates reality: "Y si dormimos, ¡qué abandonada queda la otra realidad! Nosotros les comunicamos a las cosas nuestra inquietud de día, de noche nuestra paz" (*TA* 859).

The child is also idealized in the "Fragmento Primero" (*TA* 860), for its innocence, as it was in Romantic literature (e.g. Rousseau).

Coke-Enguídanos [91–92] argues, in fact, that this type of experience is "panentheism," derived from *krausismo*: "the presence of God in all things."

11. In *Una colina meridiana* there is a poem entitled "En los espacios del tiempo" (*TA* 958).

12. For development of the figure of "mundillos unidos," see my "Algunas configuraciones" (6–18).

13. For further discussion of the fusion of "Sentido y elemento," see my Ph.D. diss. ("W. B. Y. & J. R. J." 337–38, 394).

14. There are three aposiopeses in the text: pp. 867, 877, 878. Each signifies

an aporia in the thoughts of the speaker. After the first two, a change from positive to negative is registered. After the third, the thoughts become even 'darker'.

15. Albornoz ("Estudio de la obra" 74–76), reaches much the same conclusions. For a different reading, consult Dionisio Cañas, "La oquedad creadora: Juan Ramón Jiménez y José Lezama Lima," *Insula* 426 (1982): 1, 10. Cañas sees the "hueco" as creative: "se trata de una oquedad creadora, pues aquél, el poeta, crea en ella, y al mismo tiempo, se *re-crea*, reaparece como un ser *otro*" (10).

16. The noun "cáncer" brings to mind the fact that the poet's wife, Zenobia, underwent several operations for cancer during the fifties. She finally died of cancer in 1956. Therefore, "cáncer" has a negative amatorial sememe.

17. The relationship between lovers is frequently negative throughout *Espacio*. In the "Fragmento Primero" the noun "veneno" (*TA* 854–55) is used in reference to love. In addition, as already noted, the only lovers to figure in the discourse are tragic, and sexual love is deprecated.

18. For remarks on "eterno retorno" in Juan Ramón, see my "Arbol arraigado y pleamar: respuesta a la transformación de la decadencia y la estética en Juan Ramón Jiménez," *La Torre* 29.111–14 (1981): 151–93, esp. 192.

Chapter 7

1. For greater analysis of the *Obra*'s major themes, see my "Juan Ramón Jiménez: transformación y evolución de cuatro temas fundamentales de su obra," *Cuadernos hispanoamericanos*, 376–78 (oct.-dic. 1981): 179–204.

2. The *Sonetos* begin the transformation; see chap. 3.

3. For a discussion of "desnudez," see Young (*Line* 214–30); Nemes (*Vida* 638–41); also, my "W. B. Y. & J. R. J." (280).

4. See my "'Naked' and 'Pure'" (514–16).

5. For Jiménez's struggle with the English language, see also *LP* 344; for "cielo" signifying a struggle of negative and positive, see *LP* 242, 250, 253. The negative also asserts itself in the *Diario* in the form of the "nada" and the "negro eco" (*LP* 254, 345, 364–65, 431–32, 437–38, 468). All the above poems indicate a fear of aesthetic failure, and of existential loss of control.

6. It is the last of the "Canciones de la nueva luz" (which form the second part of *La estación total*). It is one of only six poems not to appear in *Canción* in 1936; the others are *LP* 1212, 1217, 1222, 1225, 1233.

7. See Olson (138–41) for detailed analysis of this poem.

8. For analysis of this poem, see María A. Salgado, "Río-mar-desierto: Plasmación dinámica del revivir juanramoniano," *Hispania* 65 (1982): 194–99.

9. I find that some of the most original poems in *Leyenda* appear at the beginning and at the end of the anthology. The middle part is often a de-Modernizing ("reliving") of known texts. I would even go so far as to say that *Leyenda* is a rather disappointing collection of poetry. Of its 1303 poems, I estimate that about 200 are new to Jiménez's readers, by which I mean they had not appeared in either *PLP, LP, SA, TA, LIP I & II,* or *Canción.* (However, some

have appeared in the particularized editions of certain books edited by Albornoz, Gullón, Sánchez-Barbudo.) Here are the numbers of the new poems: 2–7, 15, 17, 21, 23, 25–30, 32, 34, 36–38, 42, 44, 45, 68, 84, 86–87, 93, 97, 100–01, 103–08, 110, 112, 115, 118–22, 132, 141, 146–47, 161, 167, 176, 178, 180–81, 186, 193, 196, 198, 200–02, 221, 293, 295, 298, 322–25, 330, 346–47, 357, 362–63, 365, 371, 397, 416, 419, 426, 445, 482–83, 498, 514–15, 528, 531–32, 553, 555–56, 754–56, 758–59, 764, 768–70, 854, 857, 873–74, 914, 916–22, 927, 936–37, 957, 963–64, 991, 1000, 1009–13, 1057, 1124–26, 1129–34, 1136, 1143–60, 1183–86, 1188–90, 1193–94, 1197–98, 1200–04, 1210–11, 1215, 1217, 1219, 1221, 1223–27, 1263–64, 1267–68, 1270–72, 1269, 1285–1303.

10. Compare this last stanza from Yeats's "'What then?' sang Plato's ghost. 'What then?'" (300):

> "The work is done," grown old he thought,
> "According to my boyish plan;
> Let the fools rage, I swerved in naught,
> Something to perfection brought";
> But louder sang that ghost, "What then?"

11. See Hartman (151), who uses similar terms to describe Winckelman's conception of perfect beauty.

Postscript

1. Bowie on Lacan, in Sturrock (122, 151 respectively).

2. Bowie's account of Lacan's "Symbolic" order, in Sturrock (151, 122 respectively). For extensive discussion of these issues, consult: Lacan, *Language* (e.g. pp. 159–77).

3. In "On Gide and His Journal," Barthes commented on this aspect of the artist: "Gide is a simultaneous being. To a greater or lesser degree, Nature has posited him as complete, from the very first. He has merely taken the time to reveal the various aspects of himself in succession, but we must always remember that these aspects are in fact contemporaries of each other, as are his works" (in Sontag 6).

4. This distinction stems from Johnson (99), whose psychoanalytical interpretation of the actions of Billy Budd, Claggart, and Vere I find intriguing. Billy, she says, destroys the "other" to preserve the self; Claggart kills the self to preserve the "other"; while Vere sacrifices both "for the preservation of a political order."

Works Cited

Aguirre, José María. "The Symbolism of *Arias otoñales*: A Sketch." In *Renaissance and Modern*, 58–82.

————. "The Window as Symbol in Spanish *Modernista* Poetry: Outline of a Model." In *Waiting for Pegasus*, 103–24.

Alarcos Llorach, Emilio. *Fonología espanola*. 3rd ed. Madrid: Gredos, 1961.

Albornoz, Aurora de. "Cronología de Juan Ramón Jiménez." In *Jiménez* (Escritor), 343–49.

————. "Estudio de la obra." In Jiménez, *Espacio*, 63–101.

————. "Estudio preliminar." In Jiménez, *Nueva antolojía*, 7–92.

————, ed. *Juan Ramón Jiménez* (Serie "El escritor y la crítica"). Madrid: Taurus, 1980.

Alonso, Dámaso. *Poesía española. Ensayo de métodos y límites estilísticos*. 5th ed. Madrid: Gredos, 1966.

Alonso, Dámaso, and Carlos Bousoño, *Seis calas en la expresión literaria española*. 3rd ed. Madrid: Gredos, 1963.

Azam, Gilbert. *La obra de Juan Ramón Jiménez*. Madrid: Editora Nacional, 1983.

Barthes, Roland. *A Barthes Reader*. Ed., and with an intro., by Susan Sontag. New York: Hill & Wang, 1982.

————. *Image-Music-Text*. Essays selected and trans. by Stephen Heath. Glasgow: Fontana, 1977.

————. *S/Z*. Trans. Richard Miller. New York: Hill & Wang, 1974.

————. "From Work to Text." In Harari, *Textual*, 73–81.

Beebe, Maurice. "What Modernism Was." *Journal of Modern Literature* 3.5 (1974): 1065–84.

Benveniste, Émile. *Problèmes de linguistique générale*. Paris: Gallimard, 1966.

Blasco Pascual, F. Javier. *La poética de Juan Ramón Jiménez: Desarrollo, Contexto y Sistema*. Salamanca: Universidad de Salamanca, 1981.

Bloom, Harold. *The Anxiety of Influence*. 1973. Reprint. New York: Oxford University Press, 1978.

Bly, Robert. "Spanish Leaping." *The Seventies* 1 (1972): 16–21.

Bousoño, Carlos. "La correlación en Juan Ramón Jiménez." In Albornoz, *Jiménez* (Escritor), 299–306.

Self and Image in Juan Ramón Jiménez

———. *Teoría de la expresión poética.* 5th ed. 2 vols. Madrid: Gredos, 1970.
Bowie, Malcolm. "Jacques Lacan." In Sturrock, *Structuralism*, 116–153.
Brooks, Cleanth. *The Well Wrought Urn.* New York: Harcourt Brace, 1947.
Brown, C. G. *A Literary History of Spain. The Twentieth Century.* London: Ernest Benn, 1972.
Cardwell, Richard A. *Juan Ramón Jiménez: The Modernist Apprenticeship (1895–1900).* Berlin: Colloquium Verlag, 1978.
Carreño, Antonio. *La dialéctica de la identidad en la poesía contemporánea. La persona. La máscara.* Madrid: Gredos, 1982.
Cernuda, Luis. *Prosa completa.* Ed. Derek Harris and Luis Maristany. Barcelona: Barral, 1975.
Coke-Enguídanos, Mervyn. *Word and Work in the Poetry of Juan Ramón Jiménez.* London: Támesis, 1982.
Cole, Leo R. *The Religious Instinct in the Poetry of Juan Ramón Jiménez.* Oxford: Dolphin, 1967.
Corominas, J., and J. A. Pascual, *Diccionario crítico etimológico castellano e hispánico.* Madrid: Gredos, 1980.
Culler, Jonathan. "Literature and Linguistics." In *Interrelations of Literature.* New York: Modern Language Association, 1982, 1–24.
———. *On Deconstruction: Theory and Criticism after Structuralism.* Ithaca: Cornell University Press, 1982.
———. "Problems in The 'History' of Contemporary Criticism." *Journal of the Midwest Modern Language Association* 17.1 (1984): 3–15.
———. *The Pursuit of Signs.* Ithaca: Cornell University Press, 1981.
———. *Structuralist Poetics.* London: Routledge & Kegan Paul, 1975.
Debicki, Andrew P. *Poetry of Discovery: The Spanish Generation of 1956–71.* Lexington: University Press of Kentucky, 1982.
del Río, Ángel. *Historia de la literatura española.* Vol. 2, rev. ed. New York: Holt, Rinehart & Winston, 1967.
de Man, Paul. "Action and Identity in Nietzsche." *Yale French Studies* 52 (1975): 16–30.
———. *Allegories of Reading.* New Haven and London: Yale University Press, 1979.
———. *Blindness and Insight.* New York: Oxford University Press, 1971.
———. "Hypogram and Inscription: Michael Riffaterre's Poetics of Reading." *Diacritics* 11.4 (1981): 17–35.
———. "Semiology and Rhetoric." In Harari, *Textual*, 121–40.
Derrida, Jacques. *Margins of Philosophy.* Trans. Alan Bass. Chicago: University of Chicago Press, 1982.
———. *Positions.* Trans. Alan Bass. Chicago: University of Chicago Press, 1982.
Eagleton, Terry. *Literary Theory: An Introduction.* Minneapolis: University of Minnesota Press, 1983.
Eco, Umberto. *The Role of The Reader.* Bloomington: Indiana University Press, 1979.
Eliot, T. S. *Collected Poems.* 1963. Reprint. London: Faber & Faber, 1970.

———. *Selected Essays*. 3rd ed. 1932. Reprint. London: Faber and Faber, 1969.

Fónagy, Iván. "Communication in Poetry." In Malmberg, *Readings*, 282–305.

Font, María Teresa. *Espacio: Autobiografía lírica de Juan Ramón Jiménez*. Madrid: Insula, 1972.

Forrest-Thomson, Veronica. *Poetic Artifice: A Theory of Twentieth Century Poetry*. Manchester, England: Manchester University Press, 1978.

Frenzel, Elisabeth. *Diccionario de argumentos de la literatura universal*. Trans. Carmen Schade de Caneda. Madrid: Gredos, 1976.

Freud, Sigmund. *Collected Papers*. Vol. 4. Trans. Joan Riviere. New York: Basic Books, 1959.

———. *The Complete Psychological Works of Sigmund Freud*. London: Hogarth Press, 1953.

———. *A General Introduction to Psychoanalysis*. 1924. Reprint. New York: Washington Square Press, 1968.

González, Angel. *Juan Ramón Jiménez: Estudio*. Madrid: Júcar, 1973.

Greimas, A. J., and J. Courtés *Semiotics and Language: An Analytical Dictionary*. Trans. Larry Christ and others. Bloomington: Indiana University Press, 1982.

Guillén, Claudio. *Literature As System: Essays Toward the Theory of Literary History*. Princeton: Princeton University Press, 1971.

Gullón, Ricardo. *Conversaciones con Juan Ramón Jiménez*. Madrid: Taurus, 1958.

———. *Estudios sobre Juan Ramón Jiménez*. Buenos Aires: Losada, 1960.

———. "Juan Ramón Jiménez y El modernismo." In Jiménez, *El modernismo*, 13–43.

———. *Una poética para Antonio Machado*. Madrid: Gredos, 1969.

Hamburger, Michael. *The Truth of Poetry: Tensions in Modern Poetry From Baudelaire to the 1960s*. New York: Harcourt, Brace & World, 1969.

Harari, Josué V., ed. *Textual Strategies: Perspectives In Post-Structuralist Criticism*. Ithaca: Cornell University Press, 1979.

Hartman, Geoffrey. *Criticism In The Wilderness*. New Haven: Yale University Press, 1980.

Hassan, Ihab. *Paracriticisms: Seven Speculations of the Times*. Urbana: University of Illinois Press, 1975.

Heath, Stephen. "Translator's Note." In Barthes, *Image* 7–11.

Howe, Irving, ed. *Literary Modernism*. New York: Fawcett World Library, 1967.

Iser, Wolfgang. *The Act of Reading: A Theory of Aesthetic Response*. Baltimore: Johns Hopkins University Press, 1981.

Jakobson, Roman. "'Les Chats' de Charles Baudelaire." In *L'Homme* 2 (1962): 5–21

———. "Letter to Haroldo Campos on Martin Codax's Poetic Texture." In *Russian Formalism*. Ed. S. Bann and J. E. Bowlt. New York: Barnes & Noble, 1973, 20–25.

———. "Linguistics and Poetics." In *Style in Language*. Ed. Thomas A.

Sebeok. Cambridge: MIT Press, 1960, 350–77.

———. "A Postscript To the Discussion On Grammar of Poetry." *Diacritics* 10.1 (1980): 22–35.

Jiménez, Juan Ramón. *Canción.* Madrid: Aguilar, 1961.

———. *Diario de un poeta reciéncasado.* Ed. Antonio Sánchez-Barbudo. Barcelona: Labor, 1970.

———. *El modernismo: Notas de un curso (1953).* Ed. Ricardo Gullón and Eugenio Fernández Méndez. Mexico: Aguilar, 1962.

———. *El trabajo gustoso: Conferencias.* Ed. Francisco Garfias. Mexico: Aguilar, 1961.

———. *Espacio.* Ed. Aurora de Albornoz. Madrid: Editora Nacional, 1982.

———. *Estética y ética estética: Crítica y complemento.* Ed. Francisco Garfias. Madrid: Aguilar, 1967.

———. *Leyenda (1896–1956).* Ed. Antonio Sánchez Romeralo. La Torre Abierta. Edición de Bibliófilo. Madrid: CUPSA Editorial, 1978.

———. *Libros de poesía.* Ed. Agustín Caballero. 3rd ed. Madrid: Aguilar, 1967.

———. *Libros inéditos de poesía: I.* Ed. Francisco Garfias. Madrid: Aguilar, 1964.

———. *Libros inéditos de poesía: II.* Ed. Francisco Garfias. Madrid: Aguilar, 1964.

———. *Nueva antolojía.* Ed. Aurora de Albornoz. Barcelona: Península, 1973.

———. *Poesías últimas escojidas (1918–1958).* Ed. Antonio Sánchez Romeralo. Madrid: Espasa-Calpe, 1982.

———. *Primeros libros de poesía.* Ed. Francisco Garfias. 3rd ed. Madrid: Aguilar, 1967.

———. *Segunda antolojía poética (1898–1918).* 1922. Reprint. Madrid: Espasa-Calpe, 1969.

———. *Tercera antolojía poética (1898–1953).* Madrid: Biblioteca Nueva, 1957.

Johnson, Barbara. *The Critical Difference: Essays in the Contemporary Rhetoric of Reading.* Baltimore: Johns Hopkins University Press, 1980.

Kermode, Frank. *The Sense of An Ending.* New York: Oxford University Press, 1967.

Lacan, Jacques. *The Language of the Self: The Function of Language in Psychoanalysis.* Trans. with notes and commentary by Anthony Wilden. New York: Dell Publishing Co., 1975.

Laplanche, J., and J.-B. Pontalis. *The Language of Psycho-Analysis.* Trans. Donald Nicholson-Smith. London: Hogarth Press, 1973.

Lemon, Lee T., and Marion J. Reis. *Russian Formalist Criticism.* Lincoln: University of Nebraska Press, 1965.

Lewis, Philip. "The Post-Structuralist Condition." *Diacritics* 12.1 (1982): 2–24.

Lyotard, Jean-François. *The Postmodern Condition: A Report On Knowledge.*

Trans. G. Bennington & B. Massumi. Minneapolis: University of Minnesota Press, 1984.

Machado, Antonio. *Poesías Completas*. 10th ed. Madrid: Espasa-Calpe, 1963.

Malmberg, Bertil. *Readings in Modern Linguistics: An Anthology*. The Hague: Mouton & Läromedelsförlagen, 1972.

Miller, J. Hillis. "Arachne's Broken Woof." *Georgia Review* 31 (1977): 44–60.

———. "Stevens' Rock and Criticism as Cure." *Georgia Review* 30 (1976): 5–33 & 330–48.

———. "Williams' *Spring and All* and the Progress of Poetry." *Daedalus* 99 (1970), 405–34.

Mukarovsky, Jan. "Standard Language and Poetic Language." In *A Prague School Reader On Esthetics, Literary Structure and Style*. Trans. Paul L. Garvin. Washington: Georgetown University Press, 1964, 17–30.

Nemes, Graciela Palau de. *Inicios de Zenobia y Juan Ramón Jiménez en América*. Madrid: Fundación Universitaria Espanola, 1982.

———. *Vida y obra de Juan Ramón Jiménez: La poesía desnuda*. 2nd ed., rev. 2 vols. Madrid: Gredos, 1975.

Norris, Christopher. *Deconstruction: Theory and Practice*. London: Methuen, 1982.

Olson, Paul. *Circle of Paradox: Time and Essence in The Poetry of Juan Ramón Jiménez*. Baltimore: Johns Hopkins University Press, 1967.

Pablos, Basilio de. *El tiempo en la poesía de Juan Ramón Jiménez*. Madrid: Gredos, 1965.

Paraíso de Leal, Isabel. *Juan Ramón Jiménez: Vivencia y palabra*. Madrid: Alhambra, 1976.

Pérez-Firmat, Gustavo. "Apuntes para un modelo de la intertextualidad en la literatura," *Romanic Review* 69 (1978): 1–14.

Perkins, David. *A History of Modern Poetry From 1890s to High Modernism*. Cambridge: Harvard University Press, 1976.

Perloff, Marjorie. *The Poetics of Indeterminacy*. Princeton: Princeton University Press, 1981.

Predmore, Michael P. *La poesía hermética de Juan Ramón Jiménez*. Madrid: Gredos, 1973.

Prince, Gerald. "Introduction to the Study of the Narratee." In Tompkins, *Reader*, 7–25.

Princeton Encyclopedia of Poetry and Poetics. Ed. Alex Preminger, enlarged ed. Princeton: Princeton University Press, 1974.

Renaissance and Modern Studies. *Juan Ramón Jiménez (1881–1958)*. 25 (1981).

Riffaterre, Michael. "Describing Poetic Structures: Two Approaches to Baudelaire's 'Les Chats.'" In Tompkins, *Reader*, 26–40.

———. "Flaubert's Presuppositions." *Diacritics* 11.4 (1981): 2–11.

———. "Interview." *Diacritics* 11.4 (1981): 12–16.

———. *Semiotics of Poetry*. Bloomington: Indiana University Press, 1978.

Rimbaud, Arthur. *Oeuvres complètes*. Ed. Rolland de Renéville and Jules Monguet. Paris: Gallimard, 1963.

Rorty, Richard. *Consequences of Pragmatism*. Minneapolis: University of Minnesota Press, 1982.

Sánchez-Barbudo, Antonio. *La obra poética de Juan Ramón Jiménez*. Madrid: Cátedra, 1981.

———. *La segunda época de Juan Ramón Jiménez (1916–1953)*. Vol. 1. Madrid: Gredos, 1962.

———. *La segunda época de Juan Ramón Jiménez (1916–1953)*. *Cincuenta poemas comentados*. Vol. 2. Madrid: Gredos, 1963.

Sánchez Romeralo, Antonio. "Prólogo." In Jiménez, *Poesías últimas*, 10–37.

Santos-Escudero, Ceferino. *Símbolos y Dios en el último Juan Ramón Jiménez*. Madrid: Gredos, 1975.

Scholes, Robert. *Semiotics and Interpretation*. New Haven: Yale University Press, 1982.

Siebenman, Gustav. *Los estilos poéticos en España desde 1900*. Madrid: Gredos, 1973.

Smith, Barbara Herrnstein. "Narrative Versions. Narrative Theories." *Critical Inquiry* 7 (1980): 213–36.

———. *Poetic Closure: A Study of How Poems End*. Chicago: University of Chicago Press, 1968.

Stevens, Wallace. *The Necessary Angel*. New York: Vintage, 1951.

Sturrock, John, ed. *Structuralism and Since: From Lévi-Strauss to Derrida*. Oxford: Oxford University Press, 1979.

Talens, Jenaro. *Elementos para una semiótica del texto artístico*. Madrid: Cátedra, 1978.

Tompkins, Jane P. *Reader-Response Criticism: From Formalism to Post-Structuralism*. Baltimore: Johns Hopkins University Press, 1980.

Traugott, Elizabeth Closs, and Mary Louise Pratt. *Linguistics for Students of Literature*. New York: Harcourt, Brace, Jovanovich, 1980.

Ulibarri, Sabine R. *El mundo poético de Juan Ramón Jiménez*. Madrid: Edhigar, 1962.

Villar, Arturo del. "El desdoblamiento del yo en Juan Ramón Jiménez." *Nueva Estafeta* 37 (Dec. 1981), 49–63.

Vries, Ad de. *Dictionary of Symbols and Imagery*. Amsterdam and London: North Holland Publishing Co., 1974.

Waiting for Pegasus. Ed. Roland Grass and William R. Risley. Macomb, Ill.: Western Illinois University, 1979.

Webster's Third New International Dictionary. Springfield, Mass.: G. & C. Merriam Co., 1971.

Wilcox, John C. "Algunas configuraciones espaciales en la poesía de Juan Ramón Jiménez." In *La estructura y el espacio en la novela y la poesía*. Seminario Ricardo Gullón. Sacramento, Ca.: Hispanic Press, 1980: 1–23.

———. "Etapa histórica y transformación estilística en Juan Ramón Jiménez." *Cuadernos para Investigación de la Literatura Hispánica* 4 (1982): 189–98.

————. "An Inquiry into Juan Ramón Jiménez's Interest in Walter Pater." *Studies in Twentieth Century Literature* 7.2 (1983): 185–99.

————. "Juan Ramón Jiménez and the Illinois Trio: Sandburg, Lindsay, Masters." *Comparative Literature Studies* 21.2 (1984): 186–200.

————. "The Love Poem as *vita nuova* in Juan Ramón Jiménez. A Reading of 'Subes de ti misma' (*Estío*)." In *Estudios en honor a Ricardo Gullón*. Lincoln, Nebr.: Society for Spanish and Spanish American Studies, 1984: 369–83.

————. "'Naked' versus 'Pure' Poetry in Juan Ramón Jiménez, With Remarks On The Impact of W. B. Yeats." *Hispania* 66 (1983): 511–21.

————. "W. B. Yeats and Juan Ramón Jiménez: A Study of Influence and Similarities, and A Comparison of the Themes of Death, Love, Poetics, and the Quest for Fulfilment-in-Time." Ph.D. diss. Austin: University of Texas, 1976.

Yeats, W. B. *The Collected Poems of W. B. Yeats*. Definitive ed., 1956. Reprint. New York: Macmillan, 1967.

Young, Howard T. "Juan Ramón Jiménez and The Poetry of T. S. Eliot." In *Renaissance and Modern*, 155–65.

————. *The Line in the Margin: Juan Ramón Jiménez and His Readings in Blake, Shelley, and Yeats*. Wisconsin: University of Wisconsin Press, 1980.

INDEX

Index

Index

Index

A Note on the Author

John C. Wilcox is an associate professor of Spanish at the University of Illinois, Urbana-Champaign. A native of England, he received an undergraduate degree from Bristol University. His Ph.D. is from the University of Texas at Austin. He has taught at Queens College, C.U.N.Y., and at the University of Cincinnati. Professor Wilcox was the editor, with Salvador J. Fajardo, of *At Home and Beyond: New Essays on Spanish Poets of the Twenties*. He has published a number of articles on the poetry of Juan Ramón Jiménez.